Teaching Ethics Across the Management Curriculum

Teaching Ethics Across the Management Curriculum

A Handbook for International Faculty

Kemi Ogunyemi

BEP BUSINESS EXPERT PRESS

Teaching Ethics Across the Management Curriculum: A Handbook for International Faculty
Copyright © Business Expert Press, LLC, 2015.
All rights reserved. No part of this publication may be reproduced, stored in a retrieval system, or transmitted in any form or by any means—electronic, mechanical, photocopy, recording, or any other except for brief quotations, not to exceed 400 words, without the prior permission of the publisher.

First published in 2015 by
Business Expert Press, LLC
222 East 46th Street, New York, NY 10017
www.businessexpertpress.com

ISBN-13: 978-1-60649-794-4 (paperback)
ISBN-13: 978-1-60649-795-1 (e-book)

Business Expert Press Principles of Responsible Management Education Collection

Collection ISSN: 2331-0014 (print)
Collection ISSN: 2331-0022 (electronic)

Cover and interior design by Exeter Premedia Services Private Ltd., Chennai, India

First edition: 2015

10 9 8 7 6 5 4 3 2 1

Printed in the United States of America.

Abstract

The need to embed business ethics in the teaching of management disciplines has at times given rise to a debate as to whether ethics should be taught as a standalone course or in an embedded manner. So far, the majority of opinions favor a consensus that both approaches are relevant and should be used complementarily for optimal results.

This book provides unique insights into the experience of seasoned academics regarding embedding business ethics into their teaching of the practice of management. Its multidisciplinary approach makes its content very rich, since the insights of our colleagues from within their fields are invaluable. The book therefore functions as a handbook for faculty as well as a complementary textbook for the business student (to highlight the ethical dilemmas for the different managerial functional roles). Disciplines covered include decision-making, strategy and agency theory; management accounting and macroeconomics; operations management, supply chain management and the management of information systems; marketing and consumer behavior; human resources management, career management, negotiation, managing corporate power and politics, and community and investor relations.

The *Handbook* is a platform for faculty to share their experiences of how to teach ethical profitability. This contributes to resolving the concerns that faculty may experience when they wish to incorporate ethics into their teaching but feel that they lack the preparation for doing this or ideas on how to go about it. It thus helps faculty ensure their students grasp the moral dimension of running a business when, for example, drawing up sustainable business plans, raising finance, appraising employees, executing operation strategies, buying software, or implementing a customer loyalty plan.

The chapters describe each discipline briefly, raise the typical ethical issues therein and suggest strategies for teaching and exercises or projects. Every school that wishes to teach business students to act responsibly will find this book useful. The developing country versus developed country perspectives included in each chapter may be particularly interesting to business schools that have very diverse student bodies. The book can also be used as a resource for in-company training toward attaining and sustaining an ethical culture.

Keywords

accounting, business ethics, career management, common good approach, community and investors, consumer behavior, corporate power and politics, curriculum, developed versus developing country perspectives, duty ethics, embedding ethics, ethical decision making, ethical management of human resources, ethical theories, ethics in strategy, frameworks for ethical choices, information systems, justice, macroeconomics, marketing ethics, negotiation ethics, operations management, pedagogy, PRME, rights, supply chain, teaching ethics, utilitarianism, values, virtue ethics

Contents

Foreword xi

Chapter 1   Teaching Ethics Across the Management
            Curriculum 1
            Kemi Ogunyemi

Module 1: Making Decisions 15

Chapter 2   Teaching Ethics in Business Policy
            (Strategy) Courses 17
            Michael E. Cafferky

Chapter 3   Ethical Foundations for Organizational Decision
            Making at the Operational and Strategic Levels 39
            Thomas G. Pittz and Melissa Cast

Chapter 4   Ethics and Agency Theory in Management 55
            Unsal Sigri and Umit Ercan

Module 2: Money Matters 77

Chapter 5   Embedding Ethics and Social Responsibility in
            Management Accounting Courses 79
            Jan Bell, Cathleen S. Burns, and Donna R. Sockell

Chapter 6   Ethical Dimensions in the Teaching of Economics
            and the Tradition of Critical Political Economy 119
            Patrick O'Sullivan

Module 3: On the Shop Floor 139

Chapter 7   Teaching Ethics in Operations Management 141
            Arnd Huchzermeier, Eva Kohl, and Stefan Spinler

Chapter 8   Teaching Ethics in Supply Chain Management 159
            Gerald Burch, Walter Kendall, and Joanna Shaw

Chapter 9 Teaching Ethics in Decision Making: Embedding Moral Reasoning in the Management of Information Systems 179
Olayinka David-West

Module 4: Selling the Product 199

Chapter 10 Embedding Ethical Issues in Marketing Management Classes: An Instructor's Guide 201
Uchenna Uzo

Chapter 11 Incorporating Ethics in Teaching Consumer Behavior: An Educational Strategy Based on Principles for Responsible Management Education 213
Consuelo Garcia-de-la-Torre, Gloria Camacho, and Osmar Arandia

Module 5: People Management and Soft Skills 227

Chapter 12 Teaching Ethics in Human Resources Management 229
Silke Bustamante

Chapter 13 Teaching Ethics in Career Management 245
Olusegun Babalola and Ifedapo Adeleye

Chapter 14 Ethics in Negotiation 259
Barney Jordan and David Venter

Chapter 15 Ethics in Managing Corporate Power and Politics 277
Duane Windsor

Chapter 16 Ethical Dimensions of Community and Investor Relations Communication and Governance for Sustainable Management 303
Judith Y. Weisinger and Edward L. Quevedo

Chapter 17 Future of Ethics Education in Management Curricula 323
Emeka Enwere and Uchenna Uzo

Chapter Summaries 331
About the Authors 343
Index 357

Foreword

The conversation on whether and how to teach ethics in business schools has already gone on for several decades and I do not expect it to come to an end soon. There are many reasons for this, not the least important of which is that one's views on these issues depend critically on more fundamental positions about matters like the ultimate purpose of business, human flourishing, and the connection between human fulfillment, however conceived, and professional activity; all matters on which there is no reason to expect that we will ever secure universal agreement.

Still, this is not the end of the story. Often we can provide the outlines of solutions that answer such questions to our own satisfaction, and this is already a great achievement. After all, when we wrestle with ethical issues our main objective should be to obtain guidance on how to live our own lives and, secondarily, how to help those who seek our advice, not necessarily, nor primarily, how to devise theories that will in fact secure universal agreement. (It goes without saying that this is one of the many questions on which there is no universal agreement.)

A less basic, but in practice perhaps even more important, reason why there is a continuing argument on whether and how to teach business ethics is that it is very difficult to teach ethics well. In my experience, many business school professors are reluctant to confront ethical issues in the classroom simply because they have very little idea how to it competently. In so far as this is the case, an effective way of overcoming such reluctance is to simply show them a practical and sensible way of doing it. This is precisely what this book seeks to do. A great advantage of this procedure is that a great many false arguments are thereby avoided. If a professor of, say, marketing objects to teaching her students the ethics of marketing on the basis that it is not for her to tell people how to live their lives, perhaps it is not a good idea to respond with a spirited defense of the Aristotelian notion of *eudaimonia* and its relationship to an objective view of human nature; it may be much better to just say that all one would like her to do is to help her students to see why engaging in deceptive or sexist advertising or in predatory pricing are not very good ideas. As it is most likely that this is already her own view, all that is left to do is to suggest some way of doing this in an effective way and without consuming too much of the always short time available to any professor. And in this way, which is the way of this book, a potentially interminable discussion at very high levels of abstraction will have been avoided and hopefully one more step forward in the effort to form ethical managers will have been taken.

In my view it is also a great merit of this book that it provides practical help to extend the teaching of ethics beyond the ghetto of the compulsory (or even worse, elective) business ethics course. One of the oldest topics in the unending argument on how to teach business ethics is whether it is better to have a separate business ethics course or to embed a consideration of the relevant ethical issues in the teaching of all the standard courses. I am myself a professor of business ethics and a strong defender of the need to have a separate business ethics course, if only so that other professors may not have to repeat again and again (and perhaps not do very well) a justification of the relevant ethical principles in the discussion of each concrete ethical problem. (Remember the convenience of helping professors to conserve precious teaching time while addressing ethical issues.) However, I have no doubt that it is impossible to teach business ethics effectively if this is done *only* in an ethics module, while the rest of the sessions of the program are taught in blissful indifference to ethical concerns. When things are done in this manner, the overwhelming impression left in the minds of students is that the ethics course was placed in the curriculum only as an expression of political correctness, but that what really matters in business is to sell the stuff, or to produce it cheaply, or to make as much money as possible. In other words, one has to get results and that nothing else really matters.

However, besides being a professor of business ethics, I have also been a dean, and this experience made it very clear to me that it is by no means enough to tell other professors that they have to take responsibility for teaching their students not just how to be successful, but also to be successful in a socially constructive and personally fulfilling manner. Even if they agree to this (and, at least when the professor of business ethics is also the dean, they often do), they still need specific guidance and concrete suggestions on how to go about this, and this in my experience was by far the greatest problem in getting all faculty members aligned behind the effort to form responsible managers. It takes a lot of effort to provide that specific guidance. All I can say is that I would have been very happy to have a book like this available during my period as dean.

I would also like to point out that something I very much like about this book is that the great majority of the authors do not hold PhDs in business ethics. They are subject matter specialists who have taken the trouble to look for practical ways to incorporate ethical issues in the teaching of their bread-and-butter subjects. This is probably the most practical way of convincing other academics who are not specialists in business ethics that there is no need for them to do a second doctorate before they start addressing ethical issues in teaching their disciplines.

For all the preceding reasons, we all owe a significant debt of gratitude to Dr. Kemi Ogunyemi for having undertaken the task of putting together this book.

Prof. Juan Manuel Elegido
Vice-Chancellor and
Professor of Business Ethics
Pan-Atlantic University
Nigeria

CHAPTER 1

Teaching Ethics Across the Management Curriculum

Kemi Ogunyemi

Lagos Business School, Pan-Atlantic University

Teaching Ethics in Management

The drive to embed business ethics in the teaching of management disciplines has at times given rise to a debate as to whether ethics should be taught as a standalone course or in an embedded manner. So far, the majority of the opinions favors a consensus that both approaches are relevant and should be used complementarily for optimal results (Crossan et al. 2013; Rasche, Gilbert, and Schedel 2013). What is incontrovertibly clear is that there are still numerous challenges to the effective teaching of business ethics through the existing curricula and structures in many schools. According to Rasche, Gilbert, and Schedel (2013), ethics-related courses in business schools increased in number by 100 percent over the five years leading up to 2009. Yet, the authors at the end of this empirical study found that the integration of ethics into the actual MBA curriculum remains acutely problematic. As Cant and Kulik emphasize, echoing numerous calls for the integration of ethics teaching into all management disciplines, "coursework-as-usual is insufficient, or at least irresponsible, because they cover material independent of ethics" (2009, 232). There is a need to train future business managers and leaders to apply ethical reasoning in all the different business situations in which they find themselves, whether they are dealing with issues of human resource management (HRM), financing and investment strategy, operations management, organizational politics, marketing plans, and so forth. It is thus that they will be empowered to act responsibly, going beyond the demands of legal compliance to adopt decision-making styles rooted in integrity.

According to Enderle (2011), wealth creation is more than production: It includes distribution, it includes public wealth as well as private wealth, it includes spiritual as well as material wealth, and it must be sustainable. To attain this, a high level of ethical sensitivity is demanded from those who are saddled with the responsibility of wealth creation. As maintained by Melé, Argandoña, and Sánchez-Runde (2011, 1), we are currently faced with problems of "faulty human behavior and moral character." One of the key questions to answer is that of the purpose of business itself, or what may equally be referred to as the calling of those who are in the business profession. Attempting to answer this question, Wishloff (2014, 31) speaks about the purpose of business as being the common good and its contribution as being the provision of "goods and services that contribute to human flourishing". Rivas and Rivas (2003) assert that the vocation of a business leader is a call to serve. In this context, it is clear that the purpose of business can only be achieved by people—human beings who are aware of that purpose and are committed to it. The responsibility or irresponsibility of people is what is at the bottom of the responsibility or irresponsibility of corporate entities.

Scandals and Vandals: A Cheating Culture and MBAs

One of the reasons that the teaching of ethics has claimed popular attention in recent years is that the world has been shaken again and again with the evidence of the harm wrought by lack of ethical behavior among business leaders all over the globe (Cant and Kulik 2009; Waddock and Lozano 2013). Enderle and Liu (2012) describe an astonishing number of marketing scandals that took place in China over the same period, involving global companies like Walmart, Foxconn, Baxter International, Carrefour, Nestlé, HP, Toyota, Conoco Phillips, and so forth. Along with the call to business schools to examine their curricula, there have also been efforts to introduce stricter regulation (new legislation like the Sarbanes–Oxley, new and revised corporate governance codes, etc.) and an increase in ethics training within organizations. The new thinking is needed in all spheres of business and societal interaction (Melé, Argandoña, and

Sánchez-Runde 2011) and ensuring that ethics is embedded in the management classroom and in the entire business school culture is a solid contribution toward achieving that end (Crossan et al. 2013).

Managers need to have personal values and virtues to guide their work and behavior (Crossan et al. 2013; Nedelko and Potocan 2011) and if we refer to moral values rather than indifferent ones[1] and if these values are positive, then they are more likely to be able to foster ethics and responsibility in their organizations. The same idea is supported by John Broome's (2000) assertion that while other professionals need ethical awareness and sensitivity, economists need that and more—they need ethical theory. They need it in order to direct the world of business in such a way as to steer clear of causing harm to others and to create value that enables and enriches the common good of all stakeholders. They need to be able to build organizations that are ethical and responsible and therefore sustainable. This depends on their own preparation to be professionals who can achieve these goals, and their preparation depends to an extent on the orientation given to their preparation within the educational system to be business professionals. If that orientation is deficient by commission or omission, it will be no surprise if the emerging business graduate has little or no ability to apply ethical considerations to business decisions and goes on to be a hindrance for such considerations within the organizations for which he or she works. Sadly, research has shown that business students are more likely to cheat and to put their own self-interest above the common good than others who are not business students (Brown et al. 2010; McCabe, Butterfield, and Trevino 2006).

Ki, Lee, and Choi (2012) found that organizational factors affecting ethical behavior in organizations included ethical climate, support of ethical behavior from top management, and the association of ethical behavior with career success as well as a clear ethical code. Writing much earlier, Stead, Worrel, and Stead (1990) had suggested that in order to have an ethical organization, managers must model ethical behavior, establish ethical codes, train employees in ethics, establish positions and

---

[1] Innovation, which was the main value being exemplified and researched by the authors, is not a moral value—it is indifferent (neutral) as far as morality (goodness or badness) is concerned.

structures to deal with ethical issues, and reinforce ethical behavior. The first three of Ki, Lee, and Choi's factors and the practicability of Stead, Worrel, and Stead's suggestions are likely to be affected by the formation of the business students while they are in university or in business schools.

Teaching Business Ethics Across the Management Curriculum

Reflecting on the workings of the minds of the perpetrators of reprehensible business decisions in the Enron and NASA Columbia debacles, Goodpaster (2004) issues a challenge to business schools to sanitize their curricula. This and similar calls to action have galvanized business and management schools into taking action to ensure that business ethics features in their curricular. In March 2009, the European Foundation for Management Development (EFMD) MBA Directors' conference directly confronted the *accusations* that business schools are guilty of promoting unethical behavior in business at least by omission. New directions toward helping educators instill what it takes to make profit ethically through their work include the giving voice to values (GVV) approach to teaching ethical behavior, the principles for responsible management education (PRME) initiative, the 50 + 20 group, the globally responsible leaders (GRLE) group, and the humanistic management network. Approaches and frameworks also abound. One of them links leadership to virtues, values, and ethical decision making and proposes that the business school has to go beyond merely engaging the students to establish a culture within the business school itself (Crossan et al. 2013).

There are a good number of institutions already trying out different approaches; a few examples of these are given here—Lagos Business School, Pan-Atlantic University, offers a course on the nature of human beings (NHB)[2] in order to provide a counterpoint to the economic view of the human person as well as integrating ethics and sustainability ideas into the different disciplines and offering business ethics as a standalone course. Northern Illinois University uses Building Ethical Leaders Using

---

[2] This is the business school where I work, and I teach this course annually to incoming full-time MBA participants.

an Integrated Ethics Framework (BELIEF), launched in 2006 as a "systematic approach to integrating ethics into the college curriculum."[3] They also regularly hold ethics case competitions and video contests. The executive education unit of ESADE Business School started the Vicens Vives Program (VVP) in 2002 in order to raise consciousness of the environment and present the idea of leadership as service to others while emphasizing values in personal and collective life. De Paul University inaugurated, in 2007, an Ethics across the Curricula (EAC) committee that works to "Provide opportunities for all students to learn ethical systems and demonstrate ethical practice."[4] One of their first publications was the "Ethics 101: A common ethics language for dialogue" paper.[5] In the Carroll School of Management and Sociology Department, Boston, College, a Leadership for Change (LC) program ran for some years as a credit course. It was focused on helping professionals lead change for the common good and be catalysts of responsible and sustainable action in their organizations and in society. These examples show that there are already models out there to adopt in order to teach responsible management.

At the same time, the appreciation for the need to provide faculty with tools for achieving this goal continues to grow. According to Dean and Beggs (2006), faculty may at times not include ethical considerations in their teaching because they assume that some other colleague has already covered this. Also, there are faculty who would like to teach their specific business courses with attention to the ethical implications of the activities the students will carry out within their functional roles. However, they are not as prepared as ethics faculty and thus may not find it easy to identify and handle well all the ethical issues that arise in the course of their teaching. This also was a finding of Dean and Beggs (2006) and of Mintz (1990). At times they may not have the time to research to find the tools

---

[3] http://www.cob.niu.edu/belief/
[4] http://driehaus.depaul.edu/about/centers-and-institutes/institute-for-business-and-professional-ethics/teaching-and-pedagogy/Pages/ethics-across-the-curricula.aspx
[5] Available online at http://works.bepress.com/cgi/viewcontent.cgi?article=1025&context=marcotavanti

that could help them (Baetz and Sharp 2004). At other times, they may lack the time to integrate ethical reflection or embed it into their already existing course design (Dean and Beggs 2006; Jackson 2006). This book aims to contribute to resolving these challenges and help teachers to take their students beyond the stockholder and stakeholder approaches to incorporate a comprehensive moral approach (Goodpaster 2011). This is why the chapters are written by subject experts in various management disciplines incorporating their experience of embedding business ethics in their courses. It is an approach distinct from that taken by people outside the disciplines who are using the responsible management or business ethics lens to view them all. The content will also be a helpful resource for organizations that engage in developing their staff in moral reasoning, ethical decision making, and so forth in order to attain and sustain an ethical culture in the firm.

Art, Science, and Skill

The approaches, facets, and nuances of integrating business ethics vary across disciplines. The science required is also different. Each member of faculty must master the science of the principles that are needed for his or her discipline, and then learn the art of transmitting them while teaching until, becoming a skill, it is now part of the educator's personality. This book brings together the skills of educators who have developed the science and practiced the art and wish to share them with their colleagues in order to speed up the process for others.

After this introductory chapter, the book unfolds as five modules. In Module 1, *Making Decisions*, there are three chapters on ethical decision-making, business policy (strategy), and agency theory. Excellent teaching ideas are proffered by Michael Cafferky's chapter on business policy. He makes a good case for integrating business ethics into business policy courses in contrast to the way in which strategy is often viewed, and taught, as a nonmoral discipline or the way in which it is presented as merely an ostensibly moral one as, for example, when strategic stakeholder analysis is presented as if it were sufficient of itself to transform a business decision into an ethical one (Goodpaster 1991). The section titled *Advice for Instructors: Engaging Strategy Students on Ethical Issues* is particularly useful, while the suggested exercise, *Life-Cycle Case Study*, directly involves students in assuring the responsibility and sustainability of the product stories they investigate and narrate. The chapter on decision making offers a number of valuable contributions by speaking to the issue of ethical reflection at the moment of decision making. The chapter is designed to help faculty promote greater ethical sensitivity in their students. Also, a framework for ethical decision making is put forward. As a guide to case-based teaching and ethical analysis, the authors suggest five steps: recognition and awareness, fact-finding, evaluating ethical approaches, testing the decision, and reflecting on the outcome. This chapter is authored by Thomas Pittz and Melissa Cast. The chapter written by Unsal Sigri and Umit Ercan and directed toward embedding ethics in the teaching of agency theory stands out in its apt description of the issues raised by principal–agent frictions. The chapter introduces agency theory, situates it in the context of management, and highlights the issues and ethical dilemmas both principals and agents have to face as they pursue individual interests in furtherance of their collective interest of growing the company and improving performance, as well as working for the common good. The authors' discussion of agency theory's issues, cultural contexts and problems, and the teaching strategies they suggest will come in handy for people who have to teach this concept.

Module 2, *Money Matters*, has chapters on management accounting and the macroeconomic environment of business. In the former, Janice Bell, Cathleen Burns, and Donna Sockell present valuable insights into the impact of the work of the management accountant on organizational ethics. They discuss the social and ethical issues that arise in the performance of this management function and provide pedagogical material to use in confronting them. One can perceive the authors' clear and profound grasp of the moral issues relating to activity stemming from the company's accounting knowledge and management. The macroeconomics chapter, contributed by Patrick O'Sullivan, identifies the unique nature of the place of the consideration of ethics in macroeconomics. It addresses the apparent absence of ethics in economics as taught in most business schools. (Economics in business schools separates into macroeconomics— and associated fiscal/monetary policies and international trade issues— and managerial economics, basically microeconomics applied to the firm and its management.) A good explanation is provided as to why the purely positive treatment of microeconomics and macroeconomics is deficient. The discussion of normative versus positive statements in economics is particularly interesting.

The third module, *On the Shop Floor*, comprises operations management, supply chain management, and the management of information systems (MIS). The highlights of the first of the three, written by Arnd Huchzermeier, Eva Kohl, and Stefan Spinler, are its case study approach and the inclusion of real examples. These help to make the chapter content very practical and easy to adopt and adapt in teaching. Issues of sustainability are raised and discussed in depth. Morally significant nonfiduciary relationships (Goodpaster 1991) usually include those held with the suppliers of goods and services to the organization. Therefore, a consideration of ethics in supply chain management is important. A very useful framework for teaching it is proposed in Figure 8.1 in the chapter dealing with this course. The authors, Gerald Burch, Walter Kendall, and Joanna Shaw, consider six ethical concepts that complement one another. The two illustrations taken from supply chain management practice (defective or bogus parts, labor working conditions) are well developed. Dealing with the MIS, Olayinka David-West presents a comprehensive table, which is a good resource for addressing ethics and MIS issues. She demonstrates the need for ethical guidelines in the teaching and practice of MIS and empowers educators by providing a starting point in their bid to bring into their classrooms the moral dimensions of this subject.

Module 4, *Selling the Product*, contains chapters on marketing management and communications and on consumer behavior. When the spotlight turns to marketing, the ethical approach to the different aspects is thoroughly discussed—understanding the consumer, market segmentation, decisions related to the product, channels management, pricing, and communication. An ethical concern and a humanist perspective are proposed by Uchenna Uzo who says that every marketing decision has an ethical dimension and that the customer should be seen as a person. The examples given in the chapter contributed by Consuelo Garcia-de-la-Torre, Gloria Camacho, and Osmar Arandia show the ethical dilemmas that come up in teaching consumer behavior, a subdiscipline of marketing. Their practical approach to the issue is refreshing. The introductory section of the chapter provides compelling arguments making a case for considering ethics as an essential aspect of decision making in the marketing process and not as an issue that is isolated from marketing. The authors also share the interesting experience of how all teachers in a Mexican business school have to take an ethics certification course in order to be able to introduce ethical issues in their regular sessions.

The final module, *People Management and Soft Skills*, has the chapters on human resource management, negotiation, community and investor relations, career management, and managing corporate power and politics. A well-researched and easy-to-follow chapter on ethical reflection in teaching HRM is given to us by Silke Bustamante. HRM is one of the disciplines most directly related to ethics, dealing as it does with people within organizations. Issues of hiring and firing, employee rights and duties and contracts, human quality treatment of employees, fairness and justice in organizations, performance evaluation and rewards, talent development, and work–life balance challenges all require ethical reasoning and decision making. Bustamante's chapter, apart from touching on issues like the preceding which relate to employer treatment of employees, also raises issues regarding how employees are trained to behave ethically toward other stakeholders. Perspectives on career studies are contributed by Olusegun Babalola and Ifedapo Adeleye. Beginning from an introductory assumption regarding the applicability of ethics to all of life, the authors go on to make a clear distinction of ethical issues, both on a personal and a structural dimension, in career management, and to give very good examples for teaching. The dual perspective approach adopted by the authors is aimed at ensuring that career progress is undertaken in such a way as to enhance human flourishing.

In the chapter on negotiation, Barney Jordan and David Venter offer practical advice and a list of issues and suggestions to share with students. They suggest a *self-test* approach to motivate students to consider ethics in a negotiation. The examples and scenarios make the subject easily understandable. Managing corporate power and politics is an essential aspect of study in management education. There is no shortage of ethical issues in this course too. Duane Windsor offers readers a thorough coverage of literature on the topic, a teaching strategy, and some educational exercises in order to ensure a principled and responsible application of corporate power and politics. Coming right after this, Edward Quevedo and Judith Weisinger highlight the importance of transparency and clear communication in managing community and investor relations. They also offer an interesting strategy for facilitating discussions on these issues in the classroom. The teaching strategy suggested for this subject is well articulated and meaningful for readers. The ideas on teaching living cases or cases of bad practices also constitute a very useful guide for instructors.

The concluding chapter of the book discusses the future of business schools and their role in promoting sustainable development globally. Jointly contributed by Uchenna Uzo and Emeka Enwere, it looks into the trends shaping the future for the embedding of ethics into management curricula and ends by recommending that business schools should continue to implement a greater humanistic orientation into their systems.

Value of a *Handbook for Faculty*

This book provides unique insights into the experience of seasoned academics regarding embedding business ethics into their teaching of the practice of management. The chapters come from a multidisciplinary array of scholars and show how to embed ethics in the following business disciplines and others similar to them: decision making, finance, MIS, negotiation, operations management, supply chain management, marketing, management accounting, strategy, HRM, career management, and macroeconomics.

The book fits into Area 1, educator guides, of the PRME Collection as a supplementary textbook for the business student (to highlight the ethical dilemmas for all the different managerial functional roles covered in the book) and a handbook for business faculty, and promotes PRME principles 1, 2, and 3 by

1. developing the capabilities of students to be future generators of sustainable value for business and society at large and to work for an inclusive and sustainable global economy;
2. incorporating into academic activities and curricula the values of global social responsibility as portrayed in international initiatives such as the United Nations Global Compact;

3. creating educational frameworks, materials, processes, and environments that enable effective learning experiences for responsible leadership.

With a few exceptions in order to fit into peculiarities of each discipline, each chapter begins with an introduction that incorporates a justification for its inclusion and a description of the discipline. This is followed by a relation of the typical ethical issues—with examples—that come up while teaching and strategies for handling these. Some advice for teachers is then offered. Acknowledging the global dimensions of teaching business education, some developing versus developed country perspectives are offered before the summary and conclusion. This segment may be particularly interesting to business schools that have very diverse student bodies. Finally, exercises and projects are suggested.

It is expected that this book's contribution to embedding ethics in teaching management disciplines will enable ethics being seen "as an inherent dimension of human action and consequently, of economic activity" (Melé, Argandoña, and Sánchez-Runde 2011, 3).

References

Baetz, M.C., and D. Sharp. 2004. "Integrating Ethics Content into the Core Business Curriculum: Do Core Teaching Materials do the Job?" *Journal of Business Ethics* 51, no. 1, pp. 53–62.

Broome, J. 2000. "Why Economics Needs Ethical Theory." Presentation at the Meeting of the British Association for the Advancement of Science, London. http://users.ox.ac.uk/~sfop0060/pdf/Why%20economics%20needs%20ethical%20theory.pdf (accessed October 17, 2014).

Brown, T., J. Sautter, L. Littvay, A. Sautter, and B. Bearnes. 2010. "Ethics and Personality: Empathy and Narcissism as Moderators of Ethical Decision Making in Business Students." *Journal of Education for Business* 85, no. 4, pp. 203–8.

Cant, G., and B.W. Kulik. 2009. "More than Lip Service: The Development and Implementation Plan of an Ethics Decision-Making Framework for an Integrated Undergraduate Business Curriculum." *Journal of Academic Ethics* 7, no. 4, pp. 231–54.

Crossan, M., D. Mazutis, G. Seijts, and J. Gandz. 2013. "Developing Leadership Character in Business Programs." *Academy of Management Learning and Education* 12, no. 2, pp. 285–305.

Dean, K.L., and J.M. Beggs. 2006. "University Professors and Teaching Ethics: Conceptualization and Expectations." *Journal of Management Education* 30, no. 1, pp. 15–45.

Enderle, G. 2011. "Challenges for Business and Economic Ethics in the Next Ten Years." *Business and Professional Ethics Journal* 30, no. 3–4, pp. 231–52.

Enderle, G., and Q. Liu. 2012. "Discerning Ethical Challenges for Marketing in China." *Asian Journal of Business Ethics* 1, no. 2, pp. 143–62.

Goodpaster, K.E. 1991. "Business Ethics and Stakeholder Analysis." *Business Ethics Quarterly* 1, no. 1, pp. 53–73.

Goodpaster, K.E. 2004. "Ethics or Excellence? Conscience as a Check on the Unbalanced Pursuit of Organizational Goals." *Ivey Business Journal* 68, no. 4, pp. 1–8.

Goodpaster, K.E. 2011. "Goods that are Truly Good and Services that Truly Serve: Reflections On 'Caritas in Veritate'." *Journal of Business Ethics* 100, no. 1, pp. 9–16.

Jackson, K.T. 2006. "Breaking Down the Barriers: Bringing Initiatives and Reality into Business Ethics Education." *Journal of Management Education* 30, no. 1, pp. 65–90.

Ki, E.-J., J. Lee, and H.L. Choi. 2012. "Factors Affecting Ethical Practice of Public Relations Professionals within Public Relations Firms." *Asian Journal of Business Ethics* 1, no. 2, pp. 123–41.

McCabe, D.L., K.D. Butterfield, and L.K. Trevino. 2006. "Academic Dishonesty in Graduate Business Programs: Prevalence, Causes, and Proposed Action." *Academy of Management Learning & Education* 5, no. 3, pp. 294–305.

Melé, D., A. Argandoña, and C. Sánchez-Runde. 2011. "Facing the Crisis: Toward a New Humanistic Synthesis for Business." *Journal of Business Ethics* 99, no. 1, pp. 1–4.

Mintz, S. June, 1990. "Ethics in the Management Accounting Curriculum." *Management Accounting* 71, no. 12, pp. 51–54.

Nedelko, Z., and V. Potocan. 2011. "The Role of Personal Values for Managerial Work." *International Journal of Management Cases* 13, no. 4, pp. 121–31.

Rasche, A., D.U. Gilbert, and I. Schedel. 2013. "Cross-Disciplinary Ethics Education in MBA Programs: Rhetoric or Reality?" Academy of Management Learning and Education 12, no. 1, pp. 71–85.

Rivas, I.V., and D.P. Rivas. 2003. "Business as a Vocation: The Business Leadership as a Vocation." Paper presented at the Fifth International Symposium on Catholic Social Thought and Management Education, Bilbao, Spain, July 15–18. http://www.stthomas.edu/cathstudies/cst/conferences/bilbao/papers/PastorizaVelazEng.pdf (accessed June 8, 2014).

Stead, W.E., D.L. Worrel, and J.G. Stead. 1990. "An Integrative Model for Understanding and Managing Ethical Behavior in Business Organizations." *Journal of Business Ethics* 9, no. 3, pp. 233–42.

Waddock, S., and J.M. Lozano. 2013. "Developing More Holistic Management Education: Lessons Learned from Two Programs." *Academy of Management Learning and Education* 12, no. 2, pp. 265–84.

Wishloff, J. 2014. "Business Ethics: Diagnosis and Prescription in Caritas in Veritate and Vocation of the Business Leader." *Solidarity: The Journal of Catholic Social Thought and Secular Ethics* 4, no. 1, pp. 1–32. http://researchonline.nd.edu.au/solidarity/vol4/iss1/8 (accessed June 8, 2014).

MODULE 1
Making Decisions

CHAPTER 2

Teaching Ethics in Business Policy (Strategy) Courses

Michael E. Cafferky

Southern Adventist University

Introduction

This chapter will make the case that the business policy (strategy) course is not only an appropriate place to engage students in discussions of ethical issues, but it is also one of the best places to do this. To explore this topic, the chapter will first review some of the reasons why some scholars might consider ethics not appropriate for a strategy course. Representing this point of view is important when considering the scope of a typical strategy course. Next we will put forward the case that ethics is appropriate for the business strategy course. It demonstrates that ethical values cannot be separated from the strategy formulation and implementation. Last, we will see some of the ways ethics can be approached with strategy students. In this final section, we look at some approaches to teaching that can engage students on ethical issues.

The Discipline of Strategy

The discipline of strategy comprehends the entire firm interacting with its social and legal environment. This is one thing that sets it apart from the traditional functional business disciplines such as accounting and marketing. It is at the level of strategy that we are concerned about putting major assets at risk. Strategic leaders must articulate the broad functional commitments needed to achieve the firm's goals. Strategic commitments tend to have a long-run impact on the mission of the firm. It is strategy that focuses the whole of the enterprise on a few clear objectives.

As Porter (1996) and Markides (1999) say, strategy involves making difficult tradeoff prone choices. Purchasing a certain cluster of assets to make a narrow range of products such as athletic shoes means that the assets are not available to make tablet computers. Making the commitment to supply one geographic region or one market segment with a particular range of products often means that other geographic regions or other market segments are given up or other products are left to other firms to make and sell. The distribution system deemed most effective in serving the firm's target market naturally leads to tradeoffs, since the products and services meant for this segment will not be easily accessible through alternative distribution systems. The distinctive strategic position that the company establishes such that it has a competitive advantage means that there are other strategic positions for competitors to exploit for profit.

More than this, strategy is about managing the *changes* that take place in both the external and internal environment. Strategic commitment this year may be inappropriate three years from now if the environment changes. Assumptions that we make about the marketplace today may be faulty next year. Accordingly, strategic management involves ongoing leadership, planning, managerial control, organizing, and a host of other management functions and processes in a changing environment. The famed strengths-weaknesses-opportunities-threats (SWOT) framework in strategy is not just an exercise to complete once every two or three years that results in a printed report which then sits in a drawer in an office. Rather, it is an ongoing framework to continually manage the dynamics of big commitments and how these are implemented. Paradoxically, strategic management is about managing the long-term intent and assumptions of the firm. Elements of these strategic commitments may in fact be transitory.

Why Some Consider Ethics as Not Important in Strategy

Compared with other courses in the typical business curriculum, the business policy (strategy) course may not seem like a rich setting for integrating ethics into the curriculum. Several reasons can be offered for this.

Business policy is a course that seeks to help the student develop conceptual thinking skills. It is in the strategy course that we encourage students to grow from the functional thinking of accounting, marketing, finance, managerial controls, and other managerial tasks to see the organization as a whole in its larger environment. The decisions that are made at the strategic level are typically broad in scope. They leave behind the usual individual level of analysis and look at the organization as a whole. For some professors, the strategy process may be seen as neither moral nor immoral in itself, but rather as merely amoral.

Operational actions may be more interesting from an ethics point of view. Thus, even when seen as an organizational issue, ethics can be narrowly thought of as essentially and ultimately residing in the realm of individual operational behavior. And if this is so, its connection with strategy will also more likely be limited to the actions of individual managers, perhaps as they work to formulate strategic commitments and plans, but more likely limited to the actions of individuals as they implement the strategic commitments.

A chief focus of the business strategy course is what accounts for variations in performance of the entire firm or of an entire industry in a globally competitive context. But the influences on firm performance are many. In strategy, we are concerned about the drivers to competitive advantage that lie either inside the firm or outside the firm in the marketplace. We tend to think about initial conditions and strategic position with respect to competitors. In this context managers make choices. These choices lead to commitments of particular resources, particular ways to organize operational departments and divisions. Thus, when we consider just the economic dimensions of strategic thinking and strategic commitments, ethics seems to be far away from our considerations. For example, whether or not a firm chooses to strive for low-cost leadership in the market or strengthen its profitability by serving a narrowly focused, highly differentiated niche does not seem to have any direct connection with ethics.

Consider the topic of drivers to strategic performance. Drivers have a structural influence on sustainable profitability when they form the backbone of competitive advantage. A firm that, compared with competitors, has enormous scale economies will have a competitive advantage. This by itself does not seem to indicate the presence of any ethical issues worth considering. The linkages between one set of value-producing activities and another or between the value-producing activities of the firm and that of a strategic supplier are so heavily focused on the economic advantages of the strategic relationship that there hardly seems time to devote to worrying about ethical issues.

Furthermore, to isolate one dimension of possible organizational performance such as ethics and seek to understand its separate contribution to the overall performance of the firm can be a daunting task. Indeed, such an endeavor is filled with problems. Even so, this has not stopped business thinkers like Koehn (2005), Becker (2007), Paine (2000), Sen (1993), and others from trying to assess the impact of ethics on the firm as a whole. As Blowfield and Murray (2008) show, the same challenges exist when considering how to measure the impact of corporate responsibility on the firm. For some actions, it is relatively easy to measure the impact on the operational efficiency of the firm (its expenses). However, there are many other possible business impacts that are more difficult to measure objectively, such as showing the causal link between corporate responsibility and increased revenue, increased stock price, and increased demand or stronger brand.

The view that ethics is not important for a strategy course is summarized in Table 2.1.

Why Ethics Is Important in Strategy

In spite of these considerations, strategy is an important point in the business curriculum when ethics can challenge students to think critically

Table 2.1 Why some consider ethics not important in strategy

Broad scope of issues that comprise the strategy curriculum
Level of analysis is the firm rather than the individual
Operational actions seem more interesting from an ethics point of view
Chief focus of strategy: variation in performance among firms
Amoral view of business
Challenges of measuring the impact of just one influencing factor like ethical behavior on overall firm performance

about what they have learned throughout their degree program. Andrews (1989), Gilbert (1986, 1996), and Freeman, Gilbert, and Hartman (1988) have been leading supporters of integrating ethics in strategy. As Mintzberg and Lampel (1999) have pointed out, a variety of points of view (schools of thought) have characterized the field over the last two generations. The variety of perspectives suggests that strategic thinking and action is not merely a mechanistic economic action isolated from its larger social impact.

The two most dominant theoretical perspectives have been the industrial/organizational (I/O), microeconomics-based theory of the firm and the resource-based theory of the firm. Miles (1993) has considered these dominant perspectives in terms of the ethical implications and concluded that the I/O model emphasizes private gains at the expense of achieving the common good. In contrast, the resource-based view of the firm fairs better on the question of private gains and public good.

Both the I/O perspective and the resource perspective are important. Executives must take both points of view. Thus, this makes a valuable point of discussion for students in the introductory phase of a strategy course. The discussion can be widened to include the exploration of other schools of thought.

Personal and corporate values form the foundation for strategic thinking, action, and business policy formation. Ethical issues that top-level leaders face often result in actions that reinforce corporate cultural values that are seen in day-to-day operational activities. Accordingly, ethics must not be left out of the business policy course.

Competitive forces tend to put pressure on ethical behaviors. Over time, innovations tend to diffuse throughout an industry and even cross industries. Companies in a given industry over time tend to look similar. As a result, competitive advantages tend to converge. Competitive pressures push firms to continually improve. Over time, differences in operational performance decline and, with this decline, economic profits also decrease. Such convergence of competitive advantage and squeezing of performance differences and economic profits may increase competitive pressures in the industry, pressures that may impact the ethical behavior of managers.

One of the first issues to address with students is the relationship between ethical values and strategy. While several scholars have supported the connection between ethical values and strategy, some students may be skeptical that values play any significant role in the formation of strategic commitments. Such students may implicitly accept what De George (2010, 1–5) calls the myth of amoral business. This view holds that business is not concerned with ethics and that the choices that businesses make lie outside ethical concerns. Business is about making choices of what and how to buy and sell goods and services. In this view, to choose to produce and sell one product over another is not an ethical issue.

Following De George and others such as Ginsburg and Miller (1992), Pant and Lachman (1998), Guth and Tagiuri (1965), and Freeman, Gilbert, and Hartman (1988), one can propose to students arguments that counteract the viewpoint of amoral business. However, trying to argue using logic may lose some students who might learn better in the context of narrative. We feel uncomfortable when values are violated, but values are so deeply embedded in our lives that we rarely think explicitly about them. We may not even be able to articulate all the values that influence our choices.

Early calls for awareness of how important values are in strategy came from Guth and Tagiuri (1965) and a generation later by Pant and Lachman (1998). Values are important in strategy formulation for several reasons. Strategic commitments involve the employment of certain assets (and not others), leading workers to embrace the broader social purpose and goals of the organization, organizing workers in a particular way (and not another way) and monitoring strategic performance in particular ways (and not others). When making these choices, unspoken values implicitly drive the desires of the decision makers. To commit strategically means that we act intentionally in a social context with a certain degree of expectations that our actions will have an impact on the marketplace. Purposeful action requires the presence of objectives or goals that focus our expectations and efforts in a particular direction. But the presence of goals is not possible without values.

The implementation of strategic commitments also is inseparable from values. Implementation requires integration and coordination of collective social effort to achieve the overall purpose of an organization. Strategic commitments arise partially because of the nature of the products and services selected. The nature of the external environment to the organization also influences these strategic choices. The personal values of the leaders who must contend with the tradeoffs in their choices is another influence as are the shared values of others inside the organization, the organization's culture. Implementation involves ongoing tactical efforts to drive the value-laden goals through operational activities. Here, specific actions have an impact on people and because of this ethics are inseparable from business operations. We recruit and select new employees, in part, based on how well their values fit the shared values of the organization. The reporting relationships reinforce the values needed for effective performance. The leadership activities and performance motivation tactics managers use all are guided by values. The managerial control systems are driven by values.

Accordingly, when the company makes commitments to a larger environment, it establishes moral obligations to the community it serves. The community it serves will be concerned with the actions that the organization takes. One can even argue that the larger purpose of the business, which is comprehended in the firm's strategic commitments, implies awareness of fundamental, generally accepted moral principles (GAMPs).

Gert (1999, 2004) has put forward a list of what we call here GAMPs that he identifies with common morality. Two basic principles are at the root of all others and these ground all moral principles in the context of community relationships: Do not harm others and do not deprive others of their freedom. All other GAMPs (keep promises, do not cheat, do not deceive, etc.) are derivatives. In contrast to Gert, Beauchamp (2003) has a slightly different way of describing common morality, which he refers to as universally admired traits of character or virtues regardless of culture. Although Beauchamp does not describe primary and secondary virtues in his model, the root virtues seem to be integrity and faithfulness.

Other scholars have identified minimum moral standards of business behaviors in an economic system. For example, Quinn and Jones (1995) suggest four fundamental principles are followed by businesses in efficient markets: honor agreements, tell the truth, respect the autonomy of others, and avoid doing harm to others. Hosmer (2008, 33) sees being truthful and honoring contracts as the ethical basis of the free market. Hare (1998, 49) sees "honesty, truthfulness, and fair dealing" as the minimum standards.

Using another approach to identif generally accepted moral principles by surveying various organizations, Schwartz (2005) identified six principles common in many cultures: trustworthiness, respect, responsibility, fairness, caring, and citizenship. The organizations Schwartz surveyed included the United Nations Global Compact (1999), the Caux Round Table Principles for Business (1994), and the Interfaith Declaration Report (1993) produced by a group of religious organizations.

These various approaches to GAMP are shown in Table 2.2.

This table can be discussed with students using questions such as the following:

- What principles might be added to this table?
- To what degree are GAMPs applicable in developing countries?

The preceding views that promote the importance of bringing ethics into the strategy curriculum are summarized in Table 2.3.

Ethical Issues in Global Strategy

A variety of strategic ethical issues emerge when we consider business strategy in a global context. These are discussed by several scholars including Donaldson (1996), Asgary and Mitschow (2002), and Audi (2009). For example, the following are typical ethical issues encountered:

- Double standards
- Corruption
- Bribery
- Hardball competition (Barach 1985; Stalk 2006; Stalk and Lachenauer 2004)
- Opportunistic exploitation (Besanko et al. 2010; Das and Rahman 2010)
- Impact on the environment and sustainable development
- Organizational design that impacts ethical decision making
- Child labor and working conditions
- Product dumping

Table 2.2 Generally accepted moral principles: a comparison

Gert (2004)	Beauchamp (2003)	Quinn and Jones (1995)	Schwartz (2005)	Hosmer (1994)	Hare (1998)
Keep promises Do not deceive Do your duty Obey the law Do not kill, cause pain, or disable Do not cheat Do not deprive of freedom or pleasure	Trustworthiness Fidelity Truthfulness Nonmalevolence Conscientiousness Honesty Integrity Gratitude	Honor agreements Tell the truth Respect autonomy Do no harm	Trustworthiness Respect Caring Fairness Responsibility Citizenship	Honor contracts Truthfulness	Truthfulness Fair dealing Honesty

Table 2.3 Why ethics is important in strategy

Different strategy *Schools of Thought* reveals that strategy is not merely economic isolated from its larger social context.
The two dominant perspectives may influence the ethics of an organization differently.
Personal and corporate values form the foundation for all strategic thinking and action.
Competitive pressures may influence the ethics of actions inherent in the strategic commitments.
The myth of amoral business.
Strategic commitments are inseparable from values.
Presence of generally accepted moral principles.

- Counterfeit goods, brand piracy, patent infringement
- Competitor intelligence gathering (Paine 1991)
- Relationship between business and government

All of these contemporary issues provide rich settings in which to engage with students on the ethical issues surrounding strategic planning and implementation. Classroom debates on contemporary examples of these issues enliven active learning.

Developed Versus Developing Country Perspectives

Eager to stimulate additional demand for their products or lower-cost resources for products, leaders of many firms make strategic commitments to expand business operations internationally. Expansion can increase economies of scale while leveraging the expertise, resources, and comparative advantages of particular regions. In terms of the issues presented in this chapter, these strategic commitments require doing business in locations where ethical standards may appear different from their home country. Such differences can be seen when comparing how business is conducted in developing countries versus in developed countries.

The constraints of ethical, social, and legal systems vary from country to country as do the established customs and *conventions*, an integrated cluster of shared values that are commonly accepted in the market, organized labor groups, consumer groups, media groups, environmental groups, and many other stakeholders. Restraints tend to be fewer in developing countries. One of the biggest noticeable differences is the comparative lack of background or support institutions to control and guide the development and operation of business, something vital to strategic success. This lack in developing countries creates an opportunity for abuses. This makes the task of understanding the ethical challenges more difficult yet not less important.

Some of the ethical issues that make fruitful classroom discussions with strategy students include the following:

- *Double standards*: Some multinational corporations appear to adopt a double standard, doing in less developed, developing countries what would be regarded as morally wrong if done in their home country. Some practices that are legal in one country and are not considered to be unethical. Should the multinational corporation be bound by the prevailing morality of their home country? Should they follow the practices of the host country? Or, are there special ethical standards that apply when business is conducted across national boundaries? If so, what are these standards?
- *Absolutism versus relativism*: Although some bedrock concepts of right and wrong exist among people everywhere, many variations occur due to cultural, historical, political, and economic factors. Accordingly, a related debate is over the differences in moral standards when we compare one country with another. As a result, two major (extreme) points of view have developed. Absolutism considers that business ought to be conducted in the same way the world over: "When in Rome, do as you would do at home." In contrast, relativism considers that the only guide for business conduct is what is legally and morally acceptable in any given country where the firm operates: "When in Rome, do as the Romans do." Some practices may be justified where local conditions

require that corporations engage in them as a condition of doing business. "We don't agree with the Romans, but find it necessary to do things their way." Often, this argument of *necessity* is used to explain a business action is *required* when what is meant is simply that it is the most profitable way of doing business.

- *Differences in values*: Many of the ethical issues that businesses face can be seen through the lens of cultural values that differ from country to country. For example, ethical issues are interpreted differently by persons who are from an individualistic culture when compared with persons from a collectivist culture. In some countries, the ethical rules are considered to apply universally to all persons regardless of social status or position. In other countries, social rules are more flexible in their application depending on social status (see Hampden-Turner and Trompenaars 2000; House et al. 2004; Jeager and Kanungo 1990; Triandis et al. 1988).

- *Access to and distribution of resources*: Strategic commitments in developing countries sometimes involve the structure of relationships for access and control of resources. The strategic commitment of a firm in one country will lead to gaining access to a resource such as oil or natural gas underground or undersea. This often requires partnering with a local company. Here relationships with the regional or national government are important. But these relationships raise ethical issues about the country's citizens getting access to natural resources and access to the revenue that is generated from the extraction and sale of the resources.

- *Depletion of natural resources and sustainable development*: Access to and control over natural resources raises a related issue of depletion of resource. Many resources are not available in an endless supply. As the scarcity of resources becomes more of a problem, the ethical issues arise over developing these resources in ways that can be sustainable and that will minimize the impact on the environment.

Advice for Instructors Engaging Strategy Students on Ethical Issues

The business policy course is often the cap-stone course that engages the student to consider both theory and practice and case studies of actual companies and the issues they faced. Even when there are opportunities to explore ethical issues, most business strategy textbooks contain very little information about the ethics of strategy. Indeed, there is a difficult tradeoff to manage when teaching a business policy course: If the instructor devotes time to challenging students to consider ethical issues, time must be given up somewhere else in the course, time that could be spent exploring in more depth strategy principles and practice, discussing the results of simulations, or in case study discussions.

Accordingly, one way to engage students in this issue is to begin by providing a short case study of a company and its strategy. Review the cluster of strategic commitments and then discuss with the students:

- Besides earning an economic profit, what seems to be the purpose of the organization in its larger context? What is the firm trying to do for society?
- Given the strategic commitments the firm has made, what has the firm chosen not to do? In other words, what tradeoffs must be sustained if the strategic commitments are pursued over time?
- To what degree do the tradeoffs suggest possible values that underlie the choices made by top-level leaders?
- To what degree does the overall purpose of the firm suggest, or directly reveal, regarding what the leaders want to accomplish?
- In what way can we ever say that the goal that a person sets for an organization is separate from the values held by that person (or team)?
- How might strategic commitments create pressures on the operational choices that managers make?
- What essential values are at the foundation of the strategic commitments made by the firm?

Suggested Exercises and Projects

The following examples represent additional approaches to integrating ethics into a business strategy course.

A "Life-Cycle Case Study" to Teach Socially Responsible Sustainability

DesJardins and Deidrich (2003) describe how they structure a *life-cycle case study* for business ethics students and that focuses on learning social responsibility sustainability. A life-cycle case study is a study of a product or commodity learning how the product has economic, ethical, and ecological consequences throughout its life cycle. They suggest three criteria that should be used to judge models of corporate social responsibility. First, businesses need to create a sustainable economic return. Second, businesses ought to arrange their activities in a way that supports the ability of the earth to sustain life for the long run. Third, businesses should be conducted in ways that address the minimum demands of social justice (35).

The life cycle of a product shows not only the economic and ecological impact of the product. It also demonstrates that strategic commitments come with tradeoffs not only for the firm but also for society. Strategic commitments have direct implications for how society is called upon by the firm to help manage the full impact of the product on society. It is sometimes in the tradeoffs that we can see the moral implications of strategic choices.

To help students see how the impacts result from strategic commitments, give them an assignment to conduct their own research regarding the life cycle of a common product that they experience in their own life. Students are expected to study elements of the company business models that generate the economic returns from the product. They must also study the impact of the product on the larger biosphere environment over its life cycle. Finally, students study the ways in which the companies that produce the product conduct their business in terms of social justice. Students find information in print;

they interview managers of companies to learn as much as they can from current market players. This encourages students to focus on local practices and small issues.

Students are given time for researching and writing their original case study. After writing their case study, students present it to other students for discussion. DesJardins and Deidrich offer guidelines to instructors on how to guide students in their inquiry (39). The connection with local companies gives opportunities for field trips.

When the topic of corporate social responsibility comes up during the course, students can present their written case studies for discussion. One or more class periods can be devoted to the discussion of these cases.

Red Light, Green Light Discussions

Case studies are typically used in a strategy course to engage students with the issues that the firm as a whole is facing. One way to enhance the traditional case study classroom discussion is to use what has been called the red light, green light discussion.

Reginald Litz (2003) describes the teaching technique called red light, green light. He assumes that the discussion of issues offers learning benefits. However, when students are not prepared for discussion and for this or other reasons do not participate (free riders), they do not get the benefits from discussions that they might otherwise gain.

Accordingly, Litz presents a structured way to encourage students to prepare for and engage in discussions that foster learning. He offers a five-step process:

- Students prepare a one-page preclass essay. This involves reading a case study (that is given to all students) and assigned supplemental readings. Students then prepare a one-page essay on one of the two or three case study questions given by the instructor. Students are required to deliver this short essay at least 90 minutes before class period in which they are scheduled to be discussed.

- Students attend a 15- to 20-minute preclass small group meeting before the class session. The purpose of this meeting is to facilitate the sharing of responses to the case study. This discussion primes students for the discussion that will take place in the classroom. Students also share insights they gain from the supplemental readings.
- Red, yellow, and green cards: At the beginning of the semester the instructor hands out three colored name cards for students to use during class discussions. During class discussions, the student can display a red card if the student wishes not to be called on by the instructor. The yellow card is shown if the student welcomes non-in-depth questions by the instructor. The green card indicates that the student welcomes any type of question.
- Students participate in the classroom discussion. The professor reads from the short essays (see details on this in the Litz article).
- Students write a one-page integrative postclass essay. This postclass assignment is designed to help them reflect on what they have heard during discussions.

Use Stories in Moral Development

The concept of case study can be seen in its larger context of narrative. Stories offer the settings in which moral principles can be discussed. Students can tell stories and they can read and discuss stories where the moral dimensions are either explicit or implicit. Accordingly, the strategy instructor who wishes to engage students in a dialog regarding the ethics of strategy formulation or implementation will encourage the reading, writing, and telling of stories.

Paul Vitz (1990) offers an overview of the psychological theories supporting the idea that narrative is useful for encouraging moral development. In general, this corresponds with the recommendations by Coate and Mitschow (2002). Vitz surveys the difference between propositional thinking and narrative thinking, semantic memory and episodic memory, abstract and concrete, right brain and left brain, and analog cognition and digital cognition. He asserts that moral development is rooted in our empathy and perception in interpersonal relationships.

Moral choices, he claims, present themselves to humans in terms of the character and context of the narratives of our lives. From the work of Robert Coles, Vitz draws an educational hypothesis: Introduce people to "morally challenging narratives" (1990, 716) and then ask them to reflect on these. Vitz says, "One may view narratives as the laboratory of moral life... Of course, this experience should not be left without moral reflection, guided by a teacher and others ... just as music is far more than music theory and football is more than books on it, so the moral life is far more than abstract dilemmas and propositions" (718). "All this is not to say that moral education should consist exclusively of narratives..." (718). The use of "reasoned reflection on the moral significance of stories" is also important. Using reason to reflect on narratives, students can arrive at generalizations and fundamental principles of morality. It is the integration of different types of thinking where "the highest forms of moral knowledge are developed" (718). Vitz's recommendation is consistent with what Kenneth Andrews wrote in 1989: "Great literature can be a self-evident source of ethical instruction, for it informs the mind and heart together about the complexities of moral choice. Emotionally engaged with fictional or historical characters who must choose ... we expand our own moral imaginations as well" (100).

Ultimately, it can be argued, the strategic commitments that a firm makes are a narrative creating process. As the firm's leaders first choose strategic directions and then implement these operationally, the narrative of this emerges in the competitive market. For example, if a firm chooses to be a low-cost leader in its market, a particular narrative is created. If, on the other hand, the firm chooses to differentiate itself from competitors on one or more attributes, this creates a different narrative. Stories about corporations and their strategic choices (often considered in the form of case studies in business school) offer students the setting to explore economic context, and operational resources, as well as the moral dimensions that might be slightly different from one type of strategy to another or one type of firm to another.

Stories can be used in the teaching–learning process in two different ways: (a) having students read and reflect on stories that others have written and (b) having students write their own stories and reflect on what they write.

References

Andrews, K.R. 1989. "Ethics in Practice." *Harvard Business Review* 67, no. 5, pp. 99–104.

Asgary, N., and M.C. Mitschow. 2002. "Toward a Model for International Business Ethics." *Journal of Business Ethics* 36, no.3, pp. 239–46.

Audi, R. 2009. "International Trade and Cross-cultural Standards." In *Business Ethics and Ethical Business*, 109–28. New York: Oxford University Press.

Barach, J.A. 1985 "The Ethics of Hardball." *California Management Review* 27, no. 2, pp. 132–9.

Beauchamp, T.L. 2003. "A Defense of the Common Morality." *Kennedy Institute of Ethics Journal* 13, no. 3, pp. 260–1.

Becker, G. 2007. "The Competitive Edge of Moral Leadership." *International Management Review* 3, no. 1, pp. 50–71.

Besanko, D., D. Dranove, M. Shanley, and S. Schaefer. 2010. *Economics of Strategy*. 5th ed. Hoboken, NJ: John Wiley & Sons.

Blowfield, M. and Murray, A. 2008. *Corporate Responsibility: A Critical Introduction*. New York: Oxford University Press.

Coate, C.J., and M.C. Mitschow. 2002. "Business Ethics, Business Practices, and the Power of the Parable." *Teaching Business Ethics* 6, no. 1, pp. 127–35.

CRT (Caux Round Table). 1994. *Caux Round Table Principles for Business*. The Hague, Netherlands: CRT.

Das, T.K., and N. Rahman. 2010. "Determinants of Partner Opportunism in Strategic Alliances: A Conceptual Framework." *Journal of Business Psychology* 25, pp. 55–74.

De George, R. T. 2010. *Business Ethics*. 7th ed. Upper Saddle River, NJ: Pearson Prentice Hall.

DesJardins, J.R., and E. Diedrich. 2003. "Learning What It Really Costs: Teaching Business Ethics with Life-cycle Case Studies." *Journal of Business Ethics* 48, no. 1, pp. 33–42.

Donaldson, T. 1996. "Values in Tension: Ethics Away from Home." *Harvard Business Review* 74, no. 5, pp. 48–62.

Freeman, R.E., D.R. Gilbert, Jr., and E. Hartman. 1988. "Values and the Foundations of Strategic Management." *Journal of Business Ethics* 7, no. 11, pp. 821–34.

Gert, B. 1999. "Common Morality and Computing." *Ethics and Information Technology* 1, no. 1, pp. 53, 58–64.

Gert, B. 2004. *Common Morality: Deciding What to Do.* New York: Oxford University Press.

Gilbert, D.R., Jr. 1986. "Corporate Strategy and Ethics." *Journal of Business Ethics* 5, pp. 137–50.

Gilbert, D.R., Jr. 1996. *Ethics through Corporate Strategy.* New York: Oxford University Press.

Ginsburg, L., and N. Miller. 1992. "Value-driven Management." *Business Horizons* 35, no. 3, pp. 23–27.

Guth, W.D., and R. Tagiuri. 1965. "Personal Values and Corporate Strategy." *Harvard Business Review* 43, no. 5, pp. 123–32.

Hampden-Turner, C.M., and F. Trompenaars. 2000. *Building Cross-cultural Competence: How to Create Wealth from Conflicting Values.* New Haven, CT: Yale University Press.

Hare, R.M. 1998. "One Philosopher's Approach to Business Ethics." In *Business Ethics: Perspectives on the Practice of Theory*, eds. C. Cowton and R. Crisp. New York: Oxford University Press.

Hosmer, L.T. 1994. "Strategic Planning as if Ethics Mattered." *Strategic Management Journal* 15, pp. 17–34.

Hosmer, L.T. 2008. *The Ethics of Management.* 6th ed. New York: McGraw-Hill Irwin.

House, R.J., P.J. Hanges, M. Javidan., P.W. Dorfman, and V. Gupta. 2004. *Culture, Leadership, and Organizations: The GLOBE Study of 62 Societies.* Thousand Oaks, CA: Sage Publications.

Interfaith Declaration. 1993. *Interfaith Declaration: A Code of Ethics on International Business for Christians, Muslims and Jews.* http://institute.jesdialogue.org/fileadmin/bizcourse/INTERFAITHDECLARATION.pdf.

Jeager, A.M., and R.N. Kanungo. 1990. *Management in Developing Countries.* New York: Routledge.

Koehn, D. 2005. "Integrity as a Business Asset." *Journal of Business Ethics* 58, pp. 125–36.

Litz, R.D.A. 2003. "Red Light, Green Light and Other Ideas for Class Participation-intensive Courses: Method and Implications for Business Ethics Education." *Teaching Business Ethics* 7, no. 4, pp. 365–78.

Markides, C.C. 1999. "A Dynamic View of Strategy." *Sloan Management Review* 40, no. 3, pp. 55–63.

Miles, G. 1993. "In Search of Ethical Profits: Insights from Strategic Management." *Journal of Business Ethics* 12, no. 3, pp. 219–25.
Mintzberg, H., and J. Lampel. 1999. "Reflecting on the Strategy Process." *Sloan Management Review* 40, no. 3, pp. 21–30.
Paine, L.S. 1991. "Corporate Policy and the Ethics of Competitor Intelligence Gathering." *Journal of Business Ethics* 10, no. 6, pp. 423–36.
Paine, L.S. 2000. "Does Ethics Pay?" *Business Ethics Quarterly* 10, no. 1, pp. 319–30.
Pant, P.N., and R. Lachman. 1998. "Value Incongruity and Strategic Choice." *Journal of Management Studies* 35, no. 2, pp. 195–212.
Porter, M.E. 1996. "What is Strategy?" *Harvard Business Review* 74, no. 6, pp. 61–78.
Quinn, D., and T. Jones. 1995. "An Agent Morality View of Business Policy." *Academy of Management Review* 20, no. 1, pp. 22–42.
Schwartz, M.S. 2005. "Universal Moral Values for Corporate Codes of Ethics." *Journal of Business Ethics* 59, no. 1–2, pp. 27–44.
Sen, A. 1993 "Does Business Ethics Make Economic Sense?" *Business Ethics Quarterly* 3, no. 1, pp. 45–54.
Stalk, G., Jr. 2006. "Curveball Strategies to Fool the Competition." *Harvard Business Review* 84, no. 9, pp. 114–22.
Stalk, G., Jr., and R. Lachenauer. 2004. "Hard Ball: Five Killer Strategies for Trouncing the Competition." *Harvard Business Review* 82, no. 4, pp. 62–71.
Triandis, H.C., R. Bontempo, M.J. Villareal, M. Asai, and N. Lucca. 1988. "Individualism and Collectivism: Cross-cultural Perspectives on Self-Ingroup Relationships." *Journal of Personality and Social Psychology* 54, no. 2, pp. 323–38.
United Nations. 1999. *United Nations Global Compact.* https://www.unglobalcompact.org/
Vitz, P.C. 1990. "The Use of Stories in Moral Development." *American Psychologist* 45, no. 6, pp. 709–20.

Further Reading

Akers, J.F. 1989. "Ethics and Competitiveness: Putting First Things First." *MIT Sloan Management Review* 39, no. 2, pp. 69–71.
Bowman, E.H. 1975. "A Strategic Posture toward Corporate Social Responsibility." *California Management Review* 18, no. 2, pp. 49–58.
Carlson, P., and M.S. Blodgett. 1997. "International Ethics Standards for Business: NAFTA, CAUX Principles and Corporate Codes of Ethics." *Review of Business* 18, no. 3, pp. 20–23.
Davis, K. 1973. "The Case for and against Business Assumption of Social Responsibilities." *Academy of Management Journal* 16, no. 2, pp. 312–22.

Donaldson, T. 1989. *The Ethics of International Business.* New York: Oxford University Press.

Donaldson, T., and T.W. Dunfee. 1999. *Ties that Bind.* Boston, MA: Harvard Business School Press.

Gökmen, A., and A.T. Öztürk. 2012. "Issues of Business Ethics in Domestic and International Businesses: A Critical Study." *International Journal of Business Administration* 3, no. 5, pp. 82–88.

Hurn, B.J. 2008. "Ethics in International Business." *Industrial and Commercial Training* 40, no. 7, pp. 347–54.

Key, S., and S.J. Popkin. 1998. "Integrating Ethics into the Strategic Management Process: Doing Well By Doing Good." *Management Decision* 36, no. 5, pp. 331–38.

Martin, R.L. 2002. "The Virtue Matrix: Calculating the Return on Corporate Responsibility." *Harvard Business Review* 80, no 3, pp. 68–75.

Moon, C.J., and P. Woolliams. 2000. "Managing Cross Cultural Business Ethics." *Journal of Business Ethics* 27, no.1–2, pp. 105–15.

Neiman, P. 2013. "A Social Contract for International Business Ethics." *Journal of Business Ethics* 114, pp. 75–90.

O'Brien, J.C. 1992. "The Urgent Need for a Consensus on Moral Values." *International Journal of Social Economics* 19, no. 3–5, pp. 171–86.

Parnell, J.A., and D.L. Lester. 2003. "Towards a Philosophy of Strategy: Reassessing Five Critical Dilemmas in Strategy Formulation and Change." *Strategic Change* 12, no. 6, pp. 291–303.

Pedigo, K., and V. Marshall. 2004. "International Ethical Dilemmas Confronting Australian Managers." *Journal of European Industrial Training* 28, no. 2–4, pp. 183–98.

Peng, M.W. 2006. "Emphasizing Institutions, Cultures and Ethics." In *Global Strategy*, 106–44. Mason, OH: South-Western.

Porter, M.E. 1981. "The Contributions of Industrial Organization to Strategic Management." *Academy of Management Review* 6, no. 4, pp. 609–20.

Porter, M.E. 1991. "Towards a Dynamic Theory of Strategy." *Strategic Management Journal* 12, pp. 95–117.

Porter, M.E., and M.R. Kramer. 2006. "Strategy and Society: The Link between Competitive Advantage and Corporate Social Responsibility." *Harvard Business Review* 84, no. 12, pp. 78–92.

Reeves, M.F. 1990. "An Application of Bloom's Taxonomy to the Teaching of Business Ethics." *Journal of Business Ethics* 9, no. 7, pp. 609–16.

Robin, D.P., and E. Reidenbach. 1990. "Balancing Corporate Profits and Ethics: A Matrix Approach." *Business* 40, no. 4, pp. 11–15.

Sachdeva, S., P. Singh, and D. Medin. 2011. "Culture and the Quest for Universal Principles in Moral Reasoning." *International Journal of Psychology* 46, no. 3, pp. 161–76.

Singer, A.E. 2007. *Integrating Ethics with Strategy*. London: World Scientific Publishing.

Spence, L.J., A.M. Coles, and L. Harris. 2001. "The Forgotten Stakeholder? Ethics and Social Responsibility in Relation to Competitors." *Business and Society Review* 106, no. 4, pp. 331–52.

Vancil, R.F. 1976. "Strategy Formulation in Complex Organizations." *Sloan Management Review* 17, pp. 1–18.

Weaver, G.R. 2001. "Ethics Programs in Global Businesses: Culture's Role in Managing Ethics." *Journal of Business Ethics* 30, no. 1, pp. 3–15.

CHAPTER 3

Ethical Foundations for Organizational Decision Making at the Operational and Strategic Levels

Thomas G. Pittz and Melissa Cast

New Mexico State University

Introduction

The field of business ethics is routinely bifurcated along two lines—normative ethics, which guides the behavior of individuals, and descriptive ethics, which is concerned with explicating and predicting the behavior of individuals (O'Fallon and Butterfield 2005). Both aspects are important but this review utilizes normative ethics in order to provide a framework for effective teaching of the discipline.

The objective of teaching a course in ethics is to equip the student with the ability to recognize and address ethical questions, and to do so with intelligence and sensitivity to a range of personal, social, and professional considerations. In order to achieve this objective, the teacher must explore the philosophical constitution of morality and ethics, make an appeal to personal conscience, and address the management of conflicts of values in decision making. Of particular concern is the manner in which personal convictions and institutional arrangements exert ethical discipline on managers within organizations.

The reputation of business students as less ethically inclined than their peers is now received wisdom, thanks to well-publicized articles focusing on the propensity of business students to cheat (McCabe, Butterfield, and Trevino 2006) and elevate their own self-interests (Brown et al. 2010). Scholars have offered varying assessments of this problem, simultaneously faulting business schools and broader society. There are those who support the current business ethics curriculum but suggest that it be expanded to include organizational context. Otherwise, our ethically trained students are punished for applying their knowledge of a very personal, emotionally charged topic like ethics in a *real-world* environment (Moberg 2006). Others place blame squarely on the shoulders of academia, arguing that business schools are fundamentally flawed. These scholars point to a curriculum that empowers the organization as an artificially created unit of being, the care and success of which is entrusted to our students. Business students, therefore, are instructed to make the organization successful at any cost; a duty that leads to their abandonment of basic ethical tenets (Giacalone and Thompson 2006).

Along a similar vein, the arbiter of ethics in business schools is mostly silent on this issue. The gold standard of business schools, the Association to Advance Collegiate Schools of Business (AACSB), does not mandate the manner in which ethical guidance is provided (Romero 2008). Similar to the confusion over ethical perspectives themselves, this lack of advisement leads business schools to disseminate information regarding ethics in ways best befitting their curricula: seminars, dedicated courses within the business school itself, cross-disciplinary integrated courses, and so forth. (Romero 2008). Recently, the United Nations' Principles for Responsible Management Education (PRME) has sought to impact business school education by promoting the importance of three UN Global Compact topics—human rights, labor, environmental responsibility, and a general view toward anticorruption. While the initiative has partnered with the AACSB to encourage business schools to raise awareness of these issues, the accompanying principles of PRME remain mere recommendations (Alcaraz and Thiruvattal 2010).

From an educator's standpoint, perhaps the most concerning view is one that suggests that students enter business schools as inherently *broken* individuals. This argument is centered on students' predisposition to a materialistic, uncaring world that mocks those who do practice a personal ethic. Termed the "stigmatization of goodness," this phenomenon leads students into our care not with an inherent moral compass to be developed, but with a belief that those with such a compass are bad for the organization's bottom line (Giacalone and Promislo 2013). From this view, the educator's responsibility is to attempt to teach an ethic of care to students, emphasizing a world of "interconnectedness, caring, and shared interests" (Giacalone and Promislo 2013).

Recent qualitative research focusing solely on business undergraduates, however, found that such students are not *morally bankrupt*. In fact, business students are readily seeking guidance from university influences to assist them in making ethical decisions (Hanson and Moore 2013). This supports prior work suggesting that ethics is a tenet of a professional business education and that business schools should be wary of eliminating *soft* skills like ethical decision making from curricula (Trank and Rynes 2003).

Heartened by the suggestion that students are seeking guidance and relying upon our own ethic of answerability as instructors (Bakhtin 1993) as well as recent work suggesting the importance of ethics to decision making (McVea and Freeman 2005), this chapter seeks to establish a framework for ethical organizational decision making. We draw from philosophical works in the area of ethics and from some of the foundational works within operational and strategic decision making to develop and then apply this framework to a discussion of contemporary scholarly sources and illuminate relevant examples of ethical decision-making challenges. Our goal is to supply both the manager of today's complex organization and the teacher of an interested student with an ethical framework by which to guide the decision-making process.

Ethical Choice

First, let us begin by offering a basic definition for an ethical decision. In accordance with Jones (1991, 367), an ethical decision is one which is "both legal and morally acceptable to the larger community" while an unethical decision is one which is "either illegal or morally unacceptable to the larger community."

What then is an ethically *appropriate* decision? In classical terms, the answer to this question would reside within an ethical schema that described a good life (Annas 1992). From Socrates to Cynicism, from Aristotle to Epicureanism, from Plato to Stoicism, ancient philosophical schools were concerned with the vital questions of how to live a good life and how to achieve happiness by pointing out what the appropriate actions were.

Modern moral theories, conversely, deal primarily with the questions of *how one should act* or *what one should do*. These theories tend to be situation-specific and rather subjective in nature, lacking the strong commitments of earlier virtue ethics. Studies of normative ethics and ethical action encompass Kantian deontology, utilitarianism, and pragmatic and postmodern ethics and have taken on application in particular fields (e.g., biology, business, military, politics, etc.) and moral philosophy.

Entire volumes have been written demonstrating the difference between ethical schools of thought and between ancient versus modern ethical legacies. For our purposes, however, we are interested more in the synthesis of ethical thought than in a parsing out of distinctions. Scholars have shown us that both the question of *how to live a good life* and *how one should act* are inextricably intertwined and a complete ethical theory will always be concerned with both issues. Thus, in order to develop a framework for ethical decision making at both operational and strategic levels, we will lean on both classic and modern thought. As decision making is, by its nature, a situation-specific activity (Trevino 1986), an ethical process can be incorporated within it.

Organizational Decision Making: A Description of the Discipline

During the last half of the twentieth century, scholars began to re-examine the role of decision making in economic theory. Herbert Simon acknowledged "economic science has focused on just one aspect of a man's character, his reason, and particularly on the application of that reason to the problems of allocation in the face of scarcity" (Simon 1979, 494). From this recognition came a variety of alternative organizational decision-making theories that did not operate in accordance with traditional economic theory such as politics and power, bounded rationality, and garbage can theory (Eisenhardt and Zbaracki 1992).

Once empirical findings began to question the validity of the traditional economic model, the field of organizational decision making began to swing on a pendulum between bounded rationality and the purely rational process. A synthesis of the empirical work in the field confirms that organizations are primarily political systems in which the strategic decision makers have limited cognitive capability and frequently conflicting goals. According to Eisenhardt and Zbaracki (1992, 35), "Strategic decision making is best described by an interweaving of both boundedly rational and political processes."

The considerations of bounded rationality and power and politics within an organization create space for a framework of ethical decision making that did not exist in the purely rational, economic model. This is especially true when we also consider the volatility and pace of change within the modern organization. In an important work in 1989, Fredrickson and Iaquinto demonstrated the impact of environmental dynamism on the appropriateness of decision-making methodologies. They found that rational, comprehensive decision-making techniques that could be successful in a stable organizational environment with well-defined work roles often fail when applied to a more autonomous and self-directed workforce in an organization that resides in a relatively unstable industrial environment.

Building on these findings, it is evident that a codified framework of ethical guideposts marking areas beyond strictly those of legal consequence may be perfectly valid within the stable organization; however, it may demonstrate significant failings in more dynamic organizations and, in particular, entrepreneurial ventures. To be successful, the application of ethics to operational and strategic decision making ought to be malleable and consider organizational particularities in a variety of contexts intermingled with the impact of personal convictions.

Framework for Ethical Organizational Decision Making

First and foremost, a framework for ethical strategic decision making ought to emphasize its process nature. Strategic decisions have a temporal aspect (they often must be made rather quickly), occur with relative frequency, and often do not take on the appearance of a fundamental ethical truth (a categorical imperative). Furthermore and consistent with Trevino (1986), ethical decisions inherently involve interactions between the situation itself and the person making the decision. Thus, to be successful in these circumstances, the ethical framework needs to be pragmatic, reflective, nimble, and iterative.

The framework for ethical organizational decision making proposed in this chapter consists of five process steps:

1. Recognition and awareness

    (a) Could this decision be damaging to someone or some group?
    (b) Is this decision about more than what is legal or most efficient?

2. Fact-finding

    (a) Do we have all of the facts?
    (b) What individuals or groups have a stake in the outcome?
    (c) Have all of the pertinent stakeholders been consulted?
    (d) Have we considered all options and attempted creative solutions?

3. Evaluating ethical approaches

    (a) Which option will produce the most good and do the least harm (utilitarian approach)?
    (b) Which option best represents the rights of all stakeholders (rights approach)?
    (c) Which option treats people equally (justice approach)?
    (d) Which option best serves the community as whole, not just certain members (common good approach)?
    (e) Which option leads me to act in accordance with the kind of person I want to be (virtue approach)?
    (f) Other ethical approaches exist but it is useful to limit the conversation to the aforementioned since they represent the most commonly used approaches within organizational decision making.

4. Testing the decision

    (a) Which approach best fits the strategic decision?
    (b) If the decision was *shown the light of day* to people we respect, would they agree with our decision and our process?

5. Reflecting on the outcome

    (a) How can the decision be implemented in a manner that is sensitive to the concerns of all of the stakeholders?
    (b) How did the decision turn out and what did we learn from it?

Typical Ethical Concerns in Organizational Decision Making

Ethical concerns in organizational decision making are many and varied. They encompass the full spectrum of business activities from accounting (do we recognize the revenue from a preorder in the current period when our business is at stake due to investor requirements?), to human resources (do we compromise our ethical standards in order to bring in an employee who fits a hard-to-fill organizational need?), to marketing (our product is not quite ready but once orders come in, we will have the money to complete it—do we say that it is ready to go?), to operations (who owns the ideas that are conceived of while on or not on the company's payroll?).

Strategy for Teaching

Considering the fast pace of the modern business world and the myriad ethical choices facing today's leaders, teaching ethical decision making is best achieved through creating ethical awareness, developing ethical critical thinking skills, and providing students and managers with an ethical decision-making framework that is sufficiently malleable to be applicable to wide-ranging ethical dilemmas.

The optimal teaching approach is a three-step process. First, it is important to engage students and managers with ethical case studies in order to challenge and expose gaps in current ethical thinking. The second step is to produce the ethical framework discussed in this chapter as a heuristic for future operational and strategic decision making. Finally, step three is to reintroduce the case study format accompanied by the ethical decision-making framework to demonstrate its effectiveness and encourage its use. This will help to ossify the consistent use of the methodology in the minds of students and managers.

Advice for Teachers

Contemporary philosophical pedagogy contains an unfortunate expectation that teachers will present a variety of moral theories and potential applications neutrally, without advocating for a particular point of view. Instead, we encourage teachers to choose which theories they favored and how they could be applied in particular cases, either drawn from literature, film, biography, or even their own or their students' lives. While we are not suggesting that teachers present their view as the privileged view to the exclusion of any other, we are suggesting that teachers acknowledge that they are members of society and, as such, cannot help but have feelings and thoughts about ethical situations. This may actually make those students concerned with sharing their thoughts more comfortable, as the *all-knowing* teacher becomes just another person struggling with ethics. In other words, educational institutions and their students would benefit from a multidisciplinary discussion about the proper framework for ethical decision making that makes a conscious choice among alternatives and maintains agency—just as we advocate for the businesses we study—regarding the direction of the organization.

Developed Versus Developing Economy Perspectives

With the expansion of business activities on a global scale, the importance of ethical consideration of organizational decisions has never been greater. The need for ethical consistency goes beyond the qualitative moral imperative and has direct impact on economic performance since business relationships rely on a shared understanding of what are acceptable standards of behavior in order to be fruitful. The following is a brief summary of the key ethical impacts on organizational decision making of globalization. While a full discussion of the characteristics of all stakeholders and their salience is beyond the scope of this chapter, the most commonly identified stakeholders include the following:

- Shareholders: Lack of regulation in global capital markets creates opportunity for ethical, if not legal, malfeasance.

- Employees: Outsourcing production raises the potential for exploitation of employees and poor working conditions.
- Suppliers: Do our suppliers share our organizational values around ethics, sustainability, and fair business practices?
- Customers: Cheaper prices can be created by globalization but are they at the cost of local cultural degradation (if not the outright perception of western imperialism)?
- Environment: The production and transportation of products can cause pollution and increasing problems of waste disposal can cause environmental catastrophes.
- Governments: Globalization can weaken the governments of developing economies and increase corporate responsibility for jobs and welfare of local employees. Are corporations up for the task?

Suggested Exercise

Following is a case study example used as a part of the ethics assessment for all business majors at New Mexico State University. It was originally adopted from Lockheed Martin orientation and training materials and has been reprinted here with the permission of the Department of Management in the College of Business. Consistent with the PRME initiative, this study presents a form of experiential learning in which students may take on a *real-life* scenario in order to apply course principles (Alcaraz and Thiruvattal 2010).

In the following text, we briefly illustrate how the framework proposed in this chapter may be used to analyze the case prior to or in tandem with answering case questions. As with any case, we recognize that student answers may not exactly match what is provided as an example.

Step 1—Recognition and awareness: Students may acknowledge that this decision could be damaging to high-usage customers, themselves as employees, or the organization more broadly. They may also note that this is not a legal decision per se, as the rule regarding usage was developed in-house by the organization. Further, the decision is not one of efficiency, as it may not be considered efficient by some decision

New Product Release

Your team is responsible for testing a new product. Under company guidelines, you put the product through the most rigorous testing procedure possible involving hundreds of individual tests. Two-thirds (67 percent) of the time, the product withstood the extreme conditions of the tests. Your company demands that all products pass the tests with a 70 percent success rate under the conditions of *heavy use* (i.e., extreme conditions). Your customers are eagerly awaiting the new product release and you expect that your company will generate significant sales revenue from it. You know that everyday customer use will never amount to the extreme conditions of your test. Do you ship the product?

Assignment Questions

1. Describe the aspects of the ethical dilemma in this situation.
2. Is there more to this decision than company policy?
3. Who are the stakeholders that are affected by any decision that is to be made?
4. Identify at least three alternative decisions that might be made to address this problem.
5. Apply the five different ethical approaches to justify your alternative decisions from question 3. (As a reminder, the approaches are: utilitarian, rights, justice, common good, and virtue ethics.)
6. Which alternative decision would you select and why?

Framework Steps

1. Recognition and awareness
2. Fact finding
3. Evaluating ethical approaches
4. Testing the decision
5. Reflecting on the outcome

makers to delay a product release for failing to achieve an arbitrary standard.

Step 2—Fact-finding: Students may point out that we do not have all of the facts. In fact, many students may suggest *passing the buck* on this decision to a supervisor, as they feel unprepared to make a decision based on the information provided. For example, they may dislike not knowing how the rule regarding usage was developed. Students will likely have no issue recognizing pertinent stakeholders, however, since, in our experience, they routinely exceed expectations in this aspect of the query. They may note the following as stakeholders: customers, the organization, their own work team, themselves as individuals, the broader community (i.e., friends and family of high-usage customers), and so forth. In fact, the instructor may be surprised by the number and creativity of options generated.

Students may suggest a second test to ensure that the product is not failing, a re-evaluation of the rule itself, a commitment to get the product to market but with a warning label, or even an extended warranty to protect against product malfunction. In all cases, instructors should be prepared to point out the underlying assumptions of each suggested solution. For example, what would a second product test cost the company? Would it cost less than a product malfunction?

Step 3—Evaluating ethical approaches: For many students, answering the question of which ethical approach to take is quite personal and emotionally charged. The instructor should be prepared to guide the discussion with sensitivity knowing that this represents an opportunity to engage students in critical thinking in a *safe* environment if accomplished correctly. The majority of the class may easily and confidently match a particular option with a particular approach; there is typically a fraction of students who disagree based on the alternatives generated. Students will typically note the following:

> *Utilitarian*: Sending the product to market as it will do the most good since the organization, its employees, and customers in general will benefit. Students will likely point out that because a small percentage of customers exhibit high usage, their concerns can essentially be sacrificed for the greater good.

Rights: Students will again likely select to send the product to market using this approach. They may, however, expand on this alternative by mandating the use of a warning label. Their reasoning typically includes the idea that only one stakeholder group would suffer a violation of rights under this approach, and that the inclusion of a warning label negates that violation.

Justice: Students adopting the justice approach typically suggest delaying the products' release until it complies with the organization's testing rule. The reasoning is typically that this is the only option that treats everyone equally in terms of safety.

Common good: Students will typically suggest the delay of the product under this approach. The discussion customarily involves the need to subjugate the organization to the broader community. Concepts of corporate responsibility and being a good *corporate neighbor* may fit here.

Virtue: This is the most personal approach and students will likely weave discussions of upbringing and religion into their responses. The instructor should be prepared to moderate discussion of this approach while gently assisting students in evaluating the potential outcomes of taking the moral high road, as this is what the majority of students will declare as their decision. For example, students should consider how individuals are sometimes regarded when they act in accordance with their ethical selves to the detriment of the organization. Further discussion of organizational culture and whistle blowing are appropriate here.

Step 4—Testing the decision: Students here will offer a variety of reasons for selecting a particular approach, especially as they tie the approach selected to the *light of day* test. Be prepared for students to list a wide range of persons they would wish to help evaluate their decision—everyone from religious, political, and organizational leaders to very personal family leaders (e.g., "what would my mom say?").

Step 5—Reflecting on the outcome: Since this is an artificial scenario, instructors may opt to leave the case open-ended and elect to not provide an outcome. Alternatively, they may choose to create an outcome to provide students with closure. In that case, students will react to the outcome (again, be prepared for lively discussion, particularly if the outcome is controversial). The key to this step is the learning that takes place from the outcome. For example, consider the following: The organization pushes the product on the market without any warning label despite its test failure and one customer is seriously harmed six months later. The subsequent media coverage is detrimental to the organization's stock price and current sales. What is learned from this outcome?

On the other hand, consider an alternative in which the product is pushed to market despite its test failure and no subsequent harm occurs. What is learned in this case? It is important to note that ethical decisions cannot be evaluated solely in terms of the outcome. Rather, a consideration of the process itself, including what was learned about oneself, colleagues, other stakeholders, the organization and its policies and procedures, and so forth, is important.

Concluding case note: It is imperative that the instructor set aside one to two full class periods in order to cover the ethical perspectives, the framework, and its application. It may also be useful to place the students in small teams and create props, and so forth, to make the case more experiential. In any case, students will need a chance to process the case. Instructors may find it useful to refer to Dennehy, Sims, and Collins (1998) for suggested debriefing practices.

Conclusion

This chapter offers two primary contributions. First, we demonstrate that the movement of the field of organizational decision making away from a purely rational, economic model to incorporate concepts such as bounded rationality, politics, and power has created a space for normative ethics to flourish. Second, we offer practical advice for those teaching business ethics in decision-making courses. We encourage teachers to challenge students' current ethical conceptions to promote greater awareness, we provide a five-step framework for approaching ethical decisions, and we offer a case study example to employ the framework and promote a new way of ethical thinking.

References

Alcaraz, J.M., and E. Thiruvattal. 2010. "An Interview with Manuel Escudero: The United Nations' Principles for Responsible Management Education: A Global Call for Sustainability." *Academy of Management Learning & Education* 9, no. 3, pp. 542–50.

Annas, J. 1992. "Ancient Ethics and Modern Morality." *Philosophical Perspectives* 6, pp. 119–36.

Bakhtin, M.M. 1993. *Toward a Philosophy of the Act*. Austin, TX: University of Texas Press.

Brown, T., J. Sautter, L. Littvay, A. Sautter, and B. Bearnes. 2010. "Ethics and Personality: Empathy and Narcissism as Moderators of Ethical Decision Making in Business Students." *Journal of Education for Business* 85, pp. 203–8.

Dennehy, R.F., R.R. Sims, and H.E. Collins. 1998. "Debriefing Experiential Learning Exercises: A Theoretical and Practical Guide for Success." *Journal of Management Education* 22, no. 1, pp. 9–25.

Eisenhardt, K., and M. Zbaracki. 1992. "Strategic Decision Making." *Strategic Management Journal* 13, pp. 17–37.

Fredrickson, J., and A. Iaquinto. 1989. "Inertia and Creeping Rationality in Strategic Decision Processes." *Academy of Management Journal* 32, no. 3, pp. 516–42.

Giacalone, R.A., and M.D. Promislo. 2013. "Broken When Entering: The Stigmatization of Goodness and Business Ethics Education." *Academy of Management Learning & Education* 12, pp. 86–101.

Giacalone, R.A., and K.R. Thompson. 2006. "Business Ethics and Social Responsibility Education: Shifting the Worldview." *Academy of Management Learning & Education* 5, pp. 266–77.

Hanson, W., and J. Moore. 2013. "Business Student Moral Influencers: Unseen Opportunities for Development?" *Academy of Management Learning & Education*. Published online before print, doi: 10.5465/amle.2012.0325.

Jones, T.M. 1991. "Ethical Decision Making by Individuals in Organizations: An Issue-Contingent Model." *Academy of Management Review* 16, no. 2, pp. 366–95.

McCabe, D.L., K.D. Butterfield, and L.K. Trevino. 2006. "Academic Dishonesty in Graduate Business Programs: Prevalence, Causes, and Proposed Action." *Academy of Management Learning & Education* 5, pp. 294–305.

McVea, J.F., and R.E. Freeman. 2005. "A Names-and-faces Approach to Stakeholder Management How Focusing on Stakeholders as Individuals Can Bring Ethics and Entrepreneurial Strategy Together." *Journal of Management Inquiry* 14, pp. 57–69.

Moberg, D.J. 2006. "Best Intentions, Worst Results: Grounding Ethics Students in the Realities of Organizational Context." *Academy of Management Learning & Education* 5, pp. 307–16.

O'Fallon, M., and K. Butterfield. 2005. "A Review of the Empirical Ethical Decision-Making Literature: 1996–2003." *Journal of Business Ethics* 59, no. 4, pp. 375–413.

Romero, E.J. 2008. "AACSB Accreditation: Addressing Faculty Concerns." *Academy of Management Learning & Education* 7, pp. 245–55.

Simon, H. 1979. "Rational Decision Making in Business Organizations." *The American Economic Review* 69, no. 4, pp. 493–513.

Trank, C.Q., and S.L. Rynes. 2003. "Who Moved Our Cheese? Reclaiming Professionalism in Business Education." *Academy of Management Learning & Education* 2, pp. 189–205.

Trevino, L.K. 1986. "Ethical Decision Making in Organizations: A Person-Situation Interactionist Model." *Academy of Management Review* 11, no. 3, pp. 601–17.

Further Reading

Ashkanasy, N., C. Windsor, and L. Trevino. 2006. "Bad Apples in Bad Barrels Revisited: Cognitive Moral Development, Just World Beliefs, Rewards, and Ethical Decision-Making." *Business Ethics Quarterly* 16, no. 4, pp. 449–73.

Tenbrunsel, A.E., and K. Smith-Crowe. 2008. "Ethical Decision-making: Where We've Been and Where We're Going." *Academy of Management Annals* 2, pp. 545–607.

CHAPTER 4

Ethics and Agency Theory in Management

Unsal Sigri

Baskent University, Ankara, Turkey

Umit Ercan

Turkish Military Academy, Defense Science Institute, Ankara, Turkey

Introduction

The use of agency theory remains highly controversial among business ethicists. While some regard it as an essential tool for analyzing and understanding the recent spate of corporate ethics scandals, others argue that these scandals might not even have occurred had it not been for the widespread teaching of agency theory in business schools. (Heath 2009)

This chapter focuses on agency theory or principal–agent problem, a topic that is widely discussed in economics and management, and becoming a concern in business ethics today. Organizational theories concern with the structures of the organizations and the roles of the people in the organizations. The owner and the manager is not the same person in today's business world, which is quite different from the classical model of entrepreneurship that the owner and the manager is the same person. Actually with the monumental work of Berle and Means (1932). *The Modern Corporation and Private Property*, ownership and control of the corporation has been separated. This separating is the result of the modern corporation but also the reason of many problems as well.

Agency theory, as one of the organizational theories, is interested in the sharing of power, control, information, money, efficiency, and other instruments between principals (as owners, shareholders, stakeholders) and the agents (CEOs, managers, board of directors, employees, etc.). In an agency relation, one party acts on behalf of another (Shapiro 2005) and the bilateral relations, control mechanisms, and ethical issues are the main points of this relation.

"Rooted from economics and finance" (Fama 1980; Fama and Jensen 1983), the agency theory becomes one of the tenets of the corporate governance. Then, "the control and self-interest-oriented assumptions" (Davis 2005), "political aspect" (Mitnick 1992), "sociological" (White 1985), and "legal theories" (DeMott 1998; Lan and Heracleous 2010) of the firm are discussed under agency theory. Beginning with the economics paradigm, social science, business, political, law, and sociology paradigm the ethics of the theory is the only subject that is not to be changed. The institutions, roles, forms of social organization, social control strategies, and other problems should be discussed under the ethical aspect. The ethics of the agent–owner relation of the agency theory should be discussed as theory and cases. The ethics of the theory should be taught by the academics to the business management students to decrease the ethical problems of the theory and to improve the performance of the organizations with less friction between the parties.

The theory tries to explore, explain, rule, and arrange the relations of two sides—the principals and the agents. Relations between these two sides might be on the economic base of "rational action," which means either of the two parties cares firstly for their own interests. Another problem is that two sides try to "maximize their own profits" against the other side. Besides this, the theory has some other certain types of problems to be solved by the agents and principals such as information asymmetry (Sharma 1997), profession, trust (Granovetter 1985), goal conflicts, opportunism, monitoring, insurance, risk, and agency costs (Shapiro 2005).

Description of Discipline

Economists have long been concerned with the incentive problems that arise when decision making in a firm is the province of managers who are not the firm's security holders (Fama 1980). Different from the classical model of entrepreneurship, the owner and the managers are not the same person in the modern organizations. The one who controls the organization and the owner is separated. The literature has moved toward theories that reject the classical model of firm but assume classical forms of economic behavior on the part of agents within the firm. The firm is viewed as a set of contracts among factors of production, with each factor motivated by its self-interest (Fama 1980).

An organization is the nexus of contracts, written and unwritten, among owners of factors of production and customers. These contracts or internal "rules of game" specify the rights of each agent in the organization, performance criteria on which agents are evaluated, and the payoff functions they face (Fama and Jensen 1983). An agency relation is based on a high level of trust and also strict confidentiality. The relation between an agent and principal involves clear duty "to serve the interests of another" (Hannafey and Vitulano 2013). The agency theory has two sides: the agents who achieve on behalf of others and the principals who control and lead the agents' behavior (Mitnick 1998). The agency relation can be of use to ethical theory by providing a model for understanding some of the roles that people occupy in business and the duties and rights that attend these roles (Boatright 1992).

Even though some scholars assess that agency theory is very different from organization theories (Perrow 1986), agency theory has several links to mainstream organization perspectives (Eisenhardt 1989) like cooperative behavior (Bernard 1938), political model of organization (Pfeffer 1981), information processing approach to contingency theory (Chandler 1962), and transaction cost perspective (Williamson 1975). The relation of agency theory with these theories is generally summed up under the problems of self-interest, goal conflict, bounded rationality, information asymmetry, and preeminence of efficiency, risk aversion, and information as a commodity.

The heart of principal–agent theory is the trade-off between the cost of measuring behavior and the cost of measuring outcomes and transferring risk to the agent (Eisenhardt 1989). These problems of the theory are also closely related with the ethical aspects of it. In the effort to understand and solve the ethical problems of the agency theory, the problems between the agent and the principal should be examined. The solutions to the agency problems are also the answers to the ethical issues. Before discussing the agency problems and their relations with ethical issues, we should clarify what ethics and professional ethics are.

The dictionary explanation of ethics is "the basic concepts and fundamental principles of decent human conduct. It includes the study of universal values such as the essential equality of all men and women, human or natural rights, obedience to the law of the land, concern for health and safety and for the natural environment" (BusinessDictionary 2013a). Parallel to the dictionary definition of ethics, professional ethics can be defined as "professionally accepted standards of personal and business behavior, values and guiding principles. Codes of professional ethics are often established by professional organizations to help guide members in performing their job functions according to sound and consistent ethical principles" (BusinessDictionary 2013b). So agency problems and agency rules should be related with ethics rules for the good of both the agent and the principal. In the next section, we will try to discuss the agency problems and their possible relations with ethics.

Agency Problems

According to Eisenhardt (1989), "agency theory is concerned with resolving two problems that can occur in agency relationships." The first problem is "the desires or goals conflicts of the principal and agent." The second problem is "difficulty or expense for the principal to verify what the agent is actually doing." It is not easy for the principal to "verify that the agent has behaved appropriately." Additionally, the problem of risk sharing arises when the principal and agent have different ethics and control mechanisms are limited. Ethics may be the answer of these questions about different attitudes toward risk (Eisenhardt 1989). Agency problems arise because contracts are not costless to write and to enforce. Agency costs include the costs of structuring, monitoring, and bonding a set of contracts among agents with conflicting interests (Fama and Jensen 1983). The level of agency problems may vary related to the size, structure, complexity, and owner(s) of the contract, and to being profit or nonprofit types of organizations.

Despite the fact that agency theory can be explained from the aspects of different disciplines, agency problems are generally common. These problems can be listed as goal conflict (Shapiro 2005), issues of professionalism (Sharma 1997), information asymmetry, adverse selection, moral hazard (Eisenhardt 1989), agent opportunism, embeddedness and trust (Granovetter 1985; Cook 2001), fiduciaries, and opportunism. Eisenhardt (1989) has divided these problems in different groups, saying that "the principal–agent relationship has assumptions about people—of agency relation—(self-interest, bounded rationality, risk aversion), organizations (goal conflict among members), and information (information is a commodity which can be purchased)."

Goal conflict: In the classical agency relation paradigm, goal conflict occurs when the benefits of the agent and the principal conflict (Shapiro 2005). Agents firstly take into consideration of their own goals even if they are against the goal of the principal. But according to the ethical rules, the agent should balance the benefits of his or her own interests with the interest of the person(s) whom he or she serves. Opportunism is one possible result of the goal conflict: Every side of the agency relation acts firstly for their own interests. Ethical rules are the main rules to balance the goal conflict and opportunism.

Risk sharing: One of the main points of the agency theory is risk sharing among the individuals and groups (Eisenhardt 1989). The management of an organization of any size includes different kinds of risks. The one who leads the organization should have the responsibilities of managing and pride of the gains. Unlike the classical family firms, in modern organizations and management systems, the owners and the managers are different persons. So *the risk-sharing problem* arises when cooperating parties have different attitudes toward risk. Specifically, agency theory is directed at the ubiquitous agency relationship, in which one party delegates work to another, who performs that work (Jensen and Meckling 1976; Eisenhardt 1989).

Moral hazard: This refers to a lack of effort on the part of the agent. The argument here is that the agent may simply not put forth the agreed-upon effort (Eisenhardt 1989), especially if the agent(s) works for his or her own priority instead of the organization's common wellness. It is not easy for the principal(s) to detect or recognize it. This is the reason for building in control mechanisms for the principal(s) to check and control the efforts of agent, to know whether he or she acts according to the previously decided rules or contract signed at the beginning of the agency relation. Even when all of the details have not been decided before the contract is signed between the parties, the universal rules of contracts (we can identify these as ethical rules) should be the guiding principles against the moral hazard.

Transparency and accountability: Modern organizations need transparent management and account systems to build up an accounting structure. These two factors are the main tenets of a healthy agency mechanism (Lambright 2009). The principal(s) can use different control mechanisms to monitor and check the work of the agent(s). But for building the proper control mechanisms, the transparency and accountability structure of the organizational management is essential. Additionally, it is not only an essential but also a legal necessity of modern management structure. Ethical behavior is closely related to accountability, and when managers are accountable for their actions they are more likely to behave ethically (Ang 1993). Accountability is the first characteristic of responsible agents and a morally responsible person is a person whose actions reflect a consideration for the impact of his or her actions on others (Goodpaster and Matthews 1982).

Professionalism: This is related with experience and information asymmetry. Principals choose their agents with regard to their special knowledge and experiences. Agents have the professional knowledge but they also need clear contracts to strengthen their position in the organization (Sharma 1997). One of the main features of professionalism is the ethical behavior of both sides—the agent and the principal. Contractual fidelity, working for the good of both sides, bona fide, working for the common wealth of the organization are some examples of being professional.

Embeddedness: This has to do with problems of trust, choosing, monitoring, and controlling of agents. Embedded agent relations aim to prevent adverse selections. Principals choose agents who have common values, beliefs, and area of interests. The features of ethical behaviors can be explained as embedded agent behavior. The principal will choose the best agent and must monitor his or her behaviors by using different tools consisting of the ethical rules.

Fiduciaries: Agency theory depends on the assumption that all the agents are fiduciary. No principal gives any kind of responsibility to anyone who is not trustworthy and trust is the main scope of agency relation. So the agent should be a model of trustability and other ethical behaviors for the principal(s) and the general benefits of the organization he or she leads. As a result of acting on behalf of others, the agent should at least balance his own benefits with the benefits of the principal(s).

Adverse selection: This is the misrepresentation of ability by the agent (Eisenhardt 1989). Principals are generally unable to verify the skills and abilities of the agents especially with regard to high level of skill and ability needed missions. In the face of unobservable behavior (moral hazard or adverse selection), the principal has two options. One is to discover the agent's behavior by investing in information systems such as budgeting, reporting procedures, boards of directors, and additional layers of management. The other option is to base the contract on the outcomes of the agent's behavior. Such an outcome-based contract motivates ethical behavior by alignment of the agent's preferences with those of the principal, but at the price of transferring risk to the agent (Eisenhardt 1989). These are the monitoring mechanisms for the principals to control their agents. If the ethical rules can be applied well to the agency relation, the adverse selection and monitoring problems will be solved easier. Adverse selection and moral hazard are part of the terminology of agency theory (Heimer 1985) and moral issues are closely related with the ethical rules.

In an agency relation, the problems of selection costs, adverse selection, wrong references, pay and monitoring costs, insurance and goal conflicts, (Mitnick 1992) and the other problems that we listed, only the important ones can be defined as agency costs. There are other problems that are not listed here but happen. In the agency relation, both sides of the contract must bear these costs and, to decrease the number and effects of these problems, ethical rules are one of the most important tools that organizations can apply.

Agency theory re-establishes the importance of incentives and self-interest in organizational thinking (Perrow 1986) and reminds us that much of organizational life, whether we like it or not, is based on self-interest (Eisenhardt 1989). So the ethical rules and professional ethics become the main focus of the organization to prevent or control the self-interest based acts of the agents.

Typical Ethical Issues in Agency Theory

One of the main ethical claims of scholars is that agency theory relies on an assumption of self-interested agents who seek to maximize personal economic wealth while minimizing personal effort (Bruce, Buck, and Main 2005; Lubatkin et al. 2007). Principals typically want growth in profits and stock prices, while agents are usually concerned with growth in their salaries and positions in the hierarchy. The self-interest of the manager is apparently in conflict with the manager's duty to owners (Bowie and Freeman 1992). In modern organizations, professional managers lead the organization and the principal(s) need control mechanisms to check if their agents behave and act as per their contract.

> The spectacular corporate scandals and bankruptcies have served as a powerful reminder of the risks that are involved in the ownership of enterprise. As the recent wave of corporate scandals has demonstrated once again, it can be extraordinarily difficult for shareholders to exercise effective control of management, or more generally, for the firm to achieve the appropriate alignment of interests between managers and owners. After all, it is shareholders who were the ones most hurt by the scandals at Enron, Tyco, Worldcom, Parmalat, Hollinger, and elsewhere. (Heath 2009)

A short explanation and evaluation about the *Enron case* is discussed in the box at the end of the chapter.

Agency theory provides a series of instructive parables concerning the system's consequences of unreservedly opportunistic behavior. Due to a mutual lack of trust, some otherwise mutually beneficial exchanges do not take place. Even when exchanges do take place, there are dead-weight losses due to monitoring costs and inefficient risk sharing. Therefore, in ex ante terms, everyone may be better off if they mutually agree to restrain their opportunistic behavior. Unfortunately, by its very nature, opportunistic behavior is not readily observed. Thus, an agreement (i.e., ethical code) to abstain from opportunistic behavior cannot be effectively enforced by external rewards or sanctions; instead, the sanctions for unethical behavior must be internalized (Noreen 1988).

One of the central tasks of theoretical business ethics is to provide a conceptual framework that allows one to articulate more precisely the intuitive sense that *nest-feathering* and similar forms of conduct are unethical. Business ethicists should look into and clarify agency theory—the relationship between owners and managers, deception and misappropriation of funds by the agent, types of moral hazard problems, and the endemic features of principal–agent relations (Heath 2009). After the economic crisis caused by the agent (or agency) problems, the United States government, the leading country of the free market economy theory of Adam Smith, began to change its economic approach and to build up the control systems of the agent–principal relation. This example also implies that the agency theory does not only have an economic aspect or effects but also managerial, sociological, and legal aspects and effects.

Ethics Teaching Strategy for Agency Theory

It is a characteristic of nearly all modern business firms that the principals (the owners and shareholders) are not the same people as the agents (the managers who run the firms for the principals). This separation causes situations in which the goals of the principals and the agents are not the same. As already mentioned above, the principals want growth in profits and stock price, while agents want growth in salaries and positions in the hierarchy. Their self-interests are in conflict. This happens in all areas of business. Academic programs on business management need to be designed to emphasize the challenge of ethical problems based on principal–agent frictions. As a result of such activities, many advocates of ethics teaching have called for increasing ethics teaching in business schools. Gilbert (1992) and Feldman and Thompson (1990) offer the following questions that are important in teaching business ethics: what, why, who, where, when, and how.

Experiential learning exercises—lecture, case study, role play, behavioral modeling, and business simulations—can play an important role in teaching ethics focused on the principal–agent problems. Many ethical problems do not have specific *correct* solutions like the problems presented in a number of courses in business schools (i.e., accounting, operations, statistics, etc.). To address this problem, business students need to have an experiential awareness of the types of ethical dilemmas they will face (i.e., relevancy), and they need to be able to evaluate and identify possible courses of action when confronted by ethical dilemmas. Black and Mendenhall (1989) have noted that experiential training methods such as simulations, field trips, and role plays are more rigorous and engage the participants more fully than methods such as lectures and videotapes. All these pedagogical approaches emphasize high and active participation and rather than passive learning. Some of these approaches are described in the following text.

> **Case study:** This method, which will be elaborated further next, is useful for understanding the various personal factors and organizational circumstances that lead to ethical dilemmas. Students are active learners because they read the case, analyze the issues, and make recommendations based on case facts (Geva 2000). The case study presents a problem from a real-life situation for analysis and discussion. It uses problems that have already occurred in the company or elsewhere. The case study method deals with problems involving others and with an emphasis on using facts and making assumptions. With the help of case studies, students can find an opportunity to practice analyzing issues using case problems designed for business ethics courses.

Role playing: A common characteristic of many business ethics teaching initiatives is the use of business-related scenarios, statements, or case studies. In most of these instances, students are asked to assume the roles of various key stakeholders—an executive, a manager, or even a company president—and make ethical decisions relating to the stakeholders' positions. Role playing is one of the techniques advocated for teaching about ethical issues (Baetz and Carson 1999). In particular, it has been noted that role playing might help students transfer their ability to reason ethically into the business context (McDonald and Donleavy 1995).

Business simulations: Several writers have proposed using simulations to improve the learning of skills and concepts in business ethics. Simulations can provide students with hands-on experience and a better understanding of the concepts discussed in the classroom. In a simulation designed for business ethics courses, students are faced with ethical dilemmas that encourage them to react to the problems as though they were in a real-life situation. Simulations give students the chance to explore their attitudes, feelings, and communication skills. Advocates of this approach note that after participating in a simulation, students become more open minded, or at least more cognizant of important ethical issues. They may also get a better picture of the complexity involved and how individuals in organizations work through ethical dilemmas (LeClair et al. 1999).

Lectures, case analysis, and guest lectures are still very much in use, along with techniques such as role plays and simulations. Activities like role plays and business simulations can help address better the challenge that we encounter in teaching business ethics based on agency (principal–agent) problems. Effective teaching of *leadership theories* can also indirectly help students to cope with ethical problems regarding agency theory. The agent's authenticity is seen as improving profits and sustainable growth through self-awareness, self-development, leading through values, being passionate about his or her own purpose, leading with heart and head, and being himself or herself. But these features will not be able to solve the problems between the principal and the agent. The steps to teaching authentic leadership on the way to bringing solutions to agency problems should be reinforced by teaching effective organizational communication in accordance with the alignment of organizational goals.

Case Study in Teaching Ethics: Ethical Issues on Agency Theory

Case studies regarding ethical issues on agency theory are stories or scenarios, often in narrative form, created and used as a tool for the analysis and discussion of the issues. Cases with ethical issues on agency theory are often based on actual events that add a sense of urgency or reality. A good case with ethical issues on agency theory should have sufficient details to stimulate analysis from a variety of perspectives. They place the learner in the position of the problem solver within the case and students become actively engaged in the materials, discovering underlying issues, dilemmas, and conflict issues.

Examining, as a group, a case study related with the ethical issues on agency theory offers several advantages, including sharing ideas, insights, and experiences, and seeing other sides of an issue. Students also have the opportunity to reflect before responding when they practice on asynchronous discussion boards. Higher order thinking is encouraged. Solutions to cases may be ambiguous and this facilitates creative problem solving coupled with an application of previously acquired skills. They are effective devices for directing students to practically apply their skills and understandings. They have the opportunity to learn from each other.

The approach in using case study is also important. Case studies are suitable for most curricula where students would benefit from the application of facts learned to a real-world situation. They are particularly useful where situations are complex and solutions are uncertain. Setting up the case study in a specific forum requires serious preparation. A generic and practical guide for the use of case study is given in the following text.

Adaptation of case study teaching for different pedagogical levels is also an important issue. While aspects of case studies are found in all grade levels, the cognitive goals of the activity are best mated to students who are abstract thinkers. Case studies can fill the gap between the teacher-centered lecture method and pure problem-based learning.

Practical Guide: Using Case Study in Teaching Ethics on Agency Theory Problems

- Select a case study that matches your curriculum objectives with regard to agency theory problems for the course, or write one if you cannot find one that is appropriate.
- Set up a specific forum in the discussion board for the case study.
- Split students into groups to discuss the case if the class is large. Groups of about 8 to 10 should work well.
- Include the case and the initial discussion questions that students should address.
- Provide background resources for the case study, including supplementary readings and the necessary data to form an opinion about the case.
- Decide if you will ask students to do additional research as part of the case study.
- Give students guidelines about expectations for the assignment.
- Decide how you will evaluate students' work.
- Facilitate the discussion by asking questions that will extend students' thinking in relation to the educational objectives of agency theory problems.
- Consider having one or two students moderate the discussion, since this can lead to deeper learning.
- Think about whether or not you want students to complete an assignment after the group discussion, such as a summary of the issues, an individual position paper, or a research paper. If students are required to make a decision, ask them to justify their position.
- Assess the results of teaching with case study.

Assessment and evaluation should be processed properly to reach the goals in teaching ethics and ethical issues in agency theory. Assessment should be based on the teacher's prestated objectives. Some aspects of evaluation may include the following:

- Building of empathy with both sides, specifically with the agent role, evidence of consideration of all case factors
- Quality of research
- Organization of arguments
- Feasibility of solutions presented
- Intra group dynamics

An Example of a Case Study: Ethical Issues in Agency Theory—The Enron Scandal

The Texas-based energy-trading giant, once America's seventh-biggest company, declared bankruptcy and collapsed on December 2, 2001. Kenneth Lay, Enron's chairman, and his colleagues, made enough money from Enron shares, unlike their workers, whose pension funds were largely invested in Enron stock that they were unable to sell in time. Enron's demise confirms some unattractive features of American public life.

The campaign-finance system puts too many politicians under obligations to big-business donors: Enron lobbied successfully for exemption from financial regulation for its energy-trading arm, and it also helped to draw up the administration's energy policy. Executive pay and stock options have long given bosses too much for doing too little. Some companies have been at fault in encouraging workers to invest pension money in their shares; after Enron, legislation to limit this is urgently needed. But for the most part, the bankruptcy of Enron was just part of the rough-and-tumble of American capitalism.

The collapse of Enron is now raising some big questions. Andersen, the company's auditor, has admitted to an error of judgment in its treatment of the debt of one of Enron's off-balance-sheet vehicles; these vehicles led to an overstatement of profits by almost $600 million over the years 1997 to 2000. That points to the need for systemic reforms, in three areas. The first is the regulation of auditors. For years the profession has insisted that self-regulation and peer review are the right way to maintain standards. Second is the urgent need to eliminate conflicts of interest in accounting firms. Lastly come America's accounting standards (This is a summary of the article "Enron, the Real Scandal." *The Economist*, June 17, 2002).

The management style, the unethical behaviors of the agents, and the lack of control on the part of management caused billions of dollars value of scandals or bankruptcies that caused economical and sociological losses for societies. For every employee at Enron who lost a job, shareholders lost at least $4 million. In 2000, Enron had 19,000 employees and a peak market capitalization of $80 billion (Heath 2009). But just after the agency problem the organization totally collapsed and a series of other organizations collapsed after the Enron scandal.

Discussion Questions

1. How would you analyze the situation in Enron regarding the ethical issues on agency theory?
2. Describe the mismanagement of a process that ends up with agent-based ethical problems.
3. Is it possible to restore the reputation of the company? If yes, discuss your solutions to bring the company to its previous position.

Assessment

Weak: The answers just giving typical facts based on theoretical background of typical ethical issues on agency problems would be a weak resolution of the Enron case.

Moderate: The resolutions bridging the agency theory and the Enron case weakly would be a moderate resolution of the case.

Sufficient: A strong linkage between the agency theory perspectives and the Enron case would be a sufficient handling of the situation

Excellent: Novel and creative resolutions—bringing new perspectives and the ways to look at the issues with fresh eyes—would be assessed as excellent resolution of the Enron case.

Developing Versus Developed Country Perspectives

Cultural diversity is an important impact factor in agency issues. Agency theory assumes that employees and employers have different goals, act in a self-interested manner, and are willing to assume varying degrees of risk. Cultural differences may attenuate those assumptions and thereby temper agency theory predictions. Culture may align goals between employers and employees, change a company's preference for behavior versus outcome-based pay, require higher incentives before employees will accept outcome-based pay, and lower the moral hazard concerns associated with outcome-based pay (Johnson and Droege 2004).

The practices of agency theory may differ in different countries. Culture has a great impact on agency issues. "Some cultures encourage personal responsibility and a concern for others over self-interest" (Wiseman, Gloria, and Gomez-Mejia 2012) while in other cultures individualism is more important. Among the dimensions used by Hofstede (1980) to classify the national culture is the individualism–collectivism dimension that distinguishes between people who take care of themselves (individualism) versus people who are cared for by the group (collectivism). By ignoring the social or institutional context surrounding principal–agent relations, agency theory lacks validity outside a very narrow setting (Wiseman, Gloria, and Gomez-Mejia 2012).

Culture is an important factor of organizational, business, economical, and governmental systems and control mechanisms of agent–principal structure. Developing, developed, or undeveloped countries with cultural differences have different mechanisms as far as agency issues are concerned. The management control system of an organization is the structured facet of management, the formal vehicle by which the management process is executed. Agency theory and its extension, the principal–agent model, provide insights to the problem of goal congruence and suggest remedies, at least in the Western cultural context. Whether the agency theory presumptions, predictions, and prescriptions are universally applicable is an important issue in management. Their validity in different cultural contexts is largely unknown (Ekanayake 2004).

Even though the effects of cultural and managerial differences of the systems are not tested exactly by the scholars, the structure of organization may have an impact on the agency relation. The professionalism of the agents or the family organization versus professional management structure makes a certain difference in agency structure. Classical family organizations are generally common in undeveloped countries while the corporate governance system is more common in developed countries. Hence, agency theory mechanisms may be more applicable to the modern management system of developed countries.

Summary and Conclusion

Agency theory, as one of the organizational theories, is about the sharing of power, control, information, money, efficiency, and some other instruments between principals and agents. As a theory formerly rooted in economics and finance, agency theory becomes one of the tenets of corporate governance. The control and self-interest-oriented assumptions (Davis 2005), political aspects (Mitnick 1992), sociological (White 1985), and legal theories (DeMott 1998; Lan and Heracleous 2010) of the firm have been discussed under the theory of agency. The theory tries to explore, explain, rule, and arrange the relations between the two sides—the principals and the agents. One problem is that the relationship between the two sides might be on an economic base of *rational action*, which means any side of this relation—to care firstly for their own interests. Another problem is that two sides of the relations try to *maximize their own profits* generally against the other side. The theory has some other certain types of problems as asymmetric information, profession, trust, goal conflicts, opportunism, monitoring, insurance, risk, and agency costs that have close connections with ethical issues.

Ethical rules are the main focus of an organization acting to prevent and control the self-interest-based acts of the agents and the principals. Teaching the ethics of agency in business is not only for the good of economy of countries but also for the organization, management, and sociological and legal structure of countries. Otherwise the deficiencies of agency relations may cause severe problems for the systems of the countries. In this chapter, we discussed the impacts of ethical issues and their relations with agency problems.

The agency problems of modern organizations will not lose their importance in agent–principal relations. Business schools should take this into consideration and emphasize the importance of the ethics in agency relation to the future agents of organizations. Business school students, as the future managers of the firms, should be educated with the consideration that their lapses in ethics issues will affect not only the organizational agency structure but also the economic, social, and legal systems of their nations in total.

An Exercise: Example of Teaching Ethics Regarding Agency Theory Issues

Mr. A is the CEO of a worldwide leader organization on soft drinks. He is responsible for 15,000 workers from 25 different countries around the world. The firm owns 10 different factories in seven different countries. Forty percent of the shares of the firm belongs to five relatives of the founder of the firm, while the other 60 percent belongs to 6,000 shareholders.

Mr. A. is responsible for all kinds of management (marketing, distributing, planning, budgeting, selling, advertising, etc.) issues of the firm. He gives monthly reports to the board of directors and annual reports to the stock market. But he does not report the correct and detailed reports to the board of directors and hides or manipulates some information about the firm's operations.

Discussion Questions

1. Explain the activity of Mr. A by using the agency theory and ethics of the theory.
2. Explain the situation of agent and principal related to this case.
3. What kind of control mechanism should be built up to prevent agency problems?
4. Discuss the possible results of this agency relation in terms of ethics.

Assessment

Weak: Answers just giving the facts based on theoretical background of typical ethical issues in agency problems would be weak resolutions of the case.

Moderate: Resolutions bridging the theory and the case would be moderate resolutions of the case.

Sufficient: A strong linkage between agency theory perspectives and the case would be a sufficient handling of the situation.

Excellent: Novel and creative resolutions—bringing new perspectives and ways to look at the issues with fresh eyes—would be assessed as excellent resolutions of the case.

References

Ang, J.S. 1993. "On Financial Ethics." *Financial Management* 22, no. 3, pp. 32–59.

Baetz, M., and A. Carson. 1999. "Ethical Dilemmas in Teaching about Ethical Dilemmas: Obstacle or Opportunity?" *Teaching Business Ethics* 3, no. 1, pp. 1–12.

Berle, A., and G. Means. 1932. *The Modern Corporation and Private Property*. New York: Macmillan.

Bernard, C. 1938. *The Functions of the Executive*. Cambridge, MA: Harvard University Press.

Black, J., and M. Mendenhall. 1989. "A Practical but Theory Based Framework for Selecting Cross-cultural Training Methods." *Human Resource Management* 28, no.4, pp. 511–39.

Boatright, J.R. 1992. "Conflict of Interest: An Agency Analysis." In *Ethics and Agency Theory: An Introduction*, eds. N.E. Bowie and R.E. Freeman, 187–203. New York: Oxford University Press.

Bowie, N.E., and R.E. Freeman. 1992. *Ethics and Agency Theory: An Introduction*. New York: Oxford University Press.

Bruce, A., T. Buck, and B.G. Main. 2005. "Top Executive Remuneration: A View from Europe." *Journal of Management Studies* 42, no. 1, pp. 493–506.

BusinessDictionary. 2013a. "Ethics." http://www.businessdictionary.com/definition/ethics.html

BusinessDictionary. 2013b "Professional Ethics." http://www.businessdictionary.com/definition/professional-ethics.html

Chandler, A.D. 1962. *Strategy and Structure*. Cambridge, MA: MIT press.

Cook, K.S. 2001. *Trust in Society*. New York: Russell Sage Found.

Davis, G.F. 2005. "New Directions in Corporate Governance." *Annual Review of Sociology* 31, pp. 143–62

DeMott, D.A. 1998. "A Revised Prospectus for a Third Restatement of Agency." *U.C. Davis Law Review* 31, pp. 1035–63.

Eisenhardt, K.M. 1989. "Agency Theory: An Assessment and Review." *The Academy of Management Review* 14, no. 1, pp. 57–74.

Ekanayake, S. 2004. "Agency Theory, National Culture and Management Control Systems." *Journal of American Academy of Business* 4, no.1–2, pp. 49–54.

Fama, E.F. 1980. "Agency Problems and the Theory of the Firm." *Journal of Political Economy* 88, pp. 288–307.

Fama, E.F., and M.C. Jensen. 1983. "Separation of Ownership and Control." *Journal of Law and Economics* 26, pp. 301–25.

Feldman, H.D., and R.C. Thompson. 1990. "Teaching Business Ethics: A Challenge for Business Education in the 1990s." *Journal of Marketing Education* 12, no.2, pp. 10–12.

Geva, A. 2000. "The Internet and the Book: Media and Messages in Teaching Business Ethics." *Teaching Business Ethics* 4, no. 1 pp. 85–106.

Gilbert, J.T. 1992. "Teaching Business Ethics: What, Why, Who, Where, and When." *Journal of Education for Business* 68, no. 1, pp. 5–8.

Goodpaster, K.E., and J.B. Matthews. 1982. "Can a Corporation Have a Conscience?" *Harvard Business Review* 11, p. 134.

Granovetter, M. 1985. "Economic Action and Social Structure: The Problem of Embeddedness." *American Journal of Sociology* 91, pp. 481–510.

Hannafey, F.T., and L.A. Vitulano. 2013. "Ethics and Executive Coaching: An Agency Theory Approach." *Journal of Business Ethics* 115, pp. 599–603.

Heath, J. 2009. "The Uses and Abuses of Agency Theory." *Business Ethics Quarterly* 19, no.4, pp. 497–528.

Heimer, C.A. 1985. *Reactive Risk and Rational Action*. Berkeley LA: University of California Press.

Hofstede, G. 1980. *Cultures Consequences: International Differences in Work-Related Values*. Vol. 5 of *Cross Cultural Research and Methodology*. Beverly Hills, CA: Sage.

Jensen, M., and W. Meckling. 1976. "Theory of the Firm: Managerial Behavior, Agency Costs, and Ownership Structure." *Journal of Financial Economics* 3, pp. 305–60.

Johnson, N.B., and S. Droege. 2004. "Reflections on the Generalization of Agency Theory: Cross-cultural Considerations." *Human Resource Management Review* 14, no.3, pp. 325–35.

Lambright, K.T. 2009. "Agency Theory and Beyond: Contracted Providers' Motivations to Properly Use Service Monitoring Tools." *Journal of Public Administration Research and Theory* 19, no. 2, pp. 207–27.

Lan, L.L., and L. Heracleous. 2010. "Rethinking Agency Theory: The View from Law." *Academy of Management Review* 35, no. 2, pp. 294–314.

LeClair, D.T., L. Ferrell, L. Montuori, and C. Willems. 1999. "The Use of a Behavioral Simulation to Teach Business Ethics." *Teaching Business Ethics* 3, pp. 283–96.

Lubatkin, M., P.J. Lane, S. Collin, and P. Very. 2007. "An Embeddedness Framing of Governance and Opportunism: Towards a Cross-nationally Accommodating Theory of Agency." *Journal of Organizational Behavior* 28, pp. 43–58.

McDonald, G.M., and G.D. Donleavy. 1995. "Objections to the Teaching of Business Ethics." *Journal of Business Ethics* 10, no.1, pp. 829–35.

Mitnick, B.M. 1992. "The Theory of Agency and Organizational Analysis". In *Ethics and Agency Theory*, ed. N.E. Bowie and R.E. Freeman, 75–96. New York: Oxford University Press.

Mitnick, B.M. 1998. "Agency Theory." In *The Blackwell Encyclopedic Dictionary of Business Ethics*, ed. R.E. Freeman, and P.H. Werhane, 12–15. Malden, MA: Blackwell.

Noreen, E. 1988. "The Economics of Ethics: A New Perspective on Agency Theory." *Accounting, Organization and Society* 13, no.4, pp. 359–69.

Perrow, C. 1986. *Complex Organizations*. New York: Random House.

Pfeffer, J. 1981. *Power in Organizations*. Marshfield, MA: Pittman.

Shapiro, S. 2005. "Agency Theory." *Annual Review Sociology* 31, pp. 263–84.

Sharma, A. 1997. "Professional as Agent: Knowledge Asymmetry in Agency Exchange." *Academy of Management Review* 22, pp. 758–98.

White, H.C. 1985. "Agency as Control." In *Principals and Agents: The Structure of Business*, eds. J.W. Pratt and R.H. Zeckhauser, 187–212. Cambridge, MA: Harvard Business School Press.

Williamson, O. 1975. *Markets and Hierarchies: Analysis and Antitrust Implications*. New York: Free Press.

Wiseman, R.M., C. Gloria, and L.R. Gomez-Mejia. 2012. "Towards a Social Theory of Agency." *Journal of Management Studies* 49, pp. 201–23.

MODULE 2
Money Matters

CHAPTER 5

Embedding Ethics and Social Responsibility in Management Accounting Courses

Jan Bell

Babson College

Cathleen S. Burns

University of Colorado Boulder

Donna R. Sockell

SB Educational Consultants LLC

Often tasked to produce and report data for business decision making, management accountants may overlook the critical contributions they make to organizational strategy and what impact businesses have on society. As an important source of data for organizational decision making, management accountants' choices of what information to gather and report, or not to, shape the basis for business decision making. Stated more authoritatively, as March and Simon (1958) observed 55 years ago in the seminal work *Organizations*, members of organizations can exert *unobtrusive control* of the decisions made by others by tailoring the information these organizational decision makers have on which to base their decisions. Stated in simple terms, how can business decision makers be informed by the social costs of actions taken or contemplated, if management accountants do not provide data on externalities?

Therefore, in sharp contrast to the unflattering image of an accountant as just a *bean counter*, management accountants play a critical role in determining what organizational decisions will be made and how strategy will be implemented, either directly or indirectly. The sad truth is that often neither the leadership of organizations nor the accountants themselves may fully embrace their role and the impact they have on organizational ethics. Because of these oversights, leaders and management accountants need essential training to understand important relationships: the relationship between what accountants choose to report and their personal values, the relationship between the data they report and organizational decision making, and the relationship between business decision making and business impact on society. It is only then that management accountants can do their part to help organizations engage in activities that will provide greater benefits to people, profits, and the planet.

It is important to note that there are several critical perspectives that underlie the preparation of this chapter. First, a major underlying goal of this chapter, and we suspect all of the chapters in this volume, is to change the formula for business decision making from a short-term focus on immediate financial returns to a long-term focus that expands the set of relevant information on which to base decisions. This has a direct and important impact on managers' uses of accounting information and the practice of management accounting. Indeed, any thorough consideration of stakeholders' interests (Freeman 1984), including consumers, employees, the local and global community, the planet, or even many shareholders' concerns, to name a few, moves us toward a longer time horizon. As many scholars and practitioners have observed from a pragmatic perspective, we can argue cogently that lengthening this time horizon can often have a positive impact on business performance (Vogel 2005). But what also is true is that there are principled reasons for doing so, regardless of which ethical theory guides a decision maker.

Second, we view the pedagogic suggestions provided in this chapter as insufficient to fulfill an organization's obligation to train current or future employees to embrace ethics, sustainability, or corporate social responsibility (CSR) in their decision making. The importance of providing and evaluating information on CSR objectives is not just critical for upper management and management accountants. It is essential to the education of all business professionals in all functional areas who make decisions daily that reflect their values and determine how organizations will behave.

Confining ethics, sustainability, and CSR education to a single functional area—such as training just for those in a management accounting class—will not produce results sought by those who are passionate about ethics, sustainability, and CSR. If, for example, a management accountant takes great care to provide data on a business' carbon footprint or the likely impact of a plant closure on a community and then this information is discarded as irrelevant by managers and other decision makers, we have accomplished nothing to advance the cause of enhancing sustainability or a greater grasp of CSR within organizations. Similarly, in the classroom, we have observed that unless issues of ethics, sustainability, and CSR are embraced by functional areas, there is no transfer of learning from a CSR, ethics, or sustainability class to a functional area class. We heartily advocate that academic, executive education programs and business institutions adopt training in CSR, ethics, and sustainability in order to affect real change in business decision making. Indeed, this is the underlying recommendation of this volume, reflected in the diversity of functional areas covered.

Three, on a related note, to be effective, training cannot be a *one and done* experience. To have an enduring impact on how individuals and organizations make decisions, this decision making must be reinforced in many contexts and over time. Some (Sockell 2013) have referred to this approach as *scaffolded* education (vertically integrated over time in successive courses and horizontally integrated across contexts as earlier). Only through infusion of these issues throughout curricula and continuing education programs—resulting in planned repetition and reinforcement—will individuals and organizations habituate making decisions that reflect a fuller understanding of how such decisions impact society.

Finally, all organizational decision making is rooted in the decisions made by individuals; businesses do not make decisions, people do. If we are to change *business* decisions or *business decision making*, we need to focus on decisions that are made by each and every individual. And it is to the decisions that we now turn.

Description of the Management Accounting Discipline

Management accountants contribute to the achievement of an organization's goals and objectives by providing relevant information and by engaging in problem solving with managers. Management accountants should be flexible problem solvers who analyze and classify information multiple ways, for example, by product or service, by geographical location, by work activity and process, by behavior with volume changes, or by organizational structure. To influence behavior, management accounting reports must be clear and easy to decipher by managers who have little or no accounting education. A management accountant must be willing to share his or her opinion about what makes strategic sense in a constructive manner. IBM's recent international study calls management accountants "fact-based voices of reason and insight" (IBM 2013, 6).

Some examples of how managers use management accounting information include the following:

- Using accounting information to analyze alternatives and make decisions. For example, accountants provide managers analyses that show which products or services are profitable, what technology to use in production, and whether to make or buy subcomponents and services.
- Delegating oversight of organizational resources. Management accountants design and administer budget systems that lead to resource allocations. Managers trust their systems to safeguard organizational resources against theft or inefficient or ineffective use.
- Evaluating enterprise risk and proposing risk management approaches. Management accountants identify risks and develop mitigation plans for strategic, operational, geopolitical, legal, and environmental risks since all forms of risk ultimately have resource implications.

- Controlling resources by using reports that compare spending against budgets. Management accountants perform a control function, flagging results that differ from plans, so managers can take corrective action.
- Evaluating performance using accounting reports about business units and managers. Management accountants prepare scorecards with measures of key performance indicators that often serve as a basis for rewards granted by managers.
- Using accounting information to improve products and processes to achieve profitability targets. Management accountants engage in such activities as business process redesign, activity-based management, and target costing to affect managerial decision making regarding product and process design.
- Relying on management accountants to assure the integrity of information and its proper disclosure. To provide trustworthy information, management accountants design systematic data measurement and collection processes with controls that limit access to the system to authorized users. These systems provide reliable information that upper management uses for external financial reporting and for internal analysis and reports.

Ultimately, the value of management accountants' reports depends on managers' willingness to use the information provided to them. This is more likely if they trust the management accountant and the underlying information systems, can understand the data, and believe that the information is relevant to them. Relevant information and advice are used by managers to inform their future strategic and operational decisions.

Relevant information and advice have three important attributes (Ansari, Bell, and Klammer 2009):

- Technical—it enhances managers' understanding of underlying work processes, the operating results that occurred from past decisions, and areas that are problematic and require actions. It identifies the risks and opportunities that exist and forecasts results under different forward-looking scenarios.

- Behavioral—it encourages managerial actions that are consistent with an organization's strategic objectives.
- Cultural—it supports and creates a set of shared cultural values, beliefs, and mindsets in an organization and society.

As noted in our introduction, choices management accountants make about which information they will provide and advice they will offer have a critical effect on operational and strategic decision making; accordingly, management accountants assume a great deal of responsibility for how an organization functions and achieves its goals. If a management accountant fails to provide any measures of suppliers' CSR for working conditions and wage rates alongside the cost of purchased materials, management will likely be unable to make decisions that take those factors into account in a systematic way. Whether such data are gathered and reported reflect the values held by the accountant, the organization, and the societal context. What is clear is that these measures will contain vital information on behavioral impacts of actions and provide technical information about risks and opportunities. Clearly, this measurement falls within the purview of the discipline described in this section.

Our chapter next addresses how ethics, sustainability, and CSR data should be provided by management accountants to support managerial decision making and resolve conflicts among many stakeholders. The traditional management accountant might be concerned about gathering such measures, wary of the reliability of such data and whether they can be trusted to add value to the decision-making process. Management accountants may not want to be associated with social impact or CSR data because they cannot gain *comfort* about how to measure, what to measure, and who puts data into the reporting system. But management accountants cannot hide behind these fears; across the globe increasing emphasis has been placed on issues of ethics, sustainability, and CSR. Accordingly, management accountants have an imperative to tackle measurement and data collection challenges so that this critical information is available to decision makers.

Forward-thinking management accountants and organizational leaders throughout the world are experimenting with the best ways to provide reliable, consistent, and relevant nonfinancial information. The number of companies providing such information has grown exponentially. Almost each day, CSRwire, Triple Pundit, and 3BL online news services report that a new company, either within the United States or another nation, has provided a CSR report or sustainability report for the first time; moreover, the number of new companies that have dared to prepare an *integrated report*—containing financial and nonfinancial information—also is growing. South Africa, as an example of a proactive country, requires publicly traded companies to provide integrated reports if they want to participate in the stock exchange. The Global Reporting Initiative (2013) reports that 95 percent of the world's largest corporations now publish some form of sustainability report and the number of companies signatory to the UN Global Compact has risen dramatically.

Management accountants will play an increasingly important role in the planning, implementation, and evaluation of new developments in internal and external reporting. The education of current and future managers and accountants cannot ignore a changing world of expectations for business performance; the scope of the discipline has changed forever. And with these changes management accountants and other organizational decision makers face a new set of ethical dilemmas and choices. We turn to several of these challenges now.

Typical Issues Faced

Organizational decisions and actions reflect strategic choice, influenced by the values and cognitive biases of its managers (Child 1972; Hambrick and Mason 1984). To align accounting information with global interests in ethics, sustainability, and CSR, management accounting industry groups, such as the Institute of Management Accountants (IMA), and global accounting industry groups like the International Integrated Reporting Council (IIRC) recommend that accounting systems expand to include information on social contributions and externalities. As suggested earlier, some accountants avoid incorporating social and environmental information because they fear these data are messy and unreliable across industries and organizations and over time. Yet, when management accountants fail to include social and environmental information into routine accounting reports and models, they provide managers a narrow view of the organization that is not focused on long-term value creation for all stakeholders.

We now provide typical ethical and social issues that arise as management accountants perform their traditional functions of costing, planning, decision making, and controlling within organizations. Following that, we discuss ethical issues of self-interest that arise for management accountants as employees.

Corporate Level Responsibility

Costing of Products, Services, or Activities

Traditionally, externalities are excluded when providing management information about the cost of products, services, or activities. For example, when determining gross margin, there is no calculation of the social cost of substituting cheaper hydrogenated oils for healthy oils or of the cost to taxpayers of managing employees' work hours to avoid providing health benefits. Without these costs, there is no routine triggering mechanism or signal that encourages managers to propose and evaluate alternatives. This focuses managers on short-term results. When taking a long-term view of profitability, actions that result in externalities impact brand image, customers' willingness to buy, corporate reputation, laws that govern business, and the general business climate. Including externalities encourages managers to create both strategic opportunities and positive tactical solutions.

Consider the approach taken by Whole Foods. Its strategy and brand are built around CSR, causing Whole Foods to incur higher product and labor costs than other supermarkets but also generating a loyal customer base (enabling it to charge higher prices). Product displays include signs and labels explaining Whole Foods' commitment to local farmers, organic produce, animal welfare, and sustainable fishing practices. While a niche player, the strategy has paid off in return on investment for Whole Foods' shareholders. It reports gross margin and operating margin several percentage points higher than the industry median (Whole Foods Markets 2013, Investor Relations).

Planning

Strategic Planning

Progressive organizations have discovered that incorporating CSR into organizational strategies can fuel innovation and competitive advantage that also benefit society (Porter and Kramer 2006). For example, consider Pepsi's *Positive Water Balance* program in India, where they replenished more water than they consumed, a first for a beverage company (Kahani 2012). This strategy provided Pepsi with a competitive advantage while conserving local water resources.

In some organizations, the upper management encourages employees to allocate some of their paid work hours and other company resources to social and environmental issues. Traditional accounting systems typically capture those resources as product (i.e., overhead) and period (i.e., administrative) expenses, without breaking out these CSR costs in a separate reporting category. Accordingly, in these organizations managers do not fully appreciate the amount spent (and this can be material with respect to total revenue), nor do they identify specific CSR areas where they wish to make an impact. Companies create systematic reporting processes for traditional strategic initiatives, such as an initiative to reduce customer response time, to assure that they create value. Likewise, sustainability spending should focus on value creation, and managers should require the inclusion of social and environmental initiatives in the reporting structure like other strategic initiatives (Bell, Soybel, and Turner 2012).

Annual Budgeting

During the budgeting process, managers should assure that appropriate short-term goals for strategic sustainability projects are incorporated into operating budgets. For example, when Unilever identified water as an important sustainability issue for their company, they established targets for reduced water usage. As one response to this initiative, All 3X concentrated detergent was created, which uses only 64 percent of the water (a direct material cost) that its regular detergent uses. Annual budgets for that product line should reflect lower costs for direct materials and for shipping since the product weighs less. Performance metrics should also reflect reduced fossil fuel use (Martha's Circle 2007).

Decision Making

The following decision-making scenarios are typical but not exhaustive of the opportunities accountants have to influence the contributions their businesses make to society.

Product or Process Design

Management accountants can provide managers with decision support models that incorporate an organization's social and environmental goals (e.g., reducing sugars in children's drinks) along with profit goals to support product design and outsourcing decisions. For example, Levi Strauss & Co. clothing designers are using *Evaluate*, a proprietary life cycle analysis (LCA) tool, to assess the impacts of the core fabrics used in a clothing line (Westervelt 2012). This information exists alongside quality and price so managers have information to make style choices that are stylish for the customer, yield an appropriate margin for Levi Strauss, and are environmentally friendly (everyone wins).

Sourcing Decisions

When analyzing sourcing opportunities, managers should have reports that include, among other things, the cost of qualifying and monitoring suppliers so the organization does not engage suppliers that maintain unsafe working environments or use child labor. For example, as a result of catastrophic failures at plants in Bangladesh, Wal-Mart has a new program to audit and publish information about safety conditions in their suppliers' plants there. So far, they have completed only 75 audits, spent over $4 million, and have discovered that over 15 percent of the plants failed (Banjo 2013). But the ethics of these issues grow even more complicated when effects on local employment are put into the equation. The decision to improve safety in local supplier factories, for example, makes outsourcing more expensive, potentially leading to less employment in poor, developing nations.

Product Defects

Upon discovery that a product is defective and potentially harmful to users, managers need to focus on externalities and long-term organizational consequences, rather than performing an economic calculation that compares the immediate costs of redesigning and product recall against future payments to injured customers. Not only are future lawsuits and damage claims likely in such cases, public disclosures about how the company traded safety for profits will impact its reputation and erode its brand. Reputational and brand image damage can exceed warranty and legal costs by sizeable amounts (e.g., Dow Chemical and breast implants; SeaWorld and animal and employee welfare; Arthur Andersen Consulting, which became Accenture after Enron).

Bottom of the Pyramid Markets

Management accountants should engage with managers in fact-based, realistic conversations about profiting from bottom of the pyramid markets (Prahalad 2004). Many companies have entered such markets with very low-priced products and have anticipated selling enough volume to yield both a profit and provide much-needed goods and services to underserved populations. Most have been unable to make that business model work using existing business processes (Simanis 2012). Customer acquisition and retention are costly in undeveloped markets and require *high-touch*. Other operating expenses, such as distribution, are higher than they are in developed markets because of poor infrastructure and logistics. Knowing this, management accountants should push managers for innovative ways to gain customers and deliver goods and services. Without such efforts, the company should consider donating goods or engaging in other ways to benefit the communities.

Management Control

Management accountants design performance measurement systems that influence incentive pay. Systems with traditional financial performance metrics, such as sales growth, margin enhancement, asset turnover, or return on sales are unlikely to show short-term paybacks from long-term strategic sustainability initiatives. In a recent KPMG survey (2011), almost half of surveyed CEOs said that it is difficult to shift focus to sustainability initiatives from programs that provide more easily measured short-term financial results. When a company formally links its performance evaluation and compensation to sustainability efforts, employees clearly understand that there is a commitment to sustainability that goes beyond public relations.

As an example, a sustainability director of a major international food services company revealed that one of the major problems he faced was that no routine performance report showed that sustainability offerings yielded business. He had to create such a report using information from a variety of internal sources. Since this report did not emanate from the performance management system, its credibility was questioned. Clearly, this indicates that when new strategic initiatives emerge, management accountants have responsibility to revise the performance measurement system.

On a more positive note, Intel links individual compensation to environmental performance. If an Intel employee suggests an innovative environmental project and the project delivers a significant impact on pre-established performance metrics, the employee gets rewarded (Baya and Mathaisel 2011).

Individual Level Responsibility

As with all professionals, the major ethical issue facing managers and management accountants is self-interest. Self-interest, making decisions and taking actions based on your own needs and wants while ignoring the impact on others, is prohibited for accountants by codes of ethics in many countries. Yet self-interested behavior persists. The following sections provide examples of how such self-interested actions impact others.

Fairness to Others

Management accountants can act in ways that deliberately harm co-workers, suppliers, customers, and others. Examples affecting co-workers include arguing for cost allocation methods that unfairly burden a co-worker's unit while favoring one's own, taking credit for a co-worker's accomplishments, preparing a performance report that inappropriately attributes results to a subunit (product, project) to please a boss, or pushing for reductions in labor time, reductions in materials cost, or in other operating budgets while not addressing overhead expenditures of upper managers. Examples that impact customers include overbilling to cover personal expenses, such as excessive travel or entertainment, or hiding mistakes and losses in product costs rather than recognizing the additional costs as losses. Examples that negatively impact suppliers include making unreasonable demands on them for low cost or quick delivery. If a supplier is in a weak position and knows that they will lose the business unless they comply, they may agree to produce or source using unsafe working conditions. Disastrous consequences, such as those seen in Bangladesh's factories, may result. Gaining concessions on costs or delivery time from suppliers might be based on good reasons (e.g., learning curve impacts) but may also be socially harmful, self-interested behavior that makes the management accountant appear to be an effective, tough negotiator.

Performance Management

There are many ways to manage earnings that achieve short-term goals at the expense of long-term value creation. To meet short-term earning goals, accountants can suggest actions such as postponing equipment maintenance, increasing inventory levels, cancelling training or travel, reducing allowances for bad debts, shipping products earlier than ordered, or changing equipment lives to reduce depreciation expense. Misleading accounting practices are not restricted to profit seeking organizations, however. In nonprofit organizations, accountants can support (and participate in) excessive management pay and unnecessary expensive perks, and they can misclassify expenses as programmatic rather than administrative. Management accountants can allow nonprofit organizations to be run for the benefit of key managers rather than in support of the organization's mission.

Fraud

The 2012 Report to the Nations on Occupational Fraud and Abuse reported that in the United States, Europe, Africa, Canada, and Latin America, over 16 percent of all fraud cases were perpetrated by employees in the accounting department (ACFE 2012). In Asia and Oceania countries, the rates were only slightly lower (ACFE 2012, 53–54). Sadly, this is not an anomaly; in both the 2010 and 2012 studies, accountants led the list of employees who stole organizational assets. In 2012, the median loss from fraud committed by accountants was reported to be $183,000, with the smallest organizations incurring the largest losses (5). Accountants' thefts spanned all industries and were most prevalent in small businesses without good internal controls. The most common frauds that accountants committed were fictitious billing, check tampering, and skimming cash receipts (55).

As our examples illustrate, users of accounting information and management accountants have distinct ethical and social responsibilities both individually and organizationally. Education holds the promise of helping to prevent managers and accountants from engaging in fraud, and through careful crafting of lesson plans, we can demonstrate how management accountants' choices and actions impact decision making and society. We can heighten managers' and accountants' social awareness and help them make better choices. We can train managers to understand the values inherent in the accounting information they receive. We can also provide a framework for evaluating impacts and create educational opportunities for positive ways to express choices and take action and prepare them for making real-time decisions in the workplace. The next section provides advice to educators on how to accomplish these goals.

Advice for Professors

Professors, in their role as experts, have the responsibility to scaffold educational experiences (Bruner 1960; Vygotsky 1978). Scaffolds are a metaphor for professors establishing instructional structure so that higher levels of *construction* (i.e., learning) may occur. A curriculum map documents how a curriculum is scaffolded (or could be scaffolded) and is a helpful first step in designing how to accomplish learning outcomes (Jacobs 1997, 2004). Ideally, business programs scaffold students' education by providing content and decision making about ethics, sustainability, and CSR throughout the business curriculum (e.g., accounting, marketing, finance, management, and systems) and integrated into all functional areas within accounting (e.g., financial accounting, management accounting, tax accounting, and auditing) at all academic levels (e.g., first-year undergraduates through executive education).

Assume that your institution has not taken this systematic approach, and you have been assigned to teach a course in which you would like to include coverage of ethics, sustainability, or CSR without deleting functional area materials. We believe that if only one learning outcome was accomplished, it would be to make students aware of the impact that accounting has on decision making. Accordingly, we suggest that you cover the first learning activity in the exercises that follow the chapter. This exercise contrasts perceptions of accounting as a black and white set of rules with its reality, where accountants use value judgments to impact decisions.

As a second step, we suggest that as you cover assigned problems from a textbook, you ask students to reflect on the impact that their analysis might have on organizational stakeholders and how the analysis might be modified to incorporate ethical and CSR issues. Extant management accounting textbooks typically do not provide this prompt. Ethics, sustainability, and CSR materials are isolated in a chapter dedicated to this *topic* or a token ethics or CSR problem or two are included in the end-of-chapter materials. The key takeaway is that, today, textbooks will rarely provide help in strategically integrating ethics, sustainability, and CSR. As your comfort level in addressing CSR and ethics issues increases, and more commercial materials become available, you can make great progress toward integrating these topics throughout your course.

Ethics and CSR Teaching Strategy

Preassessments of students' baseline knowledge about ethics, sustainability, and CSR will be very helpful to instructors who are establishing learning outcomes for their program, course, or unit within a course. Educators also need to think about how to design assignments and assessments for desired learning levels based on a learning taxonomy. For example, Bloom et al. (1956) taxonomy is based on the perceived difficulty of the learning activity (i.e., comprehend, apply, analyze, synthesize, and evaluate). We employ the American Institute of Certified Public Accountants (AICPA) core competency framework (WolcottLynch Associates 2002; AICPA 2013) because it was developed to show how to structure assessment of accounting competencies.

Levels of cognitive complexity, as shown in Table 5.1, can be helpful to instructors who are teaching different audiences or who have an instructional goal of increasing students' cognitive complexity during the instructional period. For example, a student in an introductory management accounting course might be asked to *identify* what product costs might impact society in a negative way (level 1: low cognitive complexity) where students in an MBA program or executives in continuing education could be asked to develop a risk management *strategy* to address potential externalities with the highest likelihood and impact of occurrence (level 4: very high cognitive complexity).

One conceptual tool that can be used by educators to plan how to incorporate ethics, sustainability, and CSR topics into a program, course, or unit is the ADDIE model of instructional design (Branson et al. 1975). ADDIE is an acronym for analyze, design, develop, implement, and evaluate. The first step in instructional design is to analyze the program goals and learning needs of the target audience. The second step is to design learning goals and develop assessments. The third step is to develop learning assets. The fourth step is to create a learning implementation plan.

Table 5.1 Level of cognitive complexity and cognitive performance

Level of cognitive complexity	Cognitive performance (assessment)
1. Low	*Identify uncertainties and relevant information and make logical connections*
2. Moderate	*Explore interpretations and connections*
3. High	*Weigh alternatives and draw reasonable conclusions*
4. Very high	*Integrate, monitor, and refine strategies over time*

The last step is to evaluate if the program goals, learning goals, and learning needs of the target audience were met.

As exemplars, we provide several instructional strategies and learning activities (i.e., in a box) with teaching notes and answer keys. Two of the learning activities demonstrate the ADDIE model. Learning activities at several different cognitive levels are included for those educators who are beginning their journey to integrate ethics, sustainability, and CSR into their management accounting courses.

Developing Versus Developed Country Perspectives

While some might argue that there are vast differences between training in sustainability, ethics, and CSR in developing versus developed countries due to the sophistication of regulations governing the practice of accounting, we believe that significance is overstated. Understanding compliance rules by country (or even industry) simply is insufficient training in sustainability, ethics, and CSR. Often mistreated as synonymous with ethics training, compliance rules are external guides to conduct, which cannot keep up with the ability and creativity of humans to circumvent these rules. Further, sanctions applied in cases of violations are after-the-fact, and often the damage caused by an action (particularly in the case of a nonrenewal resource) cannot be undone. Real, disciplined, and enduring change in how decisions are made can only occur when the guides to conduct are internally driven, that is, when individuals have a well-developed moral compass by which they choose to live.

Conclusion

Management accountants, like all business actors, make decisions daily that reflect their values and, ultimately, shape the character of the organizations for which they work. These decisions, and the ethical processes used to make them, can be as small as submitting or processing a misleading expense report, or as large as collecting or neglecting to collect and report data on social or environmental externalities. A management accountant exercises professional judgment on a regular basis in contrast to the stereotypic image of an accountant who mechanically processes numbers according to black and white rules. We particularly have sought to underscore that management accountants play a critical role in framing organization decisions at the highest levels by providing the data on which organizational strategies are developed, based, and executed. By doing so, management accountants can directly or indirectly determine how decision makers in an organization treat its social and physical environment and each one of its stakeholders, that is, its level of sustainability and CSR. This role is becoming increasingly significant and challenging as society has demanded greater levels of business accountability for its actions and more positive (less negative) contributions to our world. As educators, we have a responsibility to teach students to identify the value judgments management accountants make in the performance of their duties and to encourage the inclusion of ethical, sustainability, and CSR data in management accounting analyses to address society's demand.

Problems and Cases

The first two exercises in this box demonstrate the ADDIE process of developing course materials. The last two exercises are presented without demonstrating the ADDIE process. All activities presented are classified according to the AICPA learning levels as discussed in the chapter. AICPA learning levels can be used in the design of assignment rubrics and postassessment instruments.

Instructional Strategy: Learning Activity 1

Activity: Contrast the perceived and desired roles for management accounting professionals.

We recommend this activity if an educator only has time to select one instructional activity (learning strategy) outside the textbook they are currently using because it provides the foundation for understanding how management accountants can create value for their organizations in the future.

Analyze

Overall Goal. One of the characteristics of any profession is that it has shared values of professional conduct and integrity that encourage others to trust the professional (Institute of Management Accountants [IMA] 2005, Chartered Institute of Management Accountants [CIMA] 2010). Professionals behave in ways that express their values. When students complete this learning activity, they should be able to explain how management accountants use their professional judgment to help decision makers create a more prosperous society (Pathways Commission Vision Model 2013). The desired future state gives students a more robust understanding of what management accountants do to compare to the perceptions they may have that have been engrained through various media.

Target Audience. Our assumption is that students taking cost and management accounting are MBA students and executives who have work experience.

Delivery Environment. Assume face-to-face learning but could be modified for hybrid or online environments.

Design

Learning Objectives to Accomplish Overall Goal. Contrast the perceived and desired roles for management accounting professionals.

Instructional Strategies to Support the Learning Objectives. Preassessment—Ask students to share five or six words that describe the chief financial officer or other senior-level management accounting personnel in their organizations. The words could be adjectives such as *detail-oriented* or phrases referring to what they do: "Prepare profit and loss reports for management meetings." Students should also be asked to imagine at least one example of how management accounting professionals could help create a more prosperous society through their daily work. The preassessment should take no more than 5–10 minutes. The instructor should then capture the student responses on a flipchart or board to identify common themes.

Develop

Resources Available That May Be Shared with Students.

Pathways Commission Vision Model (2013)

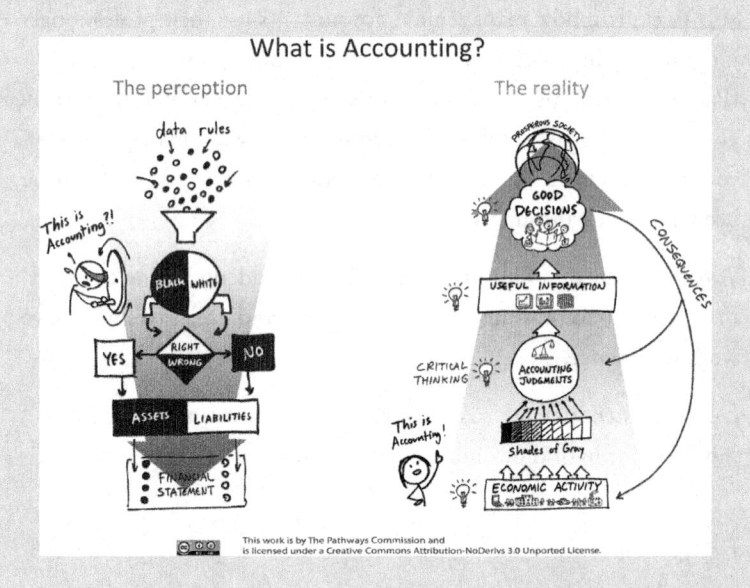

Assignment

AICPA Level 2 Moderate Cognitive Complexity: Explore Interpretations and Connections

- Recognize and control for own biases.
- Articulate assumptions and reasoning associated with alternative points of view.
- Qualitatively interpret evidence from a variety of points of view.
- Organize information in meaningful ways to encompass problem complexities.

Students should interview at least one senior-level management accounting professional in their organization or another organization. Ideally, the students would complete at least two interviews. The students should develop hypotheses based on the two models (e.g., the perception and the reality) and design questions to test the accuracy of the models. The student should not share the models with the interviewees until the questions based on the hypotheses have been answered. Once the interview questions are completed, the student should show the two models to the senior-level management accounting professional and capture their feedback on the two models. If the student completes interviews with more than one senior-level management accounting professional, how are the responses of the professionals similar or different? The interview responses could be used for a classroom discussion, online discussion board, or written assignment explaining what roles management accounting professionals play in organizations.

Implement

Delivery and Learner Support. If this learning activity is delivered in a hybrid or online environment, appropriate course management software needs to be utilized and support provided to learners on how to access and use the technology.

Evaluate

Postassessment. Repeat initial assessment to see the breadth and depth of student responses to how management accounting professionals can create a more prosperous society through their daily work.

Possible Answer Key.

1. Here are some examples of what senior-level management accounting professionals will likely share with the interviewers:

    (a) The percentage of time they spend preparing reports versus doing analytical work.

(b) How the perceptions of accountants and accounting work is negatively portrayed by the media and are not what they have experienced.
(c) Concerns about the extent to which the reports they prepare are used in decision making.
(d) Concerns about how well decision makers understand the information contained in report.
(e) The type of analyses they could prepare if only they had more employees, better technology, fewer crisis requests, and so forth.

2. The Pathways Commission Vision Model can be interpreted as a supply of information (starting at the bottom) or as the demand for information (starting at the top). The Pathways Commission Vision Model is rooted in a broadly defined set of economic activities that include environmental and social impacts throughout the supply/service chain. Professional judgment gained through accounting expertise and professional experience allows management accountants to understand the shades of gray in accounting practice that allow for many *right* answers. Management accountants provide a balanced and inclusive set of information that is useful to decision makers who anticipate how their decision-making consequences will impact the goal of a prosperous society. Possible evidence includes the following:

(a) Interviews with accountants point out that mechanical accounting procedures are being outsourced to provide more time for decision making and value creation (Lawson et al. 2014).
(b) Management accountants in countries (e.g., Germany) have a stronger profile than financial accountants (e.g., United States).
(c) IMA-MAS Task Force has completed competencies needed for management accounting that include accounting, broad management, and functional competencies (Lawson et al. 2014).
(d) The task force that created the Pathways Commission Vision Model included a broad set of accounting practitioners working in profit and nonprofit organizations.

(e) Consequences are included because the quality of decision making either enhances or detracts from the goal of a prosperous society.

(f) Elements of the model are interdependent and judgments (principles-based approach) vary along a conservative-aggressive accounting approach.

Instructional Strategy: Learning Activity 2

Activity: Contrast the perceived and desired roles for management accounting professionals.

We recommend this activity be used to supplement the make-or-buy (outsourcing) topic typically covered in a management accounting chapter dedicated to short-term decision making. Instructors should point out to students that many organizations (e.g., technology and fashion industries) rely on outsourcing as their long-term production strategy, not as a periodic decision to either make domestically in their own factory or outsource to a domestic or international factory. Make-or-buy does not just refer to manufacturing but also to services (e.g., research and development, order fulfillment, and customer support).

Discuss the traditional textbook approach to the short-term outsourcing decision-making problem. Include questions such as: What information is incorporated in textbook outsourcing problems? What information is not included in textbook outsourcing problems? If a company decided it wanted to include additional information regarding social, environmental, and governance metrics as they relate to outsourcing decisions, what recommendations could be made to expand the information collected for external reporting? What negative effects on local employment would you tolerate to increase employee welfare?

Analyze

Overall Goal. When students complete this learning activity, they should be able to explain how externalities must be included in outsourcing decisions because of the magnitude of costs that can be incurred.

Target Audience. Our assumption is that students taking cost and management accounting are second- or third-year undergraduate students. We have included a Level 1—low cognitive complexity—assignment for the students taking their first cost and management accounting course. We have also included a Level 3—high cognitive complexity—assignment that may be better suited for fourth-year students in an advanced cost accounting course or with first-year MBA students.

Delivery Environment. Assume face-to-face learning environment but could be modified for hybrid/online environments.

Design

Learning Objectives to Accomplish Overall Goal. Identify and estimate the costs of externalities in a retailer's strategy to outsource clothing production to Bangladesh or Cambodia. Prioritize mitigation strategies for the greatest risks that could yield externality costs.

Instructional Strategies to Support the Learning Objectives. Preassessment—after students have been introduced to several examples of activities outsourced by large organizations, select one activity and ask students to list three specific examples of externalities and estimate the impact (i.e., low, medium, high, catastrophic) of one of those externalities on a decision to outsource. The preassessment should take no more than 15 minutes. The instructor should then capture the student responses on a flipchart or board to identify _common themes and assessments of magnitude.

Develop

Resources Available that Need to Be Shared With Students.

- Pathways Commission Vision Model—review the desired role of management accountant to support a prosperous society. There are two videos explaining the vision model at the website (Pathways Commission Vision Model 2013) if

you want more details about this model from two faculty experts.
- Textbook presentation(s) of make-or-buy decisions (outsourcing) and where they are located in the textbooks.
- Articles from the current business press on externalities incurred in at least two industries who made outsourcing decisions.
- COSO Enterprise Risk Management and Triple Bottom Line (Faris et al. 2013).

Materials to Be Developed.

- Written assignment
- Teaching notes for instructor describing the assignment
- Grading rubrics for written assignment

Assignments (two assignments at two different cognitive learning levels targeted for different student audiences—see earlier note on "target audience")

Both assignments: Instructors can review the desired role of management accounting professionals on a flip chart (see Pathways Commission Vision Model).

Assignment #1: AICPA Level 1 Low Cognitive Complexity—Identify Relevant Information and Make Logical Connections

Students may be assigned or allowed to select an industry that outsources production or services. Students should first outline the direct costs that need to be included in the analysis.

Assignment #2: AICPA Level 3 High Cognitive Complexity—Prioritize Alternatives and Involve Others

- *After thorough analysis, develop and use reasonable guidelines for prioritizing factors and choosing among solution options.*
- *Effectively involve others, as needed, in implementing the best solution.*

In addition, students should provide a list of potential externalities and their assessment of how likely these might occur based on research they have done in the popular business press. Students should identify appropriate risk-management strategies. Then students should incorporate the costs of externalities with their direct cost analysis. Students should be able to distinguish how many of these externalities would be likely to occur in outsourced domestic production (i.e., United States or other developed country) versus outsourced domestic production in a developing economy.

Implement

Delivery and Learner Support. If this learning activity is delivered in a hybrid or online environment, appropriate course management software needs to be utilized and support provided to learners on how to access and use the technology.

Evaluate

Postassessment. Repeat initial assessment to see the breadth of externalities identified and any increased precision in the estimation of potential negative impact. Students should be able to identify appropriate risk mitigation strategies.

Answer Key. Textbook short-term outsourcing problems focus on the comparison of direct costs to make in-house versus direct costs to outsource. The first assumption is that the organization already has a production and service facility so variable direct costs are the focus. Because the cost of materials is similar, the costs of labor and overhead are typically the differential costs in a textbook outsourcing problem.

Externalities could include the following:

- Reputational damage for brand and organization
- Domestic layoffs

- Logistical costs (successful logistics and failed logistics)
- Social costs of quality of supervision, education, and training
- Loss of life and reparations for deaths
- Stockouts in a just-in-time inventory environment
- Toxic waste
- Carbon emission
- Negative impacts on employee health (e.g., drinking water, toilets, chemical contaminants)
- Discovery of underage or illegal immigrant workers
- Safety failures (i.e., building, equipment, residence)
- Cost of inspections and audits
- Cost of prequalification of multiple suppliers
- Losses due to government instability
- Losses and costs of plant seizure
- Costs of intellectual property infringement
- Lost profits and extra costs due to development of regulation

Instructional Strategy: Learning Activity 3

This activity assumes that students have identified that the action proposed in the scenario is unethical and requires students to practice discussing the issue with a supervisor. It can be taught as an additional assignment when a product costing problem is taught and is appropriate for a third-year or higher level cost accounting class.

Activity: You feel quite lucky to have landed your dream job as a programmer for Extreme Games when you graduated from college. Your assignments have been exciting and you have had the opportunity to work with some great people. You worked on Job # 4230 with a team of three other programmers. Unfortunately, you know that 100 of the 300 programming hours on the job were wasted. Your project manager (PM), juggling multiple jobs under tight time pressure, gave you and your team incorrect instructions that were followed for almost four days before your PM discovered his mistake. When he discovered what he had done, the PM told you and the other programmers to charge the wasted programming hours to the job. You know that this would hide the fact that wrong instructions were given and would prevent a bad performance review for your manager. The job is small relative to the 25,000 total billable hours the company has budgeted for the year, but as a programmer, you do not think a customer should be overcharged. You want to act but wonder what you should say, to whom you should speak, and when should you bring up your concerns.

Requirements

1. What are the values that you would like to support, encourage, and act on in the company where you work?
2. Calculate the impact of the two alternatives, bill 300 hours (the PM's position) or bill 200 hours (your position) on this year's operating profit before taxes. Assume that the cost of service is $69 per hour, and that standard billing practices specify that job costs are to be marked up by 80 percent. What percent of annual total sales revenue and profits does this job represent (see Table 5.2)?
3. Identify the stakeholders and issues that are involved in billing 300 hours compared to 200 hours (see your calculation in part 2.)
4. What arguments might the PM make to justify the overbilling and what are your most persuasive responses to these arguments (see Table 5.3)?
5. Offer strategies about who you might talk to and when an appropriate time to have the discussion with your PM might be.

AICPA Level 3 High Cognitive Complexity—Prioritize Alternatives and Involve Others

Solution

1. Responses will vary but may include statements about hyper norms of honesty and integrity:
    - Speaking openly about problems with managers
    - Providing value to customers and treating them fairly
    - Being truthful about mistakes and learning from them

2. *Table 5.2 Impact of billing alternative amounts on operating margin*

	Bill 200 hours	Bill 300 hours	Bill 25,000 hours
Revenue ($69 * 1.8)	$24,840	$37,260	$3,105,000
Cost of service ($69/hour)	$20,700	$20,700	$1,725,000
Operating margin	$4,140	$16,560	$1,415,000
Difference in margin		($4,140–$16,560)	–$12,420
% difference compared to total operating margin			Less than 1%

3. Stakeholders and issues:
   - Customer(s): The customer for the job would be overcharged; this in turn makes the cost of the video game higher. If market prices for video games are established by market conditions, this would reduce profits for the customer, decrease the return to shareholders, and might cause their employees to lose jobs.
   - Manager: It means that a manager, in need of training, is allowed to continue without any intervention. He or she is also evaluated more highly than is supported by performance.
   - Employees: Employees assigned to this manager receive the message that profitability is more important than honest, accurate information, and client billings. They also feel that they should not admit to making mistakes.
   - Programmers involved: You and others who know that this happened will feel uncomfortable and dishonest toward the client, and your morale might suffer trying to figure out what to do.
   - Upper management: Upper management will be concerned about the culture that is being created if employees are dishonest when recording their hours and PMs do not feel like they can admit mistakes. Additionally, the company's information system will not contain the proper

Table 5.3 Arguments and responses for overbilling

PM's potential argument	Response
This is a standard practice—everybody does it.	"There are always judgment calls, but I'm concerned because this is so large that it can have negative repercussions for us. I wonder if we could use this situation to our advantage to develop a better relationship with the customer. We could make it clear that although we were over-stretched with projects and spent a lot more time, we made sure that the costs weren't passed on." Another alternative: "I know that we had some issues with this job, but I think that you have an opportunity to send an extremely positive message to our customer about how we put them first and to the programmers about the pride that we at Extreme Games place in our work and service. I think you'll score a lot of points with the programmers for your leadership; it's a real opportunity." The argument should be framed in a way that doesn't accuse the PM of being unethical or dishonest, but rather to show that you want him or her to understand that you're on his side trying to figure out how to make the best out of a bad situation.
Locus of loyalty—I know this is not fair to the customer, but someone has to pay for our hours. You do not want to lose your job, do you?	"Isn't being fair and honest with our clients important for long run business relationships? I'm afraid that the customer will complain up the ladder about the extra hours, and we'll have to explain why it happened anyway. That has the potential to be worse than just acknowledging the mistake. I believe that the standard overhead charge usually includes an allowance for nonproductive hours that are worked, so why don't we just charge to that and try to be extra careful and efficient on future jobs to make up for it?"
I want my programmers to get credit for all the work you do. You guys are the best.	"Thank you for your confidence! But we feel really bad and guilty about the hours wasted on this job. Let's make this a positive learning experience and discuss how we can avoid this kind of situation in the future, and let's provide this customer great service at a fair price so we can feel good about it."

information to bid future jobs. This could adversely impact future business. Management also will not have proper information to evaluate the PM. The impact on profit is so small (less than 1 percent) that the upper management is not likely to be concerned about the loss.
4. Answers will vary; some potential responses are provided. These potential responses were developed with assistance from organizational behavior faculty members at Babson College.
5. Allow students to discuss; some might want to include fellow programmers who were involved and have a conversation over lunch with the PM. If students want to go over their PM's head to his or her boss, explain the hierarchy in the organization and the need to communicate directly with your own boss before approaching others in the organization.

Instructional Strategy: Learning Activity 4

This short case is more advanced than our other exercises and might be assigned when covering just-in-time inventory systems or supply chain management in upper division or graduate level management accounting classes. The case requires students to perform stakeholder analysis and to use an ethical framework to support their position. There is an assumption that students have been introduced to philosophical approaches to ethics somewhere else in the curriculum.

Eastern Tire Importer

[Loosely based on the article by Martin (2007)]

"I just don't understand," began Amy Wang, VP for Sourcing for Eastern Tire Importer, "why my group is getting blamed for the cost of the Chinese tires that were recalled last quarter!"

The U.S. government ordered more than 450,000 tires recalled in June, 20xx, because the tires lacked gum strips, an important safety feature that prevents the threads from separating from the tire. The tires had been manufactured by Hangzhou Zhongce in China, the company that provided tires to Eastern. The tires caused two traffic fatalities plus numerous less serious accidents in the United States. In response, the Chinese government blacklisted the tire manufacturer for creating concern about the safety of Chinese-made goods.

Amy explained to Jay Cohen, Eastern's controller, "I've complained to everyone at our manager's meetings that our engineers' late design changes and marketing's poor demand forecasting places pressure on my group to source! We had to push Hangzhou Zhongce's factory management to deliver so we could meet our price, delivery, and inventory targets. If we hadn't made our targets, we'd be below par on our performance scorecard, and nobody would have earned a bonus."

Jay, nodding, agreed. "I know, Amy, that some of our suppliers, who may already have done a poor job of production planning or have accepted orders beyond their capacity, just take on these orders and then pressure their employees to produce. The pressure to deliver on time may have outweighed their concerns about legal compliance, code compliance, and general good work practices." Jay continued, "even though you're complaining about your group being charged for the costs of the recall, your group brought that supplier to us. You are responsible for selecting quality suppliers as well as achieving your price and delivery targets."

Amy fumed, "Jay, it's the fault of our 'just-in-time' purchasing practices that you insisted on! Our buying practices are just too stressful! They are creating bad working conditions for our workers as well as our manufacturer's workers who have to work overtime at low pay rates to meet our demands! It's no wonder they just ignore manufacturing defects. In the meantime, my buyers are quitting, and I'm training new buyers. These 'just-in-time' purchasing practices undermine the brand reputation that we need to uphold. My buyers face performance incentives focused on making margins and keeping tires in stock while keeping inventory to less than two weeks supply. I don't think the buyers are likely to worry how the suppliers achieve such cheap and flexible production."

Jay shut off the conversation by saying, "Amy, you are the VP of Sourcing for an import company! Almost 70 percent of our costs are under your control. Of course your job is stressful, but you are rewarded handsomely based on your scorecard results. Just keep getting us the prices and deliveries, but chose better suppliers! If you get the company into trouble with bad vendors, your operation is going to foot the bill—no one ever wants to pay for the trouble they cause; but it's my job to trace the cost to the group that caused it."

Required

1. Supply chain management is an important part of value chain management. Evaluate Eastern Tire's management of their suppliers against what you have studied about supply chain management.
2. Following a framework for ethical decision making, determine if there is an ethical issue facing Eastern Tire Importer.
3. What changes should be made (if any) in Eastern's management accounting system to help alleviate the issues that you identified in part 2?

AICPA Level 3 High Cognitive Complexity—Prioritize Alternatives and Involve Others

Solution

1. Eastern Tire seems to be using a more traditional cost management approach that manages the external cost of supply through arm's length market transactions and focuses on finding cheaper suppliers rather than trying to cooperate with suppliers to satisfy customers' quality, cost, and time requirements. They seem to be *beating up* their suppliers to meet their changing requirements even when they know that they may be impossible.

   Eastern should forge long-term alliances with quality suppliers; this is key, since most of Eastern's costs (70 percent) are tied to suppliers' prices and delivery time. This means that Eastern needs to select suppliers who have work processes in place that assure compliance with quality standards and work laws, and who will focus on the brand image that is important to Eastern. Then, they need to share information about markets, customers, processes, and activities with their key suppliers. Eastern also needs to keep design changes to a minimum or use suppliers that design products so they have some idea of what changes to anticipate.

2. The solution to question two is evaluated from a framework used by Babson College. Substitute your institution's framework for evaluating ethical issues or introduce this framework to your class.

   (i) **Identify issues.** Determine if there are ethical issues. Is there something wrong personally, interpersonally, or socially here? How will this decision or action affect others? Define and state the ethical issues as clearly as possible. It may be useful to state these issues as questions that focus on the ethical implications of the decisions.

   The decision to push changed designs and tight time pressures on suppliers knowing that they have difficulty delivering without worrying about their production methods is problematic. This is done so the purchasing group can get their bonus under the existing system. The performance measurement and reward system in the organization is encouraging this employee behavior.

   The ethical issue is that corporate performance measurement and reward systems are causing safety concerns for society and impacting the employees' quality of working life.

   (ii) **Gather information.** Gathering information and facts that are relevant to a decision may be more difficult than it seems, as information may be unavailable or ambiguous. A critical step in gathering information is to identify the effected stakeholders and determine their interests, values, and opinions.

   Stakeholders:

   Customers—impacted by tire separations, injured, or financially impacted.

   Society—bears a risk of accident due to separating tires; uninsured accident victims are costs to society.

Employees of Eastern—pressured to perform under unfair conditions or they risk being evaluated as poor performers.

Employees of suppliers—pressured to perform under unfair conditions or they may lose their contracts.

Shareholders—suffer when brand suffers; pushing for short-term performance privileges existing shareholders over future ones.

Governments—embarrassed by actions and spend efforts controlling companies to avoid sanctions.

Managers—responding to reward systems to earn bonuses treat employees unfairly and risk the reputation of the firm.

(iii) **Brainstorm alternatives**

Alternative 1: Develop long-term relationships with a few, quality suppliers who are guaranteed a minimum amount of business per quarter each year, share design changes early and involve suppliers, and link with better information systems to suppliers so they can see anticipated needs the next quarter, in case they want to produce and carry inventory. Internally develop evaluation criteria for suppliers, prepare scorecards for suppliers, and adjust the current balanced scorecard metrics.

Alternative 2: Continue as is and push the purchasing group to continue to perform on cost, time, and inventory levels ignoring ethical and social responsibility while penalizing them when they get caught.

(iv) **Evaluate alternatives from various ethical perspectives**

The Internet provides great resources for these ethical theories (e.g., Chonko 2012). Most general education programs expose students to all frameworks, but students' values will determine which kind of framework they will ultimately use to approach ethical issues.

(a) **Deontological theories:** *Which alternative is based on a rule that you would want to apply to everyone? Which alternative respects the rights and dignity of the stakeholders?*

Alternative 1: Develop a standard way to evaluate suppliers and a supplier scorecard system that would be used on all suppliers. Suppliers must be selected and monitored regularly. Have engineering or marketing bear costs of changing design or demand estimates beyond reasonable amounts to encourage better data provision. Develop a scorecard that evaluates the purchasing group based on the quality of supply base as well as price, quality, and time.

Alternative 2 does not respect workers, society, or shareholders. In the short run, it is in the best interest of managers who may quickly leave this organization and move to another.

(b) **Utilitarianism:** *Which alternative will produce the most good and cause the least harm?*

A standard rating system will hurt some suppliers who want to exploit workers or lie to observers to appear to be qualified suppliers. Under alternative 1, workers may continue to be exploited without diligence on part of the observers (consider recent reports by Walmart as they audited their supply chain.) Alternative 1 needs an audit function.

Society should have fewer recalls and injuries with faulty products if alternative 1 is selected. They will become outraged if alternative 2 is followed and many problems occur.

In alternative 1, the job gets tougher for purchasing—they have other dimensions to incorporate that will act sometimes in opposite ways to price and time requirements. Ultimately this should be better for society and the company, however. Alternative 2 will continue to cause high turnover and a sense of unfairness.

In alternative 1, shareholders of supplier firms not selected will be hurt and will withdraw their capital support. Eastern's shareholders should benefit by having higher profitability in the long run after processes are established. In the short run, costs may go up as processes and information systems are developed, and profits may go down.

The first alternative is more consistent with *good* for society. In general, excessive pressure should not be placed on employees such that they sacrifice quality and cause harm to customers and general society.

(c) **Virtue theories:** *Which alternative develops character traits that will allow you to live peacefully with yourself and others?*

Alternative 1 creates an environment where one would be willing to work. It creates fairness in the workplace in terms of rewards and expectations. It encourages society to be more trusting of goods acquired, and does not shift costs of inferior products to society (avoids externalities).

3. Eastern's management accounting system needs to reassess the *just-in-time* purchasing and the two week inventory given their difficulty with projecting demand. The more uncertain the demand, the more inventory the company needs to maintain (from operations courses students will learn that inventory exists to overcome uncertainty). The inventory required should also consider how long it typically takes from placing an order to receiving goods.

The performance measurement and management system should include metrics for strategic factors that the company wishes to reinforce. If alliances with quality, ethical suppliers are important to the company, then metrics must be developed to operationalize those factors and the metrics have to be considered along with cost, time, and inventory levels. Otherwise this will be ignored in routine supplier selection. Management accountants should assist supply management personnel with monitoring supplier performance on metrics that go beyond price and on-time delivery. Some of the relevant items for supplier selection should be developed into performance metrics for monitoring purposes.

References

ACFE (Association of Certified Fraud Examiners). 2012. *Report to the Nations on Occupational Fraud.* http://www.acfe.com/uploadedFiles/ACFE_Website/Content/rttn/2012-report-to-nations.pdf (accessed December 17, 2013).

AICPA (American Institute of Certified Public Accountants). 2013. "Core Competency and Educational Competency Assessment Frameworks."

http://www.aicpa.org/interestareas/accountingeducation/resources/pages/corecompetency.aspx (accessed January 2, 2014).

Ansari, S., J. Bell, and T. Klammer. 2009. Strategy and Management Accounting. http://www.lulu.com/us/en/shop/jan-bell-and-shahid-ansari-and-tom-klammer/strategy-and-management-accounting/ebook/product-6001470.html (accessed January 2, 2014).

Banjo, S. 2013. "Wal-Mart: Many of Tested Bangladesh Plants Had Safety Woes." Business, *Wall Street Journal*, November 17. http://online.wsj.com/news/articles/SB10001424052702303985504579204482930379914 (accessed January 2, 2014).

Baya, V., and B. Mathaisel. 2011. "Sustainability, Moving from Compliance to Leadership." PwC, *Technology Forecast* 4, pp. 6–31. http://www.pwc.com/en_US/us/technology-forecast/2011/issue4/assets/building-sustainable-companies.pdf (accessed January 2, 2014).

Bell, J., V. Soybel, and R. Turner. 2012. "Integrating Sustainability into Corporate DNA." *The Journal of Corporate Accounting & Finance* 23, no. 3, pp. 71–81.

Bloom, B.S., M.D. Engelhart, E.J. Furst, W.H. Hill, and D.R. Krathwohl, eds. 1956. *Taxonomy of Educational Objectives: The Classification of Educational Goals. Handbook 1: Cognitive Domain*. London, WI: Longmans, Green & Co.

Branson, R.K., G.T. Rayner, J.L. Cox, J.P. Furman, F.J. King, and W.H. Hannum. 1975. *Interservice Procedures for Instructional Systems Development*. 5 vols. (TRADOC Pam 350-30 NAVEDTRA 106A). Ft. Monroe, VA: U.S. Army Training and Doctrine Command.

Bruner, J. 1960. *The Process of Education*. Cambridge, MA: Harvard University Press.

Chartered Institute of Management Accountants. 2010. *CMA Code of Ethics for Professional Accountants*. http://www.cimaglobal.com/Documents/code%20FINAL.pdf (accessed January 2, 2014).

Child, J. 1972. *Organizational Structure, Environment and Performance: The Role of Strategic Choice*. http://glennschool.osu.edu/faculty/brown/home/Org%20Theory/Readings/Child1972.pdf (accessed November 9, 2013).

Chonko, L. 2012. *Ethical Theories*. http://www.dsef.org/wp-content/uploads/2012/07/EthicalTheories.pdf (accessed January 7, 2014.)

Faris, C., B. Gilbert, B. LeBlanc, B. Ballou, and D.L. Heitger. 2013. *Demystifying Sustainability Risk: Integrating the Triple Bottom Line into an Enterprise Risk Management Program*. Durham, NC: Committee of Sponsoring Organization of the Treadway Commission (COSO) and the American Institute of Certified Public Accountants (AICPA).

Freeman, R.E. 1984. *Strategic Management: A Stakeholder Approach*. Boston, MA: Pitman.

Global Reporting Initiative. 2013. *The External Assurance of Sustainability Reporting.* https://www.globalreporting.org/resourcelibrary/GRI-Assurance.pdf (accessed December 3, 2013).

Hambrick, D. and P. Mason. 1984. "Upper Echelons: The Organization as a Reflection of its Top Managers." *Academy of Management Review* 9, no. 2, pp. 193–206.

IBM. 2013. *The New Value Integrator: Insights from the New Chief Financial Officer Study.* http://www-01.ibm.com/common/ssi/cgi-bin/ssialias?infotype=PM&subtype=XB&appname=GBSE_GB_FM_USEN&htmlfid=GBE03277USEN&attachment=GBE03277USEN.pdf (accessed January 2, 2014).

IMA (Institute of Management Accountants). 2005. *IMA Statement of Ethical Professional Practice.* http://www.imanet.org/PDFs/Public/Research/SMA/IMA%20Statement%20of%20Ethical%20Professional%20Practice.pdf (accessed November 17, 2013).

Jacobs, H.H. 1997. *Mapping the Big Picture: Integrating Curriculum and Assessment K-12.* Alexandria, VA: Association for Supervision and Curriculum Development.

Jacobs, H.H. 2004. *Getting Results with Curriculum Mapping.* Alexandria, VA: Association for Supervision and Curriculum Development.

Kahani, R. 2012. "Why Pepsi is a Global Leader in Water Stewardship and Sustainable Agriculture." *Forbes*, September 9. http://www.forbes.com/sites/rahimkanani/2012/09/14/why-pepsico-is-a-global-leader-in-water-stewardship-and-sustainable-agriculture/ (accessed January 6, 2014).

KPMG. 2011. *More U.S. Companies Reporting On Their Corporate Responsibility Activities: KPMG Research KPMG Press Release.* http://www.kpmg.com/US/en/IssuesAndInsights/ArticlesPublications/Press-Releases/Pages/More-US-Companies-Reporting-Corporate-Responsibility-Activities.aspx (accessed November 17, 2013).

Lawson, R.A., E. Blocher, P.C. Brewer, G. Cokins, J.E. Sorensen, D.E. Stout, G.L. Sundem, S.K. Wolcott, and M.J.F. Wouters. 2013. "Focusing Accounting Curricula on Students' Long-run Careers: Recommendations for an Integrated Competency-based Framework for Accounting Education." *Issues in Accounting Education* 29, no. 2, pp. 295–317.

March, J., and Simon, H. 1958. *Organizations.* New York: John Wiley and Sons.

Martha's Circle. 2007. *Sustainable is Good.* http://www.sustainableisgood.com/blog/2007/09/concentrated-la.html (accessed January 2, 2014).

Martin, A. 2007. "Chinese Tires are Ordered Recalled." World Business, *New York Times*, June 26. http://www.nytimes.com/2007/06/26/business/worldbusiness/26tire.html?n=Top/News/Business/Companies/

BRIDGESTONE%20Corporation?ref=bridgestonecorporation&_r=0 (accessed January 7, 2014).

Pathways Commission Vision Model. 2013. http://commons.aaahq.org/posts/e9e699b00f (accessed January 2, 2014).

Porter, M.E., and M.R. Kramer. 2006. "Strategy and Society: The Link between Competitive Advantage and Corporate Social Responsibility." *Harvard Business Review* 84, no. 12, pp. 78–92.

Prahalad, C.K. 2004. *Fortune at the Bottom of the Pyramid: Eradicating Poverty through Profits*. Upper Saddle River, NJ: Prentice Hall.

Simanis, E. 2012. "Reality Check at the Bottom of the Pyramid." *Harvard Business Review*. http://hbr.org/2012/06/reality-check-at-the-bottom-of-the-pyramid/ (accessed January 2, 2014).

Sockell, D. 2013. "Scaffold Learning: A Blueprint for Building Sustainable Managers." *Network for Business Sustainability*. http://nbs.net/sustainability-centres/scaffold-learning-a-blueprint-for-building-sustainable-managers/ (accessed January 3, 2014).

Vogel, D. 2005. *The Market for Virtue*. Washington, DC: The Brookings Institute.

Vygotsky, L.S. 1978. *Mind in Society: The Development of Higher Psychological Processes*. Cambridge, MA: Harvard University Press.

Westervelt 2012. *Levi's Makes Life Cycle Assessment Part of its Fabric*. http://www.greenbiz.com/blog/2012/05/22/how-levis-made-life-cycle-assessment-part-its-fabric (accessed January 2, 2014).

Whole Foods Markets. 2013. Investors Relations. http://www.wholefoodsmarket.com/company-info/investor-relations (accessed January 2, 2014).

WolcottLynch Associates. 2002. *Taxonomy of AICPA Core Competencies*. New York: American Institute of Certified Public Accountants. www.wolcottlynch.com/ (accessed January 2, 2014).

CHAPTER 6

Ethical Dimensions in the Teaching of Economics and the Tradition of Critical Political Economy

Patrick O'Sullivan

Grenoble Ecole de Management and University of Warsaw

Introduction

This book is broadly concerned with the question of how ethical concerns can be integrated into the teaching of a variety of disciplines connected to typical business curricula. The relevance of ethical concerns to disciplines such as marketing or human resource management or corporate finance is evident and the points where ethical considerations can be put before students in the teaching of these subjects are easy to see. For example, the relevance of considerations of human rights and nondiscrimination against minorities becomes directly relevant to the discussions of human resource management and to the daily decisions of human resource managers. Examples such as these have been dealt with in other chapters. However, in the case of economics the situation is rather different and this for a very simple reason: The economy is part of the broader environment in which businesses operate but on which an individual business or an individual manager can by themselves have little or no impact. There may be one or two areas where a manager or a business can have a direct *microeconomic* impact but for the most part a manager's or a business's actions cannot by themselves alone generate any significant *macroeconomic* impact; since (as we shall see in more detail) most of the big ethical questions surrounding ethics in relation to economics are concerned with *macroeconomic* issues, it follows that often there may not be that much that a teacher of economics can point to by way of concrete actions that an individual manager or business can do on a day-to-day basis to address the ethical issues raised within economics. That is not to say that raising awareness of ethical issues connected with economics is unimportant: As we shall argue later in the text, it is vital. But the practical fruit of this in the actions of individual businesses cannot be expected to be as immediate as in the case of marketing or human resource management or accounting.

Certainly there are a few cases where ethical managers should be considering the microeconomic impact of their actions such as the impact of nonpayment or avoidance of taxation. This directly reduces state receipts and so a government's ability to spend on public projects, and it has become a particularly hot topic not only in respect of tax payments by multinationals in less developed countries, it is also a burning issue in many of the European economies whose public finances are in crisis and where that is in significant part due to the failure of governments to collect the taxes theoretically due. Another area where an individual business or at least groups of businesses acting in concert can have an economic impact is in their attitude to and behavior in respect of various *corrupt* practices, this also being a scourge of many less developed economies. For example, where high-placed politicians demand for their own personal enrichment large kickbacks in return for the award of big public sector contracts and thereafter pay little or no attention to the manner of execution of those projects, such *corruption* is clearly immoral, and businesses by refusing to pay such kickbacks can contribute to ending it, particularly when they act in concert.[1] Hence, here too we find an area where a more

---

[1] I have chosen this example because I do not wish to get into the great debate about the overall effects of *corruption* and when it may or may not be immoral. The example I have chosen would be seen as immoral by pretty much any person of moral integrity since the kickback is nothing but a ruse for personal enrichment of the individual politician and will skew the distribution of income, and once paid the politician ignores the project, which may then be carried out in an irresponsible and shoddy manner to the detriment of the general public concerned. Such examples are all too frequent in less developed countries.

ethical business can have a favorable microeconomic impact and where we might wish to directly integrate some ethical considerations regarding their daily activities as (present or future) managers into the teaching of management students.

Ethics and Macroeconomics

For the most part, however, when we are teaching economics to management students that discipline constitutes a part of what is loosely called the business environment, a term in addition to the macroeconomy can also include a study of local or geopolitics, a study of nongovernmental organizations (NGOs) and their role, a study of legal systems, and studies of sustainability. The key point about these macro-environmental areas of study is that they are areas where in their daily operations individual businesses cannot be expected to have any significant impact. The business environment is rather a *given*, a parameter like the weather within which a business must operate, like it or not. To the extent that the business or an individual is powerless to change this environment and must rather accept it, it follows that there cannot be any moral decisions for the business to make in respect of the said environment since morality comes into play only when an actor is free to choose.[2]

But we may now ask: Does this mean that ethical considerations have no place whatever in the teaching of macroeconomics to management students (as part of the study of the business environment)? In fact, we find that at least in mainstream economics in particular as taught in the Anglo-American world economics in general and macroeconomics in particular have traditionally been taught in a manner that maintains a very strict and explicit ban on the consideration of *any* ethical or moral issues in the study of economics. This ban has nothing to do with the points already made earlier regarding the relative powerlessness of individual

---

[2] Of course if the environment is seriously evil there may be one very basic choice: Do we decide to do business in such a system in the first place? But once that choice is made in the affirmative together with all of the resultant moral responsibility for the decision (often conveniently but wrongfully abnegated incidentally), the system must be accepted to the extent that one business on its own cannot change it.

businesses or managers to change the macroeconomy. It is rather because of the complete banning of any consideration of normative (and hence ethical or moral)[3] questions from an economics that purports to be scientific, and that because of some epistemological considerations drawn from positivist philosophy. We will now review this longstanding ban on ethical considerations in economics and its philosophical genesis. I will argue moreover that it is highly challengeable and that ethical considerations certainly have a place even in the teaching of macroeconomics.

Tradition of Purely Positive Economics

Economics has always prided itself on being the *hardest* of the social sciences in the sense of being closest to such *hard* natural sciences as physics or chemistry in its methods. This hardness is manifest, for example, in the rigor of the econometrics present in economic modeling although there has for some time been a growing critique of the relevance to real economic questions of much of the more abstruse econometric modeling: mathematically beautiful and giving the opportunity to economists to show off their quantitative abilities but bearing little relationship to any real world economy.[4] Ever since the seminal and highly influential article on economic methodology written by Milton Friedman back in 1953, the hardness and rigor of economics is to be manifest also in a complete avoidance of any discussion of normative questions, that is, to say of questions about how the economy ought ideally to be or, more concretely, discussions of what economic policies *ought* to be followed by a government (Friedman 1953). Value judgments (such as are made all the time in normative discourse) are to be absolutely banned and economics

---

[3] Ethical and moral questions that deal with questions of how the world ought ideally to be are invariably normative in nature as opposed to purely positive factual statements of states of affairs.

[4] Ever since J.M. Keynes had long ago decried the *arid mathematical formalism* of neoclassical general equilibrium models, there has been a steady stream of critique in this vein. It is a shared point between the post-Keynesians (see Gerrard 2002) and the Austrian school (see O'Driscoll and Rizzo 1996). More recently a more general and perhaps less polemic critique of the limitations of econometrics can be found in Swann (2006).

is to be *value-free* in the sense of being devoid of value judgments. Implicitly basing himself on the epistemology of logical positivism (to which Anglo-American linguistic analysis philosophy was still to a degree in thrall in the 1950s), Friedman makes the logically valid distinction between positive discourse (statements of what is the case, so inter alia and mainly facts) and normative discourse (which makes assertions about how the world ought ideally to be). Now positive discourse can readily be checked for accuracy by comparison of the factual assertions made against independent empirical evidence or observations of the world, but normative discourse cannot be verified against factual observations in the world precisely because it is asserting how the world ought ideally to be rather than how it actually is. Drawing then on the central epistemological assertion of logical positivism as enunciated by A.J. Ayer (1946), which states that all meaningful discourse must either be tautological (purely analytic statements of definition or mathematical equivalence) or else empirically verifiable, Friedman asserts that since normative discourse is neither tautological nor empirically verifiable it is literally meaningless and so can have no place in a rigorous science. Normative discourse, also often described as the making of *value judgments*, is said to be a matter of emotion and feeling, beyond the pale of rational discourse; Friedman (1953) even goes so far as to say "about differences in fundamental values men can ultimately only fight." Ironically and even if reached by a rather different line of thinking, this is exactly the position that is taken up by Islamic Jihadists who eschew any kind of debate with depraved Western regimes and values and who hold that the only way to impose their chosen value system is by the use of military force and violence.

This stance on the epistemological status of normative discussions and hence any discussion of ethical or moral questions or of value judgments about policy has entered deeply into and now pervades the whole at least of mainstream neoclassical economics. Countless textbooks repeat the basic credo that normative discourse or value judgments have no place in a rigorous science and that the discussion of what economic policies ought to be pursued is not a matter for economists per se, that is, for politicians (oh dear!) or the people at large to determine in referenda (direct democracy). This positivist inspired approach that has been pervasive in the mainstream seems oblivious that these very same economists are certainly one of the *people* and may even be called on to give *scientific* economic policy advice by the politicians: What to do about the economy? In this latter function, they are castrated because while they may give lots of nice talk, *qua* economists they must not tell the hapless politicians what they *should* do.[5]

These self-same neoclassical economists have also for the most part been blithely oblivious to the fact that at least since the late 1950s the epistemology of Ayer's verification principle of meaning has been severely challenged and rejected by philosophers; hence, the logical foundation for eliminating normative discussion from economics is unfounded. In effect, the verification principle, however initially attractive it may seem, turns out upon examination of itself as a piece of discourse *not* to be a tautology and *not* to be empirically verifiable; in fact, it is shown to be false in empirical tests and by its own light it is therefore meaningless.[6]

If there is no good logical reason to ban normative discourse from economics, the door is opened again to normative discourse in the discipline and we may argue that indeed it has a fundamental and valuable role to play in the development of policy advice for those hapless politicians. Moreover, the rational discussion of normative issues in general (not only in economics but in many other spheres including that of religion) may allow us to avoid Friedman's drastically pessimistic and arguably irresponsible conclusion "about differences in fundamental values men may ultimately only fight."

---

[5] Of course most neoclassicals do indeed tell politicians what to do in terms of economic policies; in fact, they have a whole political agenda usually. Certainly Friedman had such an agenda.

[6] To be precise, the verification principle is clearly not just a definition of words, hence not a tautology. Hence it must be empirically testable. To test it will presuppose being able to recognize a meaningful proposition when we encounter one. We cannot just define meaningful as *tautology or empirically verifiable* since that would imply assuming the truth of what we are trying to test. Hence, some other definition of meaningful such as *intelligible to other rational beings* would have to be adopted. But it is easy to think of propositions that are certainly intelligible to others and which are not either tautological or empirically verifiable: *God is good*, or *you ought not to kill except in self-defence*, and so on. Hence, the verification principle is simply *falsified* in an empirical test of itself.

Before we pass on from this recall to the tradition of normative political economy, there is one variant of the still prevailing economic orthodoxy on positive economics that should be mentioned. In many contemporary textbooks, there is a reluctant admission that positivism as an epistemology is no longer tenable. But that, it is said, should not allow normative discourse to creep back into the hardest of the social sciences. Contemporary economists may not discard normative discourse as meaningless but they do disparage it as being merely *subjective and a matter of personal opinion* (and usually as merely emotional in nature). Such merely subjective discourse is then said to have no place in a hard science such as economics. This position is epitomized, for example, in the widely used (and rather good) basic textbook of Richard Lipsey and Alec Chrystal (2007) and it is worth quoting in detail their position because it epitomizes the contemporary orthodoxy:

> *Normative* statements depend on value judgments. They involve issues of personal opinion which cannot be settled by recourse to facts. In contrast *positive* statements do not involve value judgments. They are statements about what is, was or will be; that is statements that are about matters of fact. It is difficult to have a rational discussion of issues if positive and normative issues are confused. Much of the success of modern science depends on the ability of scientists to separate their views on *what does or might happen* in the world from their views of *what they would like to happen*. (Lipsey and Chrystal 2007)

The clear suggestion, although curiously it is not made fully explicit by the authors, is that a rational and so rigorous economic science should avoid normative discourse because such discourse is merely a matter of personal opinion and that opinion is based on emotions and wishful thinking. However, this suggestion is almost as epistemologically naïve as the positivism that it has replaced (and which had been so dominant for so long under the influence of Friedman). Unfortunately, at least since the time of Immanuel Kant (late eighteenth century) philosophers in the rationalist tradition have recognized that even in supposedly hard positive discourse based on observations of facts there is always present a subjective element to the extent that in every act of perception we construct the data of our senses in accordance with preconceived structures or frameworks that Kant had called "categories of the understanding." Hence, even positive discourse is shot through with subjectivity. Moreover, as we shall see later in this chapter when we discuss the work of Gunnar Myrdal (1959), positive discourse in the human sciences can rarely if ever be entirely value-free, a point re-echoed of course in critical social theory. Finally, there is the suggestion by Lipsey and Chrystal that in any case value judgments are just about feelings and cannot be a matter of rational discussion. There is indeed a tradition within moral philosophy that would see moral and ethical questions as ultimately a matter of sentiment and emotion but it is not the whole of moral philosophy and would indeed be severely challenged by many other if not most great moral philosophers. Ever since the time of Plato in ancient Greece (if not before in the Far East: Confucius), leading moral philosophers have sought a clear rational foundation for settling moral questions and this has indeed been seen as a way to avoid often violent conflict over such questions. The great theorists of natural law (Aquinas), of natural rights (Locke, Rousseau), as well as Bentham (utilitarianism) and of course Kant (categorical imperative) have all epitomized this effort to put moral philosophy and the discussion of moral questions on a strictly rational basis, and if the alternative is as Friedman so nicely put it that men should simply fight to the death about moral differences,[7] then surely the attempt to put moral philosophy on a strictly rational basis is highly laudable and strongly to be encouraged. In fact, it is a pointless study only to someone who is still implicitly an unreconstructed positivist in terms of epistemology.

These are considerations of high philosophy but it is important that teachers of economics be at least aware of them since a teacher who wishes to bring considerations of a moral or ethical nature into the economics classroom as things stand today in the neoclassical economics mainstream needs to be prepared to deal with the charge of being unscientific or unrigorous. At the very least, the teacher can know there is in the end

---

[7] See pg. 124 in this chapter.

no good epistemological reason to ban considerations of ethical questions from the economics classroom.

Value in Social Theory and the Tradition of Critical Political Economy

In fact, the great Swedish economist of the 20th century Gunnar Myrdal went much farther than simply demonstrating that a normative economics is possible. In his seminal work *Value in Social Theory* (1959),[8] he showed that the idea of an entirely value-judgment-free social science is an impossibility. Value judgments are inevitably present both in respect of the materials on which we as teachers or researchers *decide* to focus and also potentially in the manner in which we construct abstractions. Abstractions are inevitable if science is to progress by the construction of models. However, in human sciences the factors from which we decide to abstract are aspects of the human condition that may contain hidden value judgments about what is or is not important in human life. The clearest example of the dangers of hidden value judgments in abstractions is in respect of the mainstream economic treatment of labor as a factor of production on a par with land or capital equipment or machinery. That abstraction may be useful for the construction of production function models, and so forth, but when it comes to policy questions and applications it may all too easily lead to suggestions that firing employees in a downturn is somehow on a par with leaving machinery idle: all part and parcel of downsizing. Yet, clearly an employee who is made redundant suffers in a way that an inanimate object such as a machine certainly does not. Hence, we need to be extremely vigilant about the implicit value judgments that can lay hidden in abstract models.

Hence, we reach the conclusion that it is neither desirable nor even possible to conduct an entirely positive value judgment-free economics. Economics will always be replete with implicit value judgments and these should be made clear and explicit in Myrdal's view. Moreover, the now rehabilitated normative discussion of policy questions is not only possible, it is of utmost relevance to practical policy questions and these practical

---

[8] See in particular the introduction by Paul Streeten for a succinct summary.

questions will typically in turn be the key deciding factors in the financing and conduct of research. Scientific research as Myrdal has shown us does not occur as an entirely arbitrary lottery but rather the themes of research follow from more or less explicit judgments of what is practically useful or urgent in the social context of the community and times in which the scientist lives. To illustrate this last point in a brutally practical manner: Today research and teaching on the nature and causes of financial crises or on the development of bio-fuelled aero engines is of paramount relevance and attracts large financing, whereas research on the efficiency of a closed barter economy or on the optimal design of a horse shoe will hardly be of much relevance and so will struggle to attract funding.

However, if Myrdal thus calls us to teach and to research in economics in a manner that gives due place to and makes clearly explicit the normative and so ethical or moral parts against the tradition of purely positive economics in the mainstream, he is only calling us back to an older tradition in economic study that positive economics never managed to kill off entirely: the tradition of what I call critical political economy. It is to this very rich tradition that I would recommend that any teacher of economics who wishes to teach the subject in a manner that is aware of and open to discussion of the associated ethical issues in economics should turn to; and as we shall see from some of the examples, there is an enormous variety of perspectives available in critical political economy and it is not just the prerogative of socialist radicals (as is sometimes wrongly assumed).

Normative Political Economy in the Classroom

The tradition of going beyond the purely positive study of how economies actually work to make normative suggestions as to how the economy ought ideally to work, hence to make concrete value judgments about what economic policies ought to be pursued, stands in fact in a very noble line of economic thinking that goes right back to Adam Smith and includes all of the most famous economists. Hence, an approach to the teaching of the subject, most particularly those parts dealing with macroeconomics or policy issues, which locates the discussion within the perspective of the history of economic thought making references to the normative views of the great political economists of the past will not only broaden the horizons and stimulate the minds of the students; it also renders the subject much more interesting to students even if a bit more challenging to teachers to teach it. Classes can be encouraged to consider in relation to macroeconomic questions, for example, the very contrasting views of the classical economists (Say's law, etc.), the neoclassical development of these ideas in the works of Pigou and Wicksell, the Keynesian critique of the neoclassical adjustment mechanisms, and the new classical critique in turn of Keynesianism (not to mention the Austrian school's very own distinctive critique of all of this).[9] By exposing students to this unfolding story, its logic and its immense and contrasting implications for normative questions of the conduct of macroeconomic policy they not only become aware of the huge normative questions of policy that hinge on the contrasting theoretical understandings provided by macroeconomists, but they also grasp in a clear and concrete way the importance of the study of macroeconomics.

Let us briefly illustrate the immense variety of interesting perspectives on normative policy issues that we can find in the history of political economy and that are ours to use as teachers if we choose to teach in a way that embeds our teaching in the history of economic thought. Adam Smith did not hesitate to suggest a detailed array of economic policies to the governments of the day: The beneficence of a market system left to its own devices under perfect competition and the merits of free trade, sentiments that were to be echoed and put on an even more rigorous footing by David Ricardo. Smith in particular is very often quoted today as though he were an advocate of the ultimate in deregulation but a proper appreciation of his exact historical writing and setting will reveal a much more nuanced view in which he saw a key role for the state to promote competition and to curb monopoly power (which he saw as an all too likely temptation for businesses under pure laisser-faire capitalism). In John Stuart Mill's work, economic analysis and the political philosophy of classical 19th century liberalism sit side by side. It can be very interesting

---

[9] There are a variety of texts that tell this unfolding story of classical, neoclassical, Keynesian, and post-Keynesian macroeconomics. Among the best in my view are Ackley (1978); Kasper (2002); Trevithick (1992); Davidson (2011); and Boettke (2012).

for students to be made aware of Mill's (1864) *Essay on Liberty* and to ask them to relate its central tenets to the question of the role that the state ought to play in the economy, or indeed to questions of equality of opportunity in the workplace. In the works of Karl Marx, we find again side by side with an analysis of the dynamics of capitalist market systems a searching critique of this system that Marx believed to be destined to collapse under its own internal exploitative logic and to be replaced by a superior communist system in which the exploitation of man by man would come to an end. Given the immense role that Marxism has played in the economic and political history of the 20th century and its enduring role today as the official philosophy of Chinese communism, it is vital that students should be aware of the fundamentals of Marxism, the reasons for its (perhaps Utopian) appeal, and the question of the degree to which actual communist systems such as that of the old Soviet Union or of Chinese Communism today are or were really in line with Marx's own idealistic (and so normative) vision of a communist society. Linked to the discussions of Marxism, we can tackle the great questions of economic development and the inequality on the distribution of the world's wealth.

These great thinkers and many others of the 19th century represent the tradition of critical political economy, a tradition that did not hesitate to mix together a rigorous positive scientific analysis of economic systems with an explicitly normative discussion of what economic policy ought to be; and indeed in the 19th century the discipline was typically labelled precisely as *political economy* rather than as *economics*, and the former label was dropped only in the early 20th century.[10] The science sought to become explicitly positive and purely analytical in its approach in the 20th century until eventually normative discourse was banned as we saw in Friedman's seminal article and economists were supposed to

---

[10] It is difficult to pin down when the change in name for the discipline definitively occurred. The term *economics* had always existed and can be traced back to Aristotle for whom it signified *household management*. But because of the explicit and extensive discussion of policy issues in the 19th century, the academic discipline was styled as political economy. The first major academic work to use the *economics* label was Alfred Marshall's (1890) *Principles of Economics*. Thereafter the title economics for the subject became the norm.

be purely positive and value-free. But despite the weight of this mainstream positivism, there remained inevitably definite pockets of resistance and those not only within the Marxist tradition. In the mainstream, we can identify the quite anomalous persistence of the tradition of *welfare economics*, an explicitly normative study of a variety of policy issues based around the Pareto value judgment;[11] and of course many of the most famous economists of the 20th century have not been able to resist the temptation to give extensive policy advice. Examples such as J.M. Keynes, Friedrich von Hayek,[12] Robert Lucas, Paul Krugman, Joseph Stiglitz, and of course Milton Friedman himself come to mind. All of these economists have had distinctive and often sharply contrasting views on normative questions of appropriate short-term countercyclical macroeconomic policy, on questions of appropriate economic development, or both. Teaching of macroeconomics or of development economics in a manner that presents these contrasting views and encourages students to develop their own positions on the contrasting views will make these classes lively and stimulating, as well as demonstrating to the students the often immense practical questions of policy that hinge on positions taken in normative political economy. Political colonialism may have ended but has it given way to a new form of economic colonialism? And while Smith and Ricardo may have demonstrated conclusively that the world as a whole can gain from free trade and so in principle from globalization (potential Pareto improvement), how often and conveniently is it forgotten that for trade to benefit all attention must be paid to the distribution (or redistribution if necessary) of the gains from trade. This can lead into a searching critical and normative discussion of the impact of globalization on the less developed world, the role of the WTO, and of the Fair Trade movement. Similarly and very topically, one can present the debate about the nature of financial crises, a debate that is at once about the positive analysis and

---

[11] Any economic change that leaves some people better off while leaving nobody worse off marks an improvement in social welfare and so *ought* to be undertaken as a good policy.

[12] To be strictly fair Hayek represents the Austrian school, a dissenting offshoot of mainstream economics that has tended to reject pure positivism and has always had an explicit policy agenda.

normative political economy of financial crises, in which we can find rational expectations new classical economists (such as Robert Lucas) ranged against proponents of behavioral economics and finance (Sheila Dow, Hyman Minsky et al.) on the one hand and the Austrian school on the other in a fascinating triangular discussion of financial market regulation or deregulation. Key epicycles on this debate are concerned with the impact of globalization of the world's capital markets and freedom of financial flows on the fragile money and capital markets of the emerging economies: The Asian financial crisis of 1997 and normative lessons to be drawn from it being a key focus of this debate. Yet another fascinating and clearly normatively inspired approach to finance and financial markets is that of Islamic finance and this certainly merits discussion both for its searching ethical critique of a conventional financial system based on the charging of interest and widespread unproductive short-term speculation on various types of derivative assets, and for the fact that such a system can work and is present in some form or other in a number of successful Islamic states (Iran, Malaysia).

There are of course some even more radical perspectives on finance and on financial markets emanating from the neo-Marxian perspective of critical social theory, which we now discuss in more detail.

Critical Political Economy and Critical Social Theory

Arising from the works of Marx highly critical of market capitalism and of its ideological superstructures of false consciousness, the Frankfurt school of Horkheimer, Adorno, Marcuse, and more recently Habermas has not only maintained and revamped the Marxian critique of the internal contradictions of capitalism, it has broadened out into what is known as critical social theory. This approach applies the critical tools of Marxian thought not only to economics or political economy but rather across the whole range of sociological and political disciplines. In particular, in the field of business studies, it has given us what has come to be known as critical management studies. Allied with the epistemology of constructivism that sees the human mind as active in every act of cognition construing the world in accordance with various preconceived or a priori formats, critical social theory seeks ruthlessly to expose the ideologies by which we are kept in thrall and which ruling elites use to justify their power, their mastery over others. In such exposure, there is of course a clear normative intent that goes back to Marx's original vision: The creation of a world beyond the master–slave relationship, a world beyond exploitation and so in no need of ideology. Utopian you may say but clearly normative in intent!

Therein lies its classroom appeal! Students love at least to toy with Utopian ideas; they are typically young and idealistic, not world weary and cynical and so they are prepared to consider new ideas, to think seriously about changing the status quo, and they dare to dream about a better world. And who are we as teachers to deny them this indulgence? Indeed only by such indulgence can ideas for real social progress and transformation be born. By bringing into play the perspectives of critical social theory and the often ruthlessly radical questioning of the status quo and of its underpinning power relations and ideologies that it implies, the classroom can become a real ferment of critical discussion and debate of some of the most fundamental moral issues confronting contemporary economy and society: inequality of income and wealth, its evolution and implications especially in relation to the gap between richer developed and poorer less developed parts of the world; the interplay of the political and the economic in geopolitical relations; the challenges of corruption and the need for political as well as business ethics; the transfers of wealth implicit in financial sector bailouts; and ideological capture of leading international institutions such as the World Bank or the European commission. There is a rich and fascinating harvest of topics available to the teacher once we delve into the perspectives of critical social theory and the students will not fail to be engaged but also to begin to think for themselves on these topics. In many cases like the great German philosopher Immanuel Kant when he first read the works of the Scottish skeptical philosopher David Hume, they may even be "awakened from their dogmatic slumbers."

Ethics in the Teaching of Economics: A Conclusion

In the end therefore we reach an interesting conclusion. Bringing concerns of business ethics into the teaching and research of economics will not occur in the same easily self-evident manner as in disciplines as human resource management, accounting, or marketing where the ethical challenges in the everyday conduct of business are evident. Economics is rather a study of the business environment, which as we have seen is largely a given for business and which an individual business is largely powerless to influence whatever may be their good intentions.

But that does not mean that the teaching of economics can or should be conducted in a manner that entirely ignores ethical and moral concerns. Mainstream economics has for the past 60 years acted in just this manner seeking to dissociate itself from any kind of consideration of ethics or morality, these being dismissed on philosophical grounds as meaningless or at best as merely emotional wishful thinking. But that position we have shown to be not only philosophically challengeable, it is I have argued morally irresponsible to the extent that it bans in effect any rational discussion of normative issues. In contrast, I have instead recalled teachers and researchers in economics to the grand tradition of critical political economy in which

1. the inescapable normative presuppositions (regarding the construction of abstractions and views of what ought to be studied) of the human scientist are made fully transparent and explicit;
2. ideological positions are frankly and openly admitted for what they are;
3. important questions regarding what economic policies and forms of economic organization ought to be implemented for the well-being of the human community can be studied in depth with a view to reaching definitive normative recommendations for government and society at large.

The great 19th century thinker Thomas Carlyle once remarked that "Economics is a discipline at once dangerous and leading to occasions of sin,"[13] and the positive economists in the Friedmanite mainstream seem

---

[13] The phrase is (in) famous among economists. It first appeared anonymously in 1849 in a piece in Fraser's Magazine *for Town and Country* "Occasional Discourse on the Negro Question," Vol. XL., February 1849, London, and was later acknowledged by Carlyle.

to have taken Carlyle to heart. My argument here has been that economics does not need to go down that path to hell. A critical political economy that has no scruples about openly addressing the leading normative economic policy questions of the day can be a great force for improvement in the world, and in a world riven by financial crises and growing inequality between the richest and poorest such a political economy is arguably urgently necessary. In my own experience of teaching such a political economy over the years, it will also not fail to engage students allowing them to see the practical ethical and policy implications of a subject that all too often they find arid, boring, and irrelevant.

Some Sample Questions to Stimulate Class Debate

1. Using both economic and ethical analysis, assess the overall impact (in principle) of globalization. Upon what value judgments are you drawing in your assessment? What is the specific impact of globalization in your own country and has it been beneficial?
2. What is the ranking of your country in the world economy in terms of gross domestic product per capita (GDP per head)? What is the ranking of your country in the world economy in terms of social progress index (SPI: available at www.socialprogressimperative.org)? What conclusions can you draw from such contrast as you may find?
3. What is meant by *austerity* policies in the context of the sovereign debt crisis in the Eurozone? Are such policies the *only realistic alternative* (as the Troika tend to argue) or is that merely one ideological position among a possible array of policy options to deal with overwhelming debt? What lessons may be drawn from the Greek debt experience for economic and in particular for public finance policies in your own country? To what extent might Argentina be a role model?
4. If the future is irreducibly uncertain, can business expectations ever be said to be rational?
5. What is the ethical underpinning of the Islamic approach to finance and to what extent does it converge with the approaches

of other major religions (Christianity, Buddhism, etc.)? Can it constitute a viable alternative approach to the organization of the financial system?

6. The American neo-conservatives advocate an economy in which the role of the state is reduced to an absolute minimum (low tax low public spending economy): European social democrats advocate an extensive welfare state in which poverty is eliminated and a welfare safety net is provided for all (Nordic countries: high tax high public spending). Assess the relative merits of each in economic and in ethical terms. Which (if either) is most appropriate or attractive in your own country at its present stage of development?

References

Ackley, G. 1978. *Macroeconomic Theory and Policy*. London, UK: Macmillan.

Ayer, A.J. 1946. "The Elimination of Metaphysics." *Language Truth and Logic*. 2nd ed. 13–29. Harmondsworth, UK: Penguin.

Boettke, P. 2012. *Handbook on Contemporary Austrian Economics*. Cheltenham, UK: Edward Elgar.

Davidson, P. 2011. *Post-Keynesian Macroeconomic Theory*. 2nd ed. Cheltenham, UK: Edward Elgar.

Friedman, M. 1953. "The Methodology of Positive Economics". In *Essays in Positive Economics*. Chicago, IL: University of Chicago Press.

Gerrard, B. 2002. "The Role of Econometrics in a Radical Methodology Publisher." In *Post Keynesian Econometrics, Microeconomics and the Theory of the Firm*, eds. S.C. Dow and J. Hillard, Cheltenham, UK: Edward Elgar.

Kasper, S.D. 2002. *The Revival of Laissez-faire in American Macroeconomic Theory*. Cheltenham, UK: Edward Elgar.

Lipsey, R., and A. Chrystal. 2007. *Economics*. 11th ed. Oxford, UK: Oxford University Press.

Marshall, A. 1890. *Principles of Economics*. London, UK: Macmillan.

Mill, J.S. (1864) 2007. *On Liberty*. London, UK: Longman Green. 3rd ed. Reprinted as a Penguin Classic. Harmondsworth, UK: Penguin Books.

Myrdal, G. 1959. *Value in Social Theory*. London, UK: Routledge and Kegan Paul.

O'Driscoll, G., and M. Rizzo. 1996. *The Economics of Time and Ignorance.* London, UK: Routledge.
Swann, P. 2006. *Putting Econometrics in its Place—A New Direction in Applied Economics.* Cheltenham, UK: Edward Elgar.
Trevithick, J.A. 1992. *Involuntary Unemployment: Macroeconomics from Keynesian Perspective.* London, UK: Palgrave Macmillan.

Further Reading

Caplin, A., and A. Schotte, eds. 2008. *The Foundations of Positive and Normative Economics: A Handbook.* Oxford, UK: Oxford University Press.
Dow, S. 2011. "Cognition, Market Sentiment and Financial Instability." In Cambridge Journal of Economics 35, no. 2, pp. 233–49. https://dspace.stir.ac.uk/bitstream/1893/3059/1/2011%20cognition%20%26%20sentment%20paper.pdf
Fleurbaey, M. 2004. "Normative Economics and Theories of Distributive Justice." In *The Elgar Companion to Economics and Philosophy*, eds. J. Davis and J. Runde, 132–58. Cheltenham, UK: Edward Elgar.
Geuss, R. 1981. *The Idea of a Critical Theory: Habermas and the Frankfurt School.* Cambridge, UK: Cambridge University Press.
Haberas, J. 1972. *Knowledge and Human Interests.* London, UK: Heinemann.
Heilbronner, R. 2000. *The Worldly Philosophers.* Harmondsworth, UK: Penguin.
O'Sullivan, P. (1987) 2011. *Economic Methodology and Freedom to Choose.* London, UK: Routledge. Reprint, Routledge Revival.
Stiglitz, J. 2001. "Information and the Change in Paradigm in Economics." Nobel Prize Lecture held at Stockholm University, Sweden December, 2001. http://www.nobelprize.org/nobel_prizes/economic-sciences/laureates/2001/stiglitz-lecture.pdf.
Stiglitz, J. 2002. *Globalization and its Discontents.* Harmondsworth, UK: Penguin.

MODULE 3

On the Shop Floor

CHAPTER 7

Teaching Ethics in Operations Management

Arnd Huchzermeier, Eva Kohl, and Stefan Spinler

WHU—Otto Beisheim School of Management

Introduction

According to Al Gore, global warming represents an *inconvenient truth* mostly to businesses and policy makers, and failure to respond to this matter however is *deeply unethical* (Gore 2006). In 2013, for the first time, the concentration of CO_2 in the atmosphere exceeded 400 ppm (Gillis 2013) and keeps rising today. The consequences of climate change can already be felt as witnessed in the recent devastating typhoon hitting the Philippines (Whaley 2013), which was triggered by unusually high temperatures. Nonetheless, the latest UN climate conference that took place right afterward in Warsaw (Poland) (UNFCC 2013) ended without a binding agreement among the nations to curb emissions. On a social level, catastrophic work conditions in part of Bangladesh's textile industry, culminating in collapsing buildings, did not produce more than short-term media attention. Both industrial buyers who continue to rate Bangladesh as a key off-shoring location (McKinsey 2013) as well as consumers, intent on buying cheap textiles, failed to take appropriate action.

In this chapter, we intend to review some of the ethical issues related to operations management (OM) and how teaching can raise awareness among students for these pressing issues and trigger action for making operations more sustainable.

Description of Discipline

OM is, according to Chase et al. (2004), concerned with the strategic design and the operations, as well as the improvement of the processes, that allow the company to produce and deliver its goods and services. The strategic positioning of the firm defines the operations strategy, which in turn devises the optimal positioning within the triangle cost, quality, and time. While achieving low cost, high quality, and fast responsiveness is often mitigated by inherent trade-offs, OM provides the necessary tools to optimally balance these trade-offs, for example, pertaining to product and process design, facility layout, quality management, and inventory management. OM is tightly related to supply chain management, which might be regarded as an extension of OM thinking across the value chain and is covered in Chapter 8.

Ethics in OM can be subsumed under the principles of responsible management (Laasch and Conaway 2015), resting on the pillars of sustainable operations, responsibility, and ethics. Hence, in what follows, we shall be concerned with taking the right decisions in dilemma situations related to sustainable OM. Sustainable OM has recently been reviewed by Drake and Spinler (2013) who outline five areas where an OM lens provides value: product design, production technology, transportation systems, forward supply chains, and closed-loop supply chains. Most of these areas will be revisited in the section *Ethics Teaching Strategy* of this chapter.

Typical Ethical Issues

In OM, ethical issues refer to the impact of the production process as well as the impact of the product itself. In this context, ethical issues mainly arise when business activities that are aiming at financial short-term optimization are not compatible with sustainable, ethical business practices.

Against the background of an increasingly globalized and competitive economy, customers are becoming increasingly price-conscious. The resulting price pressure—and consequently the pressure on margins—forces companies to find more efficient and effective ways, especially in production. However, this does not necessarily result in ethical dilemmas, as many solutions are compatible with sustainable business practices (e.g., continuous improvement, process optimization, automation, staff motivation, and so on). However, there are cases where companies pursue cost-saving opportunities that have a negative social, environmental, or economic impact. Such cases of unethical behavior can flourish when there is a lack of company-internal and -external control, wrong incentive structures, bad leadership, problematic corporate values, or regulatory environments that create loopholes or doubtful opportunities.

Typical ethical issues relating to OM can occur in each of the following three dimensions: the social (people), the environmental (planet), and the economic (profits) dimension:

- In the *social dimension*, typical ethical issues are related to poor working conditions or employment practices in production. This includes issues like low pay practices, child labor, or health and safety issues in the workplace. Here, mainly blue-collar workers are affected, especially those in developing countries. In such cases, companies generate competitive advantage and increase profit margins by exploiting the employees at the bottom of the pyramid. Moreover, another typical ethical issue in this category is product safety, which refers to inferior, defective, or toxic products that might pose a risk to the workers, customers, or society at large. An example in this social category is the publicly discussed issue of working conditions in garment factories in Bangladesh, where workers are endangered by unsafe building conditions, poor health and safety conditions at work, and salaries below the legal minimum wage level (Kazmin 2013).
- Regarding the *environmental dimension*, ethical issues are linked to environmental pollution and unsustainable utilization of natural resources. In concrete, this includes issues like the usage of harmful or toxic material in production, animal testing, high CO_2 emissions, waste of water, or insufficient waste disposal. In such cases, companies are not willing to take over full responsibility for the impact of their operation and production activities. In addition, this also includes the poten-

tial negative impact of the end product on the environment. Common examples in this category are the usage of chemicals and dyes in the garment industry, the usage of pesticides in agriculture, or the issue of pollution by electronic waste.
- Concerning the *economic dimension*, ethical issues are often related to dishonorable business practices or lack of transparency toward business partners and stakeholders (i.e., suppliers, customers, employees, shareholders, or the state). This includes the major issue of corruption. In such cases, companies or individuals are being untruthful with the aim to increase their financial situation—at the stakeholders' expense. An example in this category is the bribery scandal at Siemens that was revealed in 2006, where Siemens was accused of systematically bribing government officials worldwide in order to win large-scale contracts (Schäfer 2008).

While the preceding examples are best analyzed from the perspective of deontological ethics, a consequentialist understanding of ethics would posit that ethical issues result in a situation where natural, human, or financial resources are endangered or even destroyed with a long-term negative effect.

At the company level, unethical practices pose a significant risk to the company's reputation, which can even harm the competitive position in the long run. Leading international brands have already faced reputational damage because of ethical issues at a supplier or subcontractor. This reveals that companies are held responsible for ethical issues along the whole value chain—even beyond the individual company boarders (Newing 2012).

Developing Versus Developed Countries

Developing countries are often less industrialized with a lower level of technology, infrastructure, education, and consequently also lower living standards than developed countries. Moreover, there are significant differences between the countries regarding political systems and regulations: developing countries are often characterized by lower wage levels, poor employee safety regulations, weak labor unions, lack of human rights enforcement, lack of environmental protection regulations, and a lack of governmental control. These conditions in developing countries create an attractive environment for low-cost production for some industries or product segments.

As a consequence, companies from developed countries are increasingly shifting their operations and production activities into developing countries for optimization reasons. In this way, ethical issues also are increasingly shifted or newly created in developing countries. For instance, a major share of CO_2 emissions that are produced in developing countries are actually related to the consumption of goods in developed countries (Caldeira and Davis 2010). Thus, companies in developed countries are often *outsourcing* the negative impact of production to developing countries.

However, it is a revolving system: If western companies, trade partners, and politics are addressing the ethical issues in a developing country, lessons are learned and the conditions are continuously improving. Along with that, living standards and wage levels are also increasing. As a consequence, the companies from developed countries are once again shifting the production away from these traditional low-cost production countries to even lower developed countries. In this way, ethical issues arise and are to be tackled once more from scratch (Newing 2012).

Against this background, companies are required to be proactive instead of reactive by addressing ethical issues in their operations strategy, planning, contracts, and communication, especially when producing in developing countries.

Ethics Teaching Strategy

The business ethics education literature (cf. Sims and Felton 2006; Gu and Neesham 2014) has identified reliance on an *inductive* rather than *deductive* teaching process as a key precondition for facilitating improved ethical decision making. Thus, the teaching approach outlined in the following text will be based on examples and case studies that illustrate how individuals and firms make OM decisions that may involve ethical conflicts. This teaching strategy has been developed and tested in the context of a one-semester course *Operations Strategy and Sustainability* targeted at advanced Master and MBA students. The objective pursued in this course is to illustrate how firms strategically react to constraints imposed by (natural) resource limits and regulatory frameworks (Huchzermeier 2014).

Sustainability as discussed in this particular course has at least three key focus areas:

i. Strategy deployment and execution for sustainable performance management at the firm and industry level.
ii. Creating sustainable products and services in line with the sustainability triangle.
iii. Managing closed loop supply chains to support the needs of an ever-growing world population.

The first topic addresses the issue why firms, in general, face difficulties of adapting to new market needs. The second topic exemplifies best practices for the adoption of sustainability concepts in industry and along the firm's value chain. The third topic deals with the issue of providing critical resources such as raw materials, water, and energy to a fast-growing population when efficiency improvements become harder and harder to obtain. While energy productivity can be constantly improved, water productivity cannot be improved, for example, by lower consumption levels.

Strategy Deployment and Execution for Sustainable Performance Management at the Industry and Firm Level

Policy Instruments for CO_2 Abatement

The European Union was among the first major economies to introduce emission rights trading (ec.europa.eu/clima/policies/ets). The underlying economic rationale is straightforward: Companies for whom the marginal cost of abatement is lowest will invest in clean technology and thus sell their excess emission rights to firms with high investment costs for clean technology that will not abate (Hahn 2013). This will achieve maximum industry output and profit for a targeted cap on emission levels. However, the low levels of emission right prices of currently about €5/ton of CO_2

(www.eex.com) lead, for instance in Germany, to the perverse effect that highly polluting lignite power plants become more profitable to operate than, for instance, gas-fired plants. In a Harvard simulation game for carbon emission trading, students realize that outcomes highly depend on mechanism design and the trading strategies of all market participants, including NGOs. Despite market failures, private equity investments in clean technology are at an all-time high (and surpass investments in biotechnology or software businesses). However, these investments are only a *drop in a bucket*. The ethical dimension in this example relates to the dilemma between preserving competitiveness within the European Union in terms of energy costs and at the same time limiting the amount of carbon emissions thus slowing down the projected temperature increase.

Is a market-driven approach to green investment sufficient or should the government interfere? Policy makers essentially have the choice to either regulate, for instance by curbing total emissions, or to incentivize businesses. Should firms be subsidized for engaging into research and development for green technologies or the consumer for buying green products (as is the case in many states for electric vehicles)? Should a new institution be created as an intermediary for technology transfer across regional industries? One of the authors was invited to report to a special task force on the "competitiveness of the regional state Rhineland-Palatinate" on good management practices in industry. Medium-sized firms, especially, had lobbied the government for subsidies due to high regulatory costs imposed on them (e.g., rising energy costs, additional transfer payments supporting green energy investments in the economy at large, costs for emission rights—if used at all). Jobs seemed to be at stake and there were numerous incidents where investments had already shifted to Eastern Europe or Asia for that reason. The situation is characterized by mutual distrust between policy makers, managers, and the public. Moreover, the media is mostly leading this heated discussion, often making a case for more EU regulation and company restraint to protect workers' jobs who are treated unfairly by off-shoring or outsourcing decisions (Loch, Chick, and Huchzermeier 2008). Hence, fair competition, which reflects the ethical dimension in this example, is at stake where government subsidies may interfere with market-based solutions in the interest of CO_2 reduction.

Anchoring Sustainability in the Firm's Strategy—Lessons Learned from the Industrial Excellence Award

The industry competition *Industrial Excellence Award* (IEA) rewards companies across major countries in Western Europe for their exemplary strategy deployment and execution (www.industrial-excellence-award.eu). The authors of this study find that firms differ greatly in their creativity of strategy formulation and their discipline in strategy execution. Most winners of the IEA have already created sustainable products and services and thus achieve continued output growth (= sustainable performance) at the business unit level based on high worker engagement and bottom-up initiation of strategic projects (Loch et al. 2003). Thus, these winning companies could act as role models for implementing sustainability.

Industry leaders manage productivity continuously top-down with feedback from bottom-up (and not purely delegate targets down the lines). Many companies delegate sustainability targets or objectives also top-down, that is, they subscribe to compliance management by their organization. However, the operating units often fail in their adoption and implementation, since workers cannot resolve the conflicts or perform integration tasks at the lower level of the organization alone. Like off-shoring of value chain activities, sustainability issues have to be dealt with at the strategic level first (and not only at the process or value chain level), and this is what managers fail to recognize. Like off-shoring, sustainability, when viewed *strategically*, offers the potential of cost reductions, the innovation of new products and services, the acquisition of new capabilities, and the entry into new markets. All in all, the firm's competitiveness is enhanced and not compromised!

Strengthening the competitiveness of firms and securing jobs in high-cost countries require a permanent dialog between policy makers (e.g., who make sure that skilled workers for new product and process technologies are available) and managers. What should not be done is to install yet another government-supported administrative entity that interferes in an *uncoordinated way* with firms' policy execution through undifferentiated technology push. An open issue remains though, that is, what are the key performance indicators or measures for competitive success that managers and policy makers can both agree on? If Key Performance

Indicators or measures do not change, chances are that decisions at the firm level will not be affected either. The ethical dimension in this example arises from possible divergence of interests of individual firms and the legislative bodies, for example, within the European Union again putting at stake the future competitiveness of economic zones.

Creating Sustainable Products and Processes in Line With the Sustainability Triangle

Empowering the Consumer Through Product Transparency

How can companies develop greener products while reducing their footprint along the global value chain? One approach currently being discussed in the fast-moving consumer goods industry is the adoption of more product transparency to the end customer. The GS1 organization (which is an industry organization of both manufacturers and retailers) has identified so-called *hot spots* in the life cycle of selected product categories. These hot spots are mostly independent of firms and rather symptomatic of the product. Companies then put their attention on these flagged stages to soften the impact on the planet, for example, by voluntarily banning the use of nonsustainable palm oil, lead paint in toys, or horse meat in lasagne. Currently, the information on the hot spots has not yet been married with the product information used when ordering products, since IT standards need to be agreed on by all industry partners, and legacy enterprise resource planning (ERP) systems, for example, of retailers, need to be adapted to cope with this additional information provided. In the long term, customers will receive all corporate social responsibility (CSR) related information online when making their purchasing decisions either through their own electronic devices or displays in the retail outlet. A company that has already started to collect customer-based product data is Barcoo (which is one of the most widely used apps for that matter).

To highlight the challenges with increased product (and process) transparency, the case study on Fiji Water's marketing campaign *Every Drop is Green* exemplifies how marketing claims (without actions or credible validation) are quickly viewed as green washing. By contrast, a case study about Philips explains that it has asked its international auditor firm to assume liability for both financial and sustainability reporting, that is, the adoption of joint reporting which is already a mandatory requirement to be listed on selected stock exchanges. This comes with big risks to the auditor who faces stiff legal fees in case of misreporting (not so much on the financial data though) and high costs due to a lack of standards and available data on CSR performance of the client. Students, however, strongly challenge both company-based reporting schemes as being potentially anticompetitive. Thus, the ethical dimension relates to the dilemma between greater transparency on the one hand and possible free-riding of competing firms on the other hand.

Incentive Alignment Entails Greener Products

A second approach to be followed is incentive alignment in the supply chain. The Mattel case study highlights the negative consequences of outsourcing due to cost reasons to Asian manufacturers, where ethical issues arise due to the possible cost savings that might, however, be off-set by lower quality and even harm to end customers. In 2006, Walmart adopted nine networks to tackle sustainability issues *from the farm to the fork* with varying degree of success. The supplier score card and the packaging score card are two noteworthy tools that have found broad acceptance in the industry. Green products are highly preferred due to CO_2 savings (which are not yet claimed) and licensed to other suppliers. Recently, however, the retailer has collaborated with The Wercs, a software company offering products to monitor chemical compliance, to find out about hazardous or nonsustainable substances in their suppliers' products. As soon as products have been scored as nongreen, a green store brand is put on the shelf to provide customers with an adequate alternative.

Does the Sharing Economy Enhance Sustainability?

A third approach is sharing of company assets, mostly in logistics and warehousing, to reduce CO_2 emissions through the firm's operational activities. In the private domain, car sharing services such as Zipcar in the United States and room sharing such as Airbnb are quite popular and have attracted a lot of media attention. There exist a few successful business cases in the consumer goods industry to date, but most partnerships were not continued in the medium term though (Spinler and Franklin 2011). Other industries have not adopted an asset–sharing approach as yet, nor has this approach been adopted for core manufacturing or assembly activities.

Managing Closed Loop Supply Chains to Support the Needs of an Ever-Growing World Population

Cradle-to-Cradle Approach in Industrial Ecology

The cradle-to-cradle approach stresses the importance of design for disassembly or design-for-recyclability thinking. All technical components re-enter their specific closed or recycling loop—aluminum, metals, plastics, and so forth,—whereas nontechnical components are composted and bio-degraded. An exemplary product is the Mira office chair of Herman Miller, one of the most popular office chairs in the United States. The company EPEA in Hamburg, Germany, supported the Mira chair project and has been instrumental in making the concept popular around the globe. Recently, The Netherlands has adopted the status of a *cradle-to-cradle nation*. The company MaterialConnexion in Cologne, Germany, offers bio-degradable plastics to industry. Innovative applications are bio-degradable lawns for soccer fields, for example, adopted by Real Madrid, or the entire interior decoration including seat covers for the new Airbus 380 that do not release any harmful gases which might be inhaled and absorbed by passengers.

A so-called toxic hybrid (according to cradle-to-cradle terminology) represents the Tetra Pak package (see the Tetra Pak case): While the outer skin can be recycled as high quality paper that contains long fibers used for low-quality paper as input, the interior is a nonseparable aluminum-plastics compound. In Brazil, members of the bottom-of-the-pyramid act as street collectors of the package and make sure that this nondegradable and highly popular product does not pollute the environment any longer. Over the years, Tetra Pak has trained the public (mostly children in kinder gardens) the benefits of recycling, has provided municipalities with the right recycling equipment, and kept funding of research to find a solution for the aluminum-plastic waste. In the end, a furnace technology was developed that separates the two substances into paraffin and solid aluminum. This approach shares wealth with the poor while offering an affordable and safe way of keeping food nonrefrigerated. This product stewardship shown by Tetra Pak is exceptional and a unique case of a successful implementation of an extended producer responsibility (EPR) system. This case highlights how the ethical issue that arises from, on the one hand, using recycling and thus lowering energy and material use and, on the other hand, who does the recycling, often disadvantaged groups of society, can be resolved successfully.

Dealing With Finite Natural Resources

Two resources are key inputs to operations (and to human beings' livability): energy and water. While the notion of peak oil has been around for almost 50 years, the recent fracking boom in the United States has led some to argue that (nonrenewable) energy sources are still in abundant supply. As a consequence, oil prices in the United States have remained flat recently. Fracking, however, comes at a significant cost for the environment due to large amounts of chemicals and water being injected into the shale gas reserves and significant quantities of methane being emitted. Because of its water intensity, it is doubtful whether fracking is a viable option in China where in many places water is already scarce. Progress with respect to bio-fuels, for example, see the Amyris case study, may provide a more sustainable energy future. Energy prices will likely become more volatile in the future. One reason is the subsidy that has to be paid by all for green energy such as solar and wind energy, and the other reason is the cost of keeping cold reserves, that is, traditional power plants as a backup supply resource, in place. Moreover, smart grid technology requires additional investments to make very large-scale energy nets even more robust and resilient. In the United States and elsewhere, peak load demand constantly increases and thus the danger of blackouts—which are extremely costly to the economy—increases disproportionally. As described in the Viridity case, some energy companies have started to offer smart technology for energy services and allow firms and even home owners to control and shift their energy needs, potentially even feeding energy back to the grid. Google's recent acquisition of

Nest Labs (Bradshaw 2014), specializing on smart thermostats, is a case in point. In Germany, 1.5 million home owners already generate green energy. This will certainly mitigate the need for more, mostly coal-fired, power plants. An ethical perspective thus should investigate the trade-off between higher short-term energy prices and volatility and lower long-term CO_2 emissions and thus less detrimental effects to the climate.

With regards to water, the Manila Water case shows that sustainable water can be provided even in areas with dry climates and a very low-income population. The establishment of customer demand metering zones, the constant contact of front-line personnel with customers, the use of the poor population as suppliers of water system components, the forced integration of all customers—hospitals, businesses, and wealthy individuals—onto one system, and so forth, have all led to affordable and reliable water for all.

Synthesis

The cases presented in this section illustrate that an ecosystem of the relevant stakeholders, that is, businesses, policy makers, and the public, needs to be established to solve the sustainability challenge effectively and efficiently. Importantly, a long-term perspective needs to be adopted as most measures proposed will likely incur costs in the short run but entail substantial benefits in the longer run. In essence, the notion that all stakeholders should assume responsibility for their acts must be engrained with decision makers. As the German philosopher Hans Jonas put it in his book *The Imperative of Responsibility* (1984), "Act so that the effects of your action are compatible with the permanence of genuine human life," thus complementing the categorical imperative established by Immanuel Kant. As noted previously, raising students' sensitivity toward responsibility in their decisions and actions can, in our experience, best be achieved via individual examples and case studies.

Advice for Teachers

To prepare the students for a meaningful discussion of ethical issues, the basic premises of responsible management (Laasch and Conaway 2015), that is, sustainability, responsibility, and ethics, should be reviewed. Students should be made aware of the fact that a variety of ethical lenses exist to study business ethics problems, for example, a consequentialist perspective where an act is gauged only based on its consequences and the morally right action is the one that maximizes the overall benefit. An alternative take represents the deontological view where it is posited that choices cannot be justified by their consequences but must rather be in agreement with a moral norm. Both perspectives may be employed successfully in teaching ethics in business. One challenge that we have encountered when teaching ethics in OM is the issue that students might feel overwhelmed when confronted with the global and long-term consequences that sustainability and hence business ethics entail. Given these, individual action seems to be irrelevant. However, as pointed out in the previous section, successful examples of confronting environmental and social issues do exist. The teacher should, therefore, emphasize the role of bottom-up approaches and the role of start-ups in this particular arena, as they are being nurtured in a business school environment.

Another caveat relates to the fact that different cultures will perceive and react to ethical issues in rather different ways, as one might conclude from the seminal contributions of Hofstede's cultural dimensions (Hofstede 1986) related to, for instance, power distance or short-termism. It is thus helpful to keep such variations across different cultures in mind or to explicitly deal with them in class.

Summary and Conclusion

Ethics in OM is related to the social, economic, and environmental impact of a product or process, as reflected in the consequentialist understanding. What matters equally, however, is the deontological aspect of moral norms and duties that pertain to the actions of OM stakeholders. Thus, the topic is highly complex and includes a broad range of themes and interdisciplinary perspectives. Consequently, ethics poses a really challenging topic for teachers: While young students with little work experience are mostly excited about the changing landscape in business, more senior students are often overwhelmed (and even frustrated) by the complexity of the topic. For the latter group, it is particularly important to understand that sustainability has to be dealt with strategically and along the whole value chain (as pointed out earlier).

In this context, it is recommended to use a range of learning vehicles in the classroom in order to combine theory and practical application. This includes introducing related frameworks, conducting simulation or business games, and working on real-life case studies. In addition, continuous reflection and class discussions are the key for learning in the field of ethics.

What's more, to support faculty effectiveness in the class room, it is a prerequisite that business schools wholeheartedly embrace the issues of ethics and sustainability in their own operations. To *walk the talk*, business schools should implement ethical and sustainable practices in the areas of research, teaching, outreach, and physical campus operations. For example, this includes ethics-related courses, programs, research activities, dedicated chairs and events or conferences, as well as energy efficiency in campus buildings or ethical human resource practices in the school (Kohl 2013). Failure to do so would quickly be realized by students and thus lead them to attach low priority to this field.

Suggested Exercises and Projects

There are multiple ways to engage the student. One successful example that is currently run at WHU—Otto Beisheim School of Management is a sustainability lab that stimulates students for coming up with a solution to a sustainability-related problem at a local company, for example, reducing the carbon footprint of packaging. Through multiple interactions with faculty as well as company representatives and team work among the students, solution concepts are being developed that combine the latest business thinking and industrial needs in terms of sustainability as embodied in the triple bottom line. Discussions with industry decision makers help uncover the ethical dimensions of the problem both in terms of impacts of actions and the actions themselves. The involved firms will ultimately vote on which of the proposed solutions will be further pursued.

Visits and internships with companies that have a proven track record in terms of becoming a sustainable business provide students with evidence that successful action is possible. One further way of introducing the student to the intricacies and trade-offs related to ethical issues is to apply simulation games as noted earlier for the carbon simulation.

References

Bradshaw, T. 2014. "Google Bets on 'Internet of Things' with $3.2bn Nest Deal." *Financial Times*, January 13.

Caldeira, K., and S. Davis. 2010. "Carbon Emissions 'Outsourced' to Developing Countries." Carnegie Institution of Washington, *National Academy of Sciences*, March 8. http://carnegiescience.edu/news/carbon_emissions_outsourced_developing_countries (accessed December 10, 2013).

Chase, R.B., F.R. Jacobs, and N.J. Aquilano. 2004. *Operations Management for Competitive Advantage*, 765. New York: McGraw Hill.

Drake, D.F., and S. Spinler. 2013. "OM Forum—Sustainable Operations Management: An Enduring Stream or a Passing Fancy?" *Manufacturing & Service Operations Management* 15, no. 4, pp. 689–700.

Gillis, J. 2013. "Heat-trapping Gas Passes Milestone, Raising Fears." *NY Times*, May 10.

Gore, A. *An Inconvenient Truth*. Documentary film directed by Davis Guggenheim. Paramount Classics, 2006.

Gu, J., and C. Neesham. 2014. "Moral Identity as Leverage Point in Teaching Business Ethics." *Journal of Business Ethics* 124, no. 3, pp. 527–536.

Hahn, R. October, 2013. "Ronald Harry Coase (1910–2013)." *Nature* 502, no. 7472, p. 449.

Hofstede, G. 1986. "Cultural Differences in Teaching and Learning." *International Journal of Intercultural Relations* 10, no. 3, pp. 301–20.

Huchzermeier, A. 2014. "Sustainability in Operations." In *Operations Strategy*, ed. J. Van Mieghem. London, UK: Henry Stewart Talks.

Jonas, H. 1984. *The Imperative of Responsibility: In Search of Ethics for the Technological Age*. Chicago, IL: University of Chicago Press.

Kazmin, A. 2013. "Bangladesh Factory Disasters Highlight Regulatory Failures." Business and Economics, *Financial Times*, London, April 25.

Kohl, E. 2013. "The Concept of Sustainability in the Higher Education Sector." Master Thesis, WHU—Otto Beisheim School of Management, Vallendar, October 2013.

Laasch, O., and R.N. Conaway. 2015. *Principles of Responsible Management: Global Sustainability, Responsibility, and Ethics*, 576. Stamford, CT: Cengage Learning.

Loch, C.H., S. Chick, and A. Huchzermeier. 2008. *Management Quality and Competitiveness: Lessons from the Industrial Excellence Award*. 56. Berlin, Germany: Springer.

Loch, C.H., L. Van der Heyden, L. Van Wassenhove, A. Huchzermeier, and C. Escalle. 2003. *Industrial Excellence—Management Quality in Manufacturing*, 248. Berlin, Germany: Springer.

McKinsey & Company. 2013. *The Global Sourcing Map—Balancing Cost, Compliance, and Capacity: Mckinsey's Apparel CPO Survey 2013.*

Newing, R. 2012. "Ethics: Wrong Move Can Tarnish Your Reputation." Business and Economics, *Financial Times*, London, March 19.

Schäfer, D. 2008. "Siemens to Pay €1bn Fines to Close Bribery Scandal." *Financial Times*, London, December 15. http://www.ft.com/intl/cms/s/0/1cc029de-cae9-11dd-87d7-000077b07658.html#axzz2nFhuq4eY (accessed December 12, 2013).

Sims, R.R., and E.L. Felton. 2006. "Designing and Delivering Business Ethics Teaching and Learning." *Journal of Business Ethics* 63, no. 3, pp. 297–312.

Spinler, S., and R. Franklin. 2011. "Shared Warehouses." *International Commerce Review: ECR Journal* 10, no. 1, pp. 22–31.

UNFCC (United Nations Framework Convention on Climate Change). 2013. "Warsaw Climate Change Conference—November 2013." *UNFCC*. http://unfccc.int/meetings/warsaw_nov_2013/meeting/7649.php

Whaley, F. 2013. "Philippine Typhoon Death Toll Feared in Thousands." *NY Times*. November 9.

Selected Case Studies

Airbnb, Harvard Business School, 2012.

Amyris Biotechnologies: Commercializing Biofuel, Harvard Business School, 2010.

Cradle-to-Cradle Design at Herman Miller: Moving Toward Environmental Sustainability, Harvard Business School, 2009.

Empowering the Bottom of the Pyramid via Product Stewardship: *Tetra Pak* Entrepreneurial Networks in Brazil, INSEAD, 2007.

Fiji Water and Corporate Social Responsibility—Green "Makeover" or Green Washing?, University of Western Ontario, 2011.

Integrated Assurance at *Philips Electronics N.V.* Harvard Business School, 2012.

Manila Water Company, Harvard Business School, 2007.

Unsafe For Children: *Mattel's* Toy Recalls and Supply Chain Management, Stanford University, 2008.

Viridity Energy: The Challenge and Opportunity of Promoting Clean Energy Solutions, University of Western Ontario, 2012.

Walmart's Sustainability Strategy (B): Update 2010, Stanford University, 2010.

Zipcar, Harvard Business School, 2005.

CHAPTER 8

Teaching Ethics in Supply Chain Management

Gerald Burch, Walter Kendall, and Joanna Shaw

Tarleton State University

Introduction

Strong ethical standards and actions are needed now more than ever before. Dealing with unethical and illegal activities within the business environment is a problem that no business can afford to take lightly. This is illustrated by the dramatic negative impacts on society and corporate performance due to misconduct within corporations (both intentional and unintentional) (Withers and Ebrahimpour 2012). In today's global business environment, the impact of corruption, high taxes, and intense competition is making firms more vulnerable to unethical or illegal practices both within their native country and overseas. Adding to this is a difficult economic environment where the pressure to survive (individually as well as organizationally) often results in ethical concerns being pushed away (Withers and Ebrahimpour 2012). This situation is even more pronounced where multiple companies work together to produce a good or service. This is the environment students will find themselves in when they are studying ethics, or working in the field of supply chain management.

The purpose of this chapter is to examine the role of ethics in the field of supply chain management. We begin the chapter by reviewing three disciplines—supply chain management, ethics, and curriculum techniques—needed to address the complex nature of teaching ethics and develop a concept-based ethical decision-making model that allows the student to analyze the most salient components of ethical decision making. In the next section, we offer two examples of ethical issues and use a concept-based curriculum approach to illustrate how typical ethical issues arise in supply chain management and how students can analyze, and better understand how to avoid, such situations using our model. Based on these examples, we subsequently provide recommended strategies for teaching ethics in supply chain management, give advice for teachers on integrating concepts, and outline how the state of economic development of a country can alter the ethical perspectives of supply chain decision makers.

Description of Discipline

There are three major disciplines that instructors should consider when teaching ethics in supply chain management:

- Ethics
- Supply chain management
- Concept-based curriculum

The first, and most important, is the field of ethics itself. Several ethical theories play prominent roles within the business environment. Although each theory can pertain in certain ways to the area of supply chain management, we have identified three specific theories that are most likely to align with contemporary concerns and ethical concerns within supply chain management. We have chosen contract theory based on the importance that contracts play in the establishment of agreements between supply chain partners. Care ethics was chosen to represent the need to maintain the supply chain relationships. And finally, the common good approach was selected to demonstrate the need for supply chain partners to evaluate the benefits and damages across the entire supply chain. We will look at each of these theories separately and then as a whole.

Contract theory proposes thinking about ethics in terms of agreements between people. Doing the *right thing* specifically means abiding by the agreements that the members of a rational society would choose. Contract theory is not necessarily about character, consequences, or principles. The true challenge that confronts corporate decision makers in connection with global labor conditions is often in identifying the standards by which they should govern themselves in an effort to provide greater direction in the face of possible global cultural conflicts (Hartman, Shaw, and Stevenson 2003).

Care ethics also plays a prominent role within the area of supply chain management. Care ethics mainly focuses ethical attention on relationships before other factors. As a result, acting *rightly* involves building, strengthening, and maintaining strong relationships. Acting *rightly* displays care for others, and for the relationship of which they are a part. Relationships within the theory of care ethics are fundamental to ethical thinking. In 1982, Carol Gilligan published *In a Different Voice*, a foundation text that established an ethic of care as a powerful alternative to justice as the central value around which moral theory and practice might revolve. Ethics of care starts with the perspective of viewing people as relational and interdependent (Held 2005).

The common good approach attempts to promote the common values and moral or ethical principles found in a society. This varies from place to place, based on cultural or societal beliefs. For example, the moral principles in Japan, Indonesia, China, Argentina, Mexico, or the United States will often be different from one another based on cultural variations alone. Business owners and managers often implement these principles to ensure their company's overall mission is in sync with society as a whole. The common good approach entails cooperation to promote conditions that enhance the opportunity for the human flourishing of all people within a community (Melé 2009).

Each of these three ethical theories can be viewed through their own unique *lens* in regard to an ethical situation that arises within the area of supply chain management. However, we borrow the concepts associated with all three theories to provide the conceptual framework for our model.

The second discipline that we must consider is supply chain management. A supply chain consists of all parties associated with directly, or indirectly, fulfilling a customer request (Chopra and Meindl 2010). Supply chain management therefore consists of managing the actions of every warehouse, manufacturer, supplier, transporter, retailer, and customer involved in receiving and fulfilling the customer's demand. By their very nature, supply chains are dynamic and involve the constant flow of information, raw materials, subassemblies, finished goods, and funds between multiple organizations. The overall objective of each supply chain is to maximize the total value generated by all participants (Chopra and Meindl 2010). Therefore, the success of each supply chain is built upon the close connection, design, management, and integration of all members with the objective of optimizing the whole, rather than the parts.

The final discipline needed for our discussion is the use of a concept-based curriculum. Erickson (2002) argued that the key to transferring knowledge was to identify the key concepts surrounding the topic and then to use the student's previous knowledge of the concept to accelerate learning. Current management scholars have claimed that it is the underlying game of how concepts fit together that are important for learning (Wright and Gilmore 2012). When the student considers two or more concepts simultaneously, and looks at them through the lens of the discipline, the student develops a conception (Land et al. 2005).

An example of a supply chain conception is the understanding associated with the concepts of benefit and legal as seen through the eyes of a supply chain manager. The student has a concept of benefit and a separate concept of legal that is built around their combined experience of dealing with each idea. However, supply chain management students must place themselves in the shoes of the supply chain manager and consider the legal aspects of decision making while simultaneously considering the benefits of the decision across all members of the supply chain. To help guide this discussion, we offer a concept-based ethical decision-making model (Figure 8.1).

Figure 8.1 offers six ethical concepts that should be considered by the student when evaluating decisions. These concepts come from the three ethical theories we have chosen and should be considered individually and simultaneously to ensure that the decision meets the requirements

```
                    Ethical concepts      Stakeholder lenses        Potential outcome
```

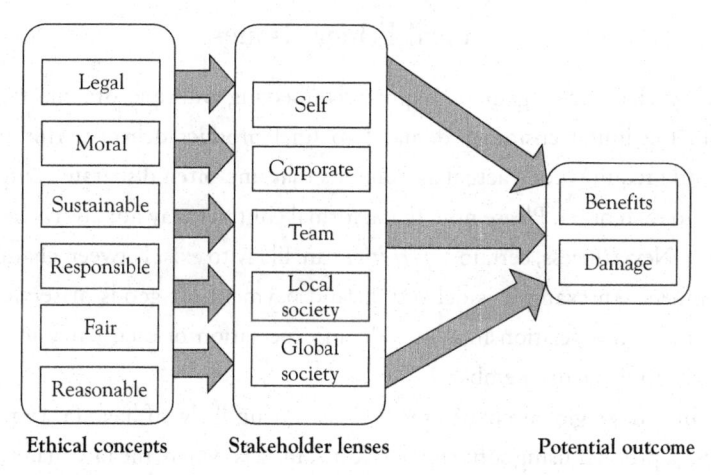

Figure 8.1 Concept-based ethical decision-making model

of all six concepts. Contract theory is built around execting transactions based on defined processes, or the law. Therefore, the concept of legality is important to consider. The remaining concepts (moral, sustainable, responsible, fair, and reasonable) are more related to care ethics and common good approach. This list of concepts is certainly not all-inclusive. They represent only those concepts the authors found applicable to these three theories. Other concepts are available and could be considered. See the review of sustainable operations management processes (Kleindorfer, Singhal, and Van Wassenhove 2005) for more examples. Further discussion about the concepts and how they are used in this model is included later in this chapter.

The model also provides the student with five lenses (self, corporate, team, local society, and global society). Decisions are made by individuals and often the benefits may only be enjoyed by the person making the decision or the company that the individual works for. Supply chains are built around teams, and benefits and damages for all team members should be examined when choosing the appropriate course of action. Added to this discussion is the increasing awareness of the effects of corporate decisions on local and global societies. Our model ensures that students consider all five of these lenses when evaluating the benefits and damages of the decision. Two examples of how students should consider all six concepts and view them through the stakeholder lenses are offered later in this chapter.

Typical Ethical Issues

Supply chain management requires connecting multiple organizations from the initial customer demand to final product delivery. This frequently requires contractual agreements that link often disparate companies to each other. Please note that a formal contract may not always be in place. Nevertheless, certain *expectations* are likely to exist between channel members. An example is delivery of and payment for goods or services. Even informal relationships include an expectation of each party to the other supply chain members.

In today's global environment, it is not unlikely to have customers order a product using software developed in Asia, where the raw materials come from North America, the final assembly is completed in Africa, and the product is delivered to a customer in Europe. Evaluating the ethical decision-making process becomes very complex since multiple companies stand to benefit from the execution of the decision. We propose that decisions are often made by the most powerful member of the supply chain and are only evaluated through the lens of that one person or one company. This phenomenon is hypothesized to be stronger in those supply chains where the balance of power is shifted more strongly to only one member. As the balance of power shifts and becomes more equitable, the decision making will move to more mutual decisions where the supply chain begins to consider the benefits and damage through the lenses of each company and also of the entire team.

This same shift is also expected in those relationships where the companies have an enduring relationship instead of a disposable one, which leads to making decisions that support both companies. In the next section, we will examine two typical supply chain examples and use these ideas and our concept-based ethical decision-making model to evaluate the decisions made by the supply chain.

Example One: Contractually Based Ethical Issues in the Supply Chain

Contractually based ethical issues present a potentially serious problem in supply chain relationships. One need not look far to find violations, either intentional or unintentional, which have had major repercussions on suppliers, manufacturers, and consumers. Examples are counterfeit aircraft parts that led to aircraft crashes and loss of life (Flight Safety Foundation 1994), lead paint in children's toys that resulted in multimillion dollar fines and costly recall campaigns, kerosene used as the liquid inside of a fake eyeball toy (Lipton and Barboza 2007), and toothpaste made with diethylene glycol, a solvent used in antifreeze, which led to the deaths of 51 people in Panama (WND 2007). Unfortunately, this list of incidents could go on (Martin and Johnson 2010; Meyer 2008).

This list of supply chain problems can be linked to contractual issues. Well-written contracts go a long way toward ensuring that the goals of all parties are met since they outline the needs and expectations of all parties. However, supply chain management problems arise when specifications are not included, incomplete, inaccurate, or not followed. Examples are the nonspecification of materials or inputs that leave the supplier to decide the appropriateness of components, and the nonspecification of industry standards or requirements that may be well understood by one supply chain partner but unknown to a supplier that is not familiar with the industry. Added to this list are those contracts where specification is incomplete or erroneous, which leads to potential harm to consumers and damage to the supply chain. These types of supply chain problems stand in contrast to the violation of contract specifications that occur either intentionally or unintentionally.

Case of Willful Violation of Regulatory Specifications

The U.S. Federal Aviation Administration (FAA), as with many national aviation regulatory bodies around the world, requires that all original and replacement aircraft parts be certified by the FAA. This usually entails manufacture to rigid specifications, identification markings on the part, and, increasingly, the ability to trace the origin of parts via Radio-frequency Identification (RFID) or other means. Most military aviation organizations have similar military specifications (MILSPEC). The obvious objective is to reduce the likelihood that counterfeit aircraft parts find their way into civil or military aircraft.

The assumption is that counterfeit parts may not meet critical standards of strength, life expectancy, or other key factors that affect safety or performance.

A recent example is the production of a two-inch, cadmium-plated steel pin with a hole drilled in one end. At first glance the pin is unimportant. However, when used to connect an aircraft control actuating rod to another movable part, such as a flight control surface, the pin is directly linked to the safety and performance of the aircraft. Even small parts that enter the supply chain without adherence to regulatory specifications can have potentially catastrophic results. There is a growing tendency to procure and use counterfeit parts based on the pressure to decrease aircraft repair and construction costs.

Evaluation of Example One

A teaching opportunity now exists to use example one to walk students through the concept-based ethical decision-making model. A discussion of decisions and outcomes may help to inform the thought process when students later find themselves in related professional situations. The situational assumptions can be varied to change the nature of ensuing discussions. The instructor is encouraged to make use of these opportunities to turn and twist the situation to provide opportunities for students to think through the model given various states and conditions.

Situation. The instructor can assume any desired starting state for the purposes of instruction. Varying the assumed relationships between the environmental inputs can introduce new problems and greatly change the situation. For this illustration let us assume the following states:

- For simplicity sake, we will consider a situation where one buyer (buyer) procures the cadmium-plated steel pins from a supplier (supplier) and then resells the pins to an aircraft repair facility (repair facility) who repairs planes for the end customer (customer).

- Both a competitive and cooperative environment exists within the supply chain. The buyer, supplier, repair facility, and customer are in an overall competitive situation where they are free to make decisions as to who they sell and buy from. This could generally be described as a cooperative agreement between supply chain partners.
- Balance of power. There is no partner with undue power or influence over the other supply chain partners.
- The purchase decision is assumed to be made by the buyer, based on the price and technical and engineering specifications for the required parts.
- The relationship quality is enduring. The supplier and buyer have a long-standing business relationship within the supply chain and expect that relationship to continue going forward.

Potential Outcome(s). While various outcomes might occur based on the environmental situation chosen by the instructor, the value of examining the supply chain participant decisions comes from the evaluation of the outcome, through the various stakeholder lenses.

Benefits: The choice to use counterfeit parts is expected to significantly reduce the cost of the pins. When viewed from the supplier, buyer, or repair facility lens, the decision to buy counterfeit parts presents a potential increase in profit. The buyer can convince themselves that the cost of evaluating the supplier's part is not needed since a long-term cooperative relationship exists between the buyer and supplier. Similarly, the repair facility can make the same claim about the buyer and the customer can make a similar claim about the repair facility.

Damage: It could be argued that damage occurs only to the customer if a pin fails or causes unexpected wear or other damage that causes injury, loss of life, or property. However, this ignores the damage to the relationship among supply chain partners that can result in the significant loss of business for each partner. Similarly, the failure of the supply chain to maintain safe aircraft can damage the local society or even global society. Loss of confidence in the aircraft repair process can cause customers to choose other transportation modes or may cause regulators to increase monitoring of aircraft repair activities, which drives up transportation costs. The actions of one buyer or one supplier in a supply chain can cause a myriad of damages when viewed through the eyes of others.

The previous discussion about benefits and damages was conducted from the focal point of companies or organizations. Students must understand that a company never makes a decision. People make decisions. Individuals or groups make decisions. The choice to buy a counterfeit part is likely done by one person. That one person could potentially be the student in their future employment.

Ethical Concept Evaluation. The concept-based ethical decision-making model shows that there are six major concepts associated with making ethical decisions.

We will evaluate example one using each of these concepts and combine the various stakeholder lenses.

Legal. For purposes of illustration and further thought, let us assume that the supplier knowingly substituted uncertified aircraft parts into the supply chain. There may or may not have been any malice. The supplier may not have even been aware of the regulatory requirements or the potential outcomes. The supplier merely saw a way to reduce costs.
It could be argued by some students that the contractual relationship (a written contract may not even exist) has not been violated by such a substitution. On the other hand, many students will see that a contract, at least of trust and spirit, even if not the letter of a written contract, has probably been violated. From the legal perspective, it could be argued that the buyer and aircraft repair facility are not legally culpable. However, in the case of government regulations it would be difficult for them to completely divorce themselves from the decisions of a supply chain partner. The question becomes "to what extent should supply chain partners trust the actions of other partners?"

Moral. Ferrell, Fraedrich, and Ferrell (2014) state that moral philosophy refers to the specific principles or rules that people use to decide what is right or wrong. This is different from legal concerns since it is associated with the cultural evaluation of what is appropriate. One warning for supply chain students is the need to understand the differences among cultures on what is right or wrong. Supply chains often cross cultural boundaries and it is possible that all partners may not have the same morals. For the purpose of evaluating example one, we believe that the supplier's decision to use counterfeit parts is immoral.

Sustainable.   Most companies are in business with the purpose of providing long-term products or services. Therefore, sustainable actions can be seen by the supplier, buyer, and repair facility as those decisions that allow them to continue their business. The supplier's choice to provide counterfeit parts could be seen as unsustainable since they would not be able to continue providing pins if they were found to be in violation of their contract. A similar situation would occur if the buyer or repair facility was aware of the counterfeit part substitution and did not take action.

Sustainability is often seen differently through the eyes of the local or global society since they often view the world through the lens of available resources or cumulative damage. Unsustainable actions are often first noticed by societies. Students must work hard to place themselves into viewing decisions through local and global societal lenses.

Responsible.   The concept of responsible is built on the belief that decisions are made by individuals and that someone must be held accountable for their actions. When viewing the decision to use counterfeit parts by the supplier, it could be easily seen by the student that the supplier did not consider themselves responsible for any damage that may occur based on their decisions. The substitution of counterfeit parts by a supply chain member makes them directly responsible for the loss of life or property, regardless of where it occurs along the supply chain. The buyer and repair facility are also responsible for entering into supply chain arrangements with credible partners since the entire supply chain is responsible for delivering goods to the consumer.

Fair.   Decisions are fair if they support the needs, requirements, and values of all stakeholders. Students will see that the supplier was not fair in their decision to use counterfeit parts since they did not share that information with the other supply chain partners.

Reasonable. The evaluation of reasonableness stems from whether the decision would be expected, or reasonable, if made by a prudent person, based on the current situation. Example one shows that the supplier's decision to use counterfeit parts would probably not be considered reasonable by most parties. However, the decision of the supplier or repair facility for not inspecting the parts before use might be considered reasonable since most people would not expect the supplier to provide counterfeit parts. Students should also be encouraged to look at reasonableness from the different cultural views of potential supply chain partners, since reasonableness will change with cultural values.

Overall evaluation of concepts. Students must understand that ethical decisions are based on the adherence to all ethical concepts. If one concept is not met, then the decision is not ethical. Similarly, decisions must be viewed as ethical through each of the stakeholder lenses. Making ethical decisions requires considerable time and energy to evaluate each of the ethical concepts and to weigh the benefits and damages that could occur to each of the stakeholders. Presenting students with contractually related situations, which may be varied at will by the instructor, should serve as a focus for insightful discussion and learning about the consequences of making ethical decisions within supply chains.

Example Two: Ethical Issues in the Supply Chain Based on Working Conditions

A growing concern in more developed countries surrounds the working conditions found with supply chain members located in less developed parts of the world. The emergence of supply chain codes of ethics, as well as supplier ethics management (SEM) and corporate social responsibility (CSR) programs like those discussed by Doorey (2011) at Levi Strauss and Nike can greatly affect the locus of responsibility for setting the ethical tone within a supply chain (Amaeshi, Osuji, and Nnodim 2008; Bendixen and Abratt 2007; Burchielli et al. 2009; Doorey 2011; Ellis and Higgins 2006; Industry Week 2008; Krueger 2008; Medford 2011; Razzaque and Hwee 2002; Smith 2011).

TEACHING ETHICS IN SUPPLY CHAIN MANAGEMENT   171

In this example, we examine the decision to use suppliers that do not maintain appropriate working conditions from the viewpoint of one or more supply chain members. While not directly connected with workforce conditions within the supply chain, instructors may also wish to examine supply chain safety issues in developing countries using the Union Carbide Corporation Bhopal disaster (Broughton 2005) as a springboard.

Making Clothes and Money

The clothing business, as with most businesses, is driven by cost. In particular, labor costs are a significant contributor to the cost of clothing. As such, it is not uncommon for clothes to be assembled in underdeveloped or developing companies. The situational assumptions can be varied by the instructor to change the nature of ensuing discussion and decisions. The instructor is encouraged to make use of these opportunities to turn and twist the situation to provide opportunities for students to think through the model given various states of being within each node. An excellent starting point is for the instructor to review the situation faced by Nike and Levi Strauss (Doorey 2011).

Situation. A major clothing manufacturer (buyer) has chosen to outsource the assembly of clothes to Asia. Several companies bid on the contract and one (supplier) was selected based on their lower cost per garment to assemble clothes. More details are offered in the following text.

- Both a competitive and a cooperative environment exist within the supply chain. While both supplier and user may be in an overall competitive situation, free to make decisions as to who to sell and buy from, the situation is one of general cooperation between supply chain partners.
- Balance of power. The buyer in this situation is in a place of significant power, at least in the supplier's eyes since the loss of the contract will result in a significant loss in business for the supplier.

> - The relationship quality is disposable since there are many suppliers that the buyer could use and no specific supplier skills are required.

Potential Outcome(s). Similar to example one, we will evaluate the benefits and damages through the various stakeholder lenses.

Benefits. The consumer, buyer, and supplier all benefit from this supply chain arrangement. The consumer pays a lower price for clothing. The buyer charges less for assembled garments and may generate a competitive advantage over their competitors, which may increase the buyer's market share. The supplier benefits by gaining a large contract to grow their business. Although not mentioned in the evaluation of example one, it is important to consider the benefit to the possibly hundreds of employees associated with the supplier.

Damage. In this situation, we assume that the supplier unbeknownst to the buyer or consumer decides to impose working conditions that might result in the use of very young workers, very long hours, or riskier working conditions. The outcome could be benign in many cases, at least as viewed through the supplier or buyer lenses. However, damages may occur if undesirable media coverage results in pressure from stockholders, consumers, and governmental and nongovernmental agencies. Damages can also be seen through the supplier lens if the pressures on the buyer result in a loss of the contract. As the pressure increases on the buyer, there could be deterioration of the relationship cultivated between the supply chain members, thereby damaging the team. Perhaps the greatest damage occurs by looking through the local and global society lenses to evaluate the working conditions for the supplier employees. We will further address these issues in the next section.

Ethical Concept Evaluation.

Legal. In many countries there are no laws concerning employee age, number of hours worked, or working conditions. In most countries, there are no laws that prohibit the use of suppliers in other countries or the working conditions for those companies. Therefore, there is nothing illegal about this decision when viewed from the supplier, buyer, or consumer perspective.

Moral.   Cultures often dictate the moral philosophy of an area. The moral beliefs in the supplier's culture may not view the working conditions as unethical. However, in most developed countries society has developed moral beliefs around the age, hours, and working condition for employees. In this situation, there may be a moral inconsistency that creates a difficult situation for the supply chain since the partners may be operating under different moral beliefs and social pressures.

Sustainable.   For a decision to be sustainable, it must use fewer resources than can naturally be replenished. Levi Strauss made the decision, under similar circumstances, to investigate and encourage better working conditions from suppliers after they determined that they could not sustain societal pressures to improve working conditions regardless of supplier locations (Doorey 2011).

Responsible.   This concept sheds considerable light on the ethical evaluation of the decision made in example two. Just because a decision is not illegal, immoral, or unsustainable, it does not mean that the decision maker is not responsible for employee safety or for creating situations that encourage over use or abuse of employees. The supplier and buyer are both responsible for the proper treatment of employees throughout the supply chain.

Fair.   This concept also demonstrates the importance for students to consider all six ethical concepts when making decisions. Students must see that the standard of living in underdeveloped or developing cultures creates situations where humans may be treated unfairly, at least as viewed through the lenses of global or more developed countries. In this case the criteria being considered is the working conditions for suppliers; however, it could be a myriad of other things.

Reasonable. The emergence of a global economy has created the situation where labor is often divided across countries based on the country's available resources. Perhaps the greatest resource for developing countries is the availability of inexpensive labor. It is reasonable for companies inside these countries to use the resources that they have. However, students should be aware of the effects on other ethical concepts.

The preceding examples give concrete examples for instructors to teach ethics and also a model for them to guide the student through the ethical decision-making process. However, perhaps the greatest benefit of using this curriculum development technique is the ability to embed the concepts of ethics throughout the entire course instead of at the end of the class. We will briefly discuss this idea in the next section.

Ethics Teaching Strategy

Students learn and categorize their worlds based on concepts and conceptions. As such, instructors should develop curriculum that forces students to hold multiple concepts in their heads while they consider new knowledge and make decisions. The six concepts of ethics presented in this chapter should provide the ethical scaffolding that the student should always consider when making decisions. Too often, the consideration of ethics is delayed until after a decision has been made. We recommend that instructors consider the following steps when teaching supply chain management:

- Introduce the idea of concepts to the student early in the course.
- Introduce the concept-based ethical decision-making model early in the course.
- Guide students through the use of concepts to make conceptions by using the model early in the course.
- Consider other ethical concepts that may have been omitted in this chapter.

- Use the ethical concepts and components of the decision-making model as often as possible throughout the course to allow the student to integrate the knowledge.
- Develop experiential learning activities that allow the student to use the decision-making model.

Ethical decision making is an activity that should be considered by business men and women at all times. Similarly, instructors should consider teaching ethics in supply chain management as an integral part of understanding the relationships and decision-making processes that are a major part of supply chain management.

Advice for Teachers

Preparing students to deal with ethical issues as they arise within their current or future organization is an important role. Using the unique case studies as outlined within this chapter and the addition of articles that support these areas within supply chain management are integral in helping students gain this knowledge. Presenting students with workplace environment situations that may be varied at will by the instructor should serve as a focus for insightful discussion and learning about the consequences of making, or conversely not making, ethical decisions within supply chains. The introduction of moral variation, external pressures, legal variation, and so forth can make this a very fruitful discussion or assignment. We also recommend team projects that require students to synthesize and analyze the scenarios with other students.

Developing Versus Developed Country Perspectives

Example two in this chapter showed how country development can affect the ethical decision-making process. Members of more developed countries often have extended legal requirements by which to judge the ethics of a decision. Similarly, the lack of resources or opportunities in developing and underdeveloped countries can affect the moral, sustainable, responsible, fair, and reasonable concepts of ethics. It is not uncommon for various supply chain members to have vastly different views of ethical concepts. However, it is the responsibility of the entire supply chain to manage the overall ethical conception.

Summary and Conclusion

Supply chains are often the amalgamation of disparate companies making decisions about the development of a product or service. This mixing of cultures creates scenarios where the balance of power may cause decisions to be made while considering the benefits and damages to the more powerful stakeholder. Similarly, the relationship quality (disposable versus enduring) may encourage one partner to consider only their lens when viewing the outcomes of the decision. This combination of effects creates situations where supply chain decisions are unethical when viewed through the eyes of others.

To address this issue, we have used three ethical theories to develop a concept-based ethical decision-making model to encourage students to simultaneously consider six ethical concepts in the evaluation of the benefits and damages by looking through the lenses of five major stakeholders. Using this model, the instructor guides the supply chain management student to consider the evaluation of decisions from multiple angles, including the potential differences associated with working with developing or underdeveloped countries.

Finally, we believe that it is this concept-based approach that is important for instructors to consider when teaching ethics and other curriculum. Students are all conceptual learners. As the breadth and depth of information increases, instructors must find ways to accelerate the delivery of information or increase teaching efficiency. Teaching students at the concept level leverages the information that the student already has about a concept. Subsequently, helping the student develop conceptions of multiple concepts, as seen through the eyes of the supply chain manager, creates enduring understandings that will guide student learning and opens the field of supply chain management as a discipline instead of simply as a course.

References

Amaeshi, K., O. Osuji, and P. Nnodim. 2008. "Corporate Social Responsibility in Supply Chains of Global Brands: A Boundaryless Responsibility?" *Journal of Business Ethics* 81, pp. 223–34.

Bendixen, M., and R. Abratt. 2007. "Corporate Identity, Ethics and Reputation in Supplier–Buyer Relationships." *Journal of Business Ethics* 76, pp. 69–82.

Broughton, E. 2005. "The Bhopal Disaster and Its Aftermath: A Review." *Environment Health: A Global Access Science Source* 4, pp. 1–6.

Burchielli, R., A. Delaney, J. Tate, and K. Coventry. 2009. "The FairWear Campaign: An Ethical Network in the Australian Garment Industry." *Journal of Business Ethics* 90, pp. 575–88.

Chopra, S., and P. Meindl. 2010. *Supply Chain Management: Strategy, Planning, and Operation*. Boston, MA: Pearson.

Doorey, D. 2011. "The Transparent Supply Chain: From Resistance to Implementation at Nike and Levi-Strauss." *Journal of Business Ethics* 103, pp. 587–603.

Ellis, N., and M. Higgins. 2006. "Recatechinzing Codes of Practice in Supply Chain Relationships: Discourse, Identity and Otherness." *Journal of Strategic Marketing* 4, pp. 387–410.

Erickson, H. 2002. *Concept-based Curriculum and Instruction*. Thousand Oaks, CA: Corwin Press.

Ferrell, O.C., J. Fraedrich, and L. Ferrell, 2014. *Business Ethics: Ethical Decision Making & Cases*. 10th ed. p. 154, Stamford, CT: Cengage Learning.

Flight Safety Foundation. 1994. "Bogus Parts—Detecting the Hidden Threat." *Flight Safety Digest* 13, pp. 1–17.

Gilligan, C. 1982. *In a Different Voice*. Boston, MA: Harvard University Press.

Hartman, L., B. Shaw, and R. Stevenson. 2003. "Exploring the Ethics and Economics of Global Labor Standards: A Challenge to Integrated Social Contract Theory." *Business Ethics Quarterly* 13, pp. 193–220.

Held, V. 2005. *The Ethics of Care: Personal, Political, and Global*. New York: Oxford University Press.

Industry Week. 2008. "How Ethical Is Your Supply Chain? Supplier Ethics Management Offers a Way to Plug Ethic Gaps." *IndustryWeek*, January 1, p. 59.

Kleindorfer, P.R., K. Singhal, and L.N. Van Wassenhove. 2005. "Sustainable Operations Management." *Production and Operations Management* 14, pp. 482–92.

Krueger, D. 2008. "The Ethics of Global Supply Chains in China—Convergences of East and West." *Journal of Business Ethics* 79, pp. 113–20.

Land, R., G. Cousin, J.H.F. Meyer, and P. Davies. 2005. "Threshold Concepts and Troublesome Knowledge (3): Implications for Course Design and Evaluation." In *Improving Student Learning Diversity and Inclusivity*, ed. C. Rust, 53–63. Oxford, England: Oxford Centre for Staff Learning and Development.

Lipton, E.S., and Barboza, D. 2007. "As More Toys are Recalled, Trail Ends in China." *New York Times*

Martin, K.D., and J.L. Johnson. 2010. "Ethical Beliefs and Information Asymetries in Supplier Relationships." *Journal of Public Policy & Marketing* 29, pp. 38–51.

Medford, R. 2011. "The Economic Value of a Sustainable Supply Chain." *Business and Society Review* 116, pp. 109–43.

Melé, D. 2009. "Integrating Personalism into Virtue-based Business Ethics: The Personalist and the Common Good." *Journal of Business Ethics* 88, pp. 227–44.

Meyer, M.W. 2008. "Editor's Forum—Made in China: Implications of Chinese Product Recalls." *Management and Organization Review* 4, pp. 157–65.

Razzaque, M., and T. Hwee. 2002. "Ethics and Purchasing Dilemma: A Singaporean View." *Journal of Business Ethics* 25, pp. 307–26.

Smith, N. 2011. "Responsible Consumers and Stakeholder Marketing: Building a Virtuous Circle of Social Responsibility." *Universal Business Review* 30, pp. 68–79.

Withers, B., and M. Ebrahimpour. 2013. "The Effects of Codes of Ethics on the Supply Chain: A Comparison of LEs and SMEs." *Journal of Business & Economic Studies* 1, no 1, pp. 24–40.

WND (WorldNetDaily). 2007. "Florida Company Recalls 'Toxic' China toothpaste."

Wright, A.L., and A. Gilmore, A. 2012. "Threshold Concepts and Conceptions Student Learning in Introductory Management Courses." *Journal of Management Education* 36, pp. 614–35.

CHAPTER 9

Teaching Ethics in Decision Making: Embedding Moral Reasoning in the Management of Information Systems

Olayinka David-West

Lagos Business School, Pan-Atlantic University

Introduction

Information and communication technologies (ICTs) are significant in business and social contexts as a result of the commoditization of computing, the commercialization of the Internet, the convergence of voice, data, and media, and digital trends like social networking, cloud computing, and mobility. Commonly known as the digital or information age, this era is characterized by ICTs, volumes of digitized information (digital content), and information workers.

In the business-context, ICTs are typically deployed to enhance productivity and improve performance. The ability of ICTs to meet business-oriented goals requires the integration of human and organizational capabilities to form a holistic systems-view and complementary management practices. The management practices guide information systems (IS) initiative choices, resources and capabilities acquisitions, operational management, and value delivery methods. Though adequate for organizational deployment of ICTs, management practices do not sufficiently address information use and user behaviors in the information age.

The interconnectedness of computers and free access to information are benefits of the information age that warrant ethical guidelines. Ethics in the information age comprises computer ethics, ethics online (cyberethics), professional ethics, and information ethics (privacy, security) (Johnson 2000; Mason 1986). While detailed explanations are beyond the scope of this text, they remain relevant to understanding ethics in the application and management of information systems (MIS).

Objectives

The moral dimensions of MIS are the focus of this chapter that highlights ethical dilemmas relating to information use and user behaviors in the planning, development, management, governance, and application of IS. The chapter highlights MIS ethical dilemmas and demonstrates the application of ethical principles in decision making.

This chapter introduces the following:

- The MIS lifecycle of activities
- IS ethical principles and sample MIS dilemmas
- Embedded MIS-ethics teaching strategies
- Ethical IS decision making

The chapter comprises five sections. Following the introduction, the key concepts of MIS are presented. This is followed by an explanation of the key IS ethical principles and examples of ethical dilemmas. The section *Integrating Business Ethics in MIS* features a teaching strategy that demonstrates the application of ethical principles to IS decisions. The concluding section summarizes the relevance of ethical principles to MIS work and decision making.

ISs and Their Management

ISs are the combination of human (people), organizational (processes), and digital (systems) resources and capabilities deployed to meet diverse business and organizational needs.

Management of IS

MIS takes a business approach to IS development. MIS practices generate answers to the following questions: How can ICT contribute to organizational goals? What ICT resources and capabilities need to be acquired? What management practices must be imbibed for effective ICT maintenance? Are ICTs properly utilized and are organizational goals met? MIS activities—strategic planning, systems development, management, governance, and effective use—are deployed toward the actualization of business value.

Strategic information systems planning (SISP) is the "process of deciding the objectives for organizational computing and identifying potential computer applications which the organizational should implement" (Earl 1993). SISP encompasses the identification, strategic analysis, and selection of IS initiatives that complement the attainment of business goals and objectives. Without specifying solutions to procure, SISP seeks to address the *what* question to the application of IS for strategic benefits and competitive advantage. SISP activities formulate initiatives that will ensure IS contributes to organizational goals. The process evaluates the business (strategy, industry, competitors, etc.), the IS environment (including installed systems), and benchmarks IS development among peer organizations. This in-depth analysis combined with the expertise of planners results in the generation of possible initiatives that are systematically assessed prior to development.

The application of a systems approach to information system solutions to solve business problems is known as systems development (O'Brien 2006). Where a strategic plan exists, systems development is the operationalization of that plan. The ability of organizations to deliver effective IS are hinged on effective systems development practices and decisions; hence, its complexity and relative importance cannot be understated. Systems development also encompasses project management practices that guide the activities and change management tactics that manage the changing behaviors and attitudes of users toward new work practices.

Management and Governance

Information technology (IT) management and governance activities ensure the effective operation and oversight of IS, respectively.

IS management ensures the maintenance and administration of ICT assets and services. IS management comprises technical and business management activities. The technical IS management includes the back office functions that keep systems and services operational and available for business use. The IT infrastructure library (ITIL), currently in its third version, is a best practice service management framework that "focuses on the continual measurement and improvement of quality of IT service delivered, from both a business and a customer perspective" (Cartlidge et al. 2007). IS business management focuses on information ownership and access to facilitate decision making.

IT governance "consists of the leadership and organizational structures and processes that ensure that the organization's IT sustains and extends the organization's strategies and objectives" (IT Governance Institute 2003). IT governance ensures the existence of sufficient responsibilities and practices to provide strategic IT direction, ensure business objectives are met, ascertain IT risks are managed, and verify the responsible use of IT resources.

The practices and user strategies that encourage the effective use of IS to meet business goals and deliver benefits are the scope of effective use.

MIS practices address IS contribution to organizational productivity and performance highlighting the complementary competencies required for successful IS development.

Ethical Issues

Ethical Principles in IS

Ethical principles provide managers guidance in the analysis of MIS decisions regarding information use and behaviors (user and practitioner). The section introduces and demonstrates the application of ethical principles to derive outcomes based on common good, fairness, greatest value, virtue, least harm, ownership, and repeated actions perspectives.

Immanuel Kant's categorical imperative takes an inclusive view of the proposed action. The principle seeks a decision outcome that is right for (or will cause no harm to) everyone in the organization or society (Laudon and Laudon 2006). Kant's principle can be likened to the common good principle defined by Reynolds (2011). The common good approach to decision making visualizes the society as a community whose members collectively work toward a common set of values and goals. The fairness approach treats all stakeholders equally. The approach focuses on the fair distribution of benefits and burdens among the stakeholders affected by the decision (Reynolds 2011). Also known as the golden rule principle or the pursuit of justice, the role reversal of putting oneself in the place of others permits fairness in decision making (Laudon and Laudon 2006; Mason 1995). The utilitarian approach yields outcomes with the best consequences or greatest value (Laudon and Laudon 2006; Reynolds 2011). While Kant seeks an outcome of common good, utilitarianism seeks the greatest value without consideration for the recipients or the process employed to achieve the benefits (Elegido 1996). The virtue ethics approach assumes individuals are guided by their virtues in reaching the right decision. Virtue ethics focuses on the protagonists' behavior and perception of community relationships. Also known as the pursuit of virtue (Mason 1995), the virtue ethics approach to resolving an ethical dilemma has the protagonist select the most conformable outcome or their perception of the action a role model would take. Unlike the utilitarian approach that seeks the greatest value, the risk aversion principle seeks actions that produce the least harm or lowest cost. The *no free lunch* principle acknowledges the ownership of all resources and seeks to attribute compensation or acknowledgement to the creators of resources deemed to have value. Descartes's rule of change principle bases decisions on repeated action. If the repeated implementation of an action cannot be conducted, then that action should not be considered. Descartes's principle acknowledges that even though the short-term benefits of an action may bring about a desired change, the long-term effect of repetition may bring about some damage, and the action should not be implemented.

MIS Ethical Issues

Sample ethical dilemmas associated with MIS practices are illustrated in subsequent paragraphs.

SISP activities are somewhat subjective and dependent on the knowledge and experience. The ability to conduct a thorough SISP on the one hand is based on the agent's ability to evaluate both the IS and business landscapes, provide fair judgment on the internal state of IT, and conceptualize IT initiatives for business-IT alignment. The interest and scrutiny of the business executives and their ability to question and test the proposed IS initiatives are essential. Judgment, an ethical SISP dilemma results in the inability to formulate big, hairy, and audacious initiatives. This is exemplified when an internal IT manager is assigned to formulate the SISP but is unable to disclose the full complement of ICT assets for fear of self-exposure. Another SISP challenge is proffering solutions as opposed to conceptual initiatives due to bias, pre-existing relationships with vendors, or following competition. When applied to SISP, ethical principles guarantee objectivity and process rigor that ultimately derive favorable outcomes.

Systems development ethical dilemmas are embedded in the various decisions and lifecycle practices. For instance, the downsizing threat of computerization is a common ethical challenge associated with the introduction of software applications. Even though computers cannot replace humans, attention to human issues, changing work practices, digital competencies, and so forth can potentially reduce threats and fears of job losses, which may also curtail employee sabotage. The decision to maintain status quo or replace current practices with new ICT systems may be motivated by intrinsic benefits unrelated to the decision. This is common in developing countries where decisions to replace applications are accompanied by spurious and expensive foreign trips, in some cases by unqualified personnel. In spite of the availability of countless packaged software applications, the weights assigned to selection decision criteria may be flawed favoring lower ranked criteria like local representation instead of availability of competencies to address the business problems. When consultants are employed in vendor evaluation and selection decisions, pre-existing relationships may introduce bias and cloud objectivity. In cases where software applications require a multitiered enterprise architecture that warrants various software licenses, understatement of quantities to reduce license costs is prevalent. In all, consideration of ethical principles in systems development lifecycle guarantees actions in support of the organization and stakeholders are attained.

The perceived lack of business management's interest and involvement in IS decisions are more inhibitive than moral, but moderate value return. Information issues like data protection (security and privacy) are common ethical dilemmas in the inter-networked era where internal and external breaches are norm. The story of a young lady that suspected her boyfriend of cheating explains such a breach. Without confronting him, she solicited and received mobile call logs through a friend that worked with his telecom provider. The breach —employee download and transfer of subscriber data to a third party—was never discovered, but had potentially harmful implications to the telco and the relationship. Ethical dilemmas resulting from poor IT management practices can either harm an organization's reputation or result in the imposition of penalties and fines from regulators.

IT governance responsibilities are a way to ensure measurable returns are derived from IS initiatives; however, the absence of IT knowledge among board members restricts the quality of suitability and appropriateness inquiries. The apparent lack of query is even more pertinent in public organizations where board oversight responsibilities are unknowingly abdicated. Like in SISP, the application of ethical principles in IT governance will facilitate decision objectivity and transparency.

Occupational health risks from ICT use include bodily injury to employees and warrant safeguards through the provision of ergonomic tools like keyboard support, ergonomic chairs, and antiglare screen protection. Repeated use of smartphones and tablets not only strains the thumbs but also encroaches on employee lives. Data security and privacy breaches are sustained through business-to-consumer (B2C) e-commerce where the security of personal and payment information are increasingly difficult to maintain. The resultant impact is computer and network breaches and the theft of passwords, identities, credit card information, and so forth. Systems software bugs increase insecurity and computer breaches resulting in possible data loss. Software piracy is another widespread ethical challenge. After an MIS session, I was once approached by a student who sought my confirmation of the legitimacy of the MS-Office installation on their laptop. On enquiring about the source, I was informed it came with the computer but later confirmed to have been installed by a friend. Unsuspecting users such as the student in question are oblivious of the inherent threats (IDC 2014) that increases vulnerabilities to Internet crimes. Corporate organizations implement network security policies to counter such risks and protect systems and corporate users; however, individuals often fail to acquire equivalent security applications. The free expression of speech and association in cyberspace termed net neutrality is yet another challenge that not only opposes government censorship but also fails to protect minors from inappropriate content. In sum, understanding the ICT utilization ethical dilemmas associated will reduce potential harms and risks.

The diversity of MIS activities and associated ethical dilemmas requires the application of various ethical principles in decision making that are best demonstrated by example.

Integrating Business Ethics in MIS

Embedding ethics in the MIS discipline is equivalent to the examination of user (or practitioner) behaviors when interacting with information and computers. The case study (see box) *Information Needs of Roco's Chief Executive* that describes an IS development project is used for illustrative purposes.

The ROCO case is atypical of owner-managed organizations desirous of computerization but uninterested in the process. This case discussion commences with a poll on project success. Some deem the project as successful because it was completed, installed, and in use; others argue the project failed because it did not meet John's needs. Based on John's management style, he is characterized as a micro-managing entrepreneur that makes decisions without information or little consultation. While his pricing ethics are questioned, his need for IS is not substantiated. Putting themselves in Fred's shoes, the students are asked if they would have accepted the job. To some Fred acted as any entrepreneur would, and others believed additional IS development factors should have been considered, hence questioning his professional ethics. This discussion stirs up controversy as the majority of the students believe Fred, in his capacity as a software engineer, delivered the IS that was contracted, even though the software engineers code of ethics[1] contradicts this assertion.

---

[1] See http://www.acm.org/about/se-code

As a professional, the class believes that Fred should have assessed ROCO's need for the IS and we subsequently employ the ethical principles as a guide through questions such as the following:

- Will the IS work to everyone's advantage or just serve a chosen few (common good)?
- Will the IS create and maintain equality at ROCO? Am I the best person for this job (fairness)?
- Will the IS have a good impact on all the stakeholders? Or will it bring harm to any stakeholders (greatest value)?
- Will Fred's family friendship with John remain intact (virtue)?
- Will any part of the IS harm any stakeholders (least harm)?
- What is ROCO's history with ICT projects (repeated action)?

In conclusion, the IS was appropriate for ROCO's growing business and was designed for the common good of the organization and its employees, but it maintained the culture of inequality at ROCO and increased the organization's ecological footprint and costs through frequent and bulky report printing. In addition, while the IS enhanced John's bragging rights, his jovial nature may not have impacted the family relationship; however, he would probably not refer his valued contacts to Fred. For students, this process builds the understanding of how a seemingly harmless decision may have had a different outcome had the ethical implications been considered.

John Martins, the Managing Director and owner of ROCO (Nigeria) Ltd., a firm specialized in road building, was chatting with Fred Vaughn, a computer consultant and a family friend, in the siting room of his nice house in Ikoyi.

"Look Fred, although I want to computerize my company, I am afraid of it because I fear that I would be paying too much attention to figures and miss the real decisions...."

John's style of management is in many ways unpredictable, and generally based on oral communications from his contacts in the government circles with regard to contracts and from his employees in matters related to the company. In his chat with Fred, he was summarizing his management career as follows:

"I have made mistakes, but I have learned from them. I have made many decisions involving millions of Naira in a matter of seconds. I give a lot of importance to my nose, especially in serious decisions. I like taking risks, and so far I have succeeded," he proudly added.

Although a foreigner, John has been living in Nigeria for decades, and considers himself a Nigerian. He now enjoys a comfortable position to a great extent due to the acquisition of ROCO.

The Company

When John Martins decided to buy FMO (Nigeria) Ltd. Construction Company, he knew he was doing a good business. He changed the company's name to ROCO (Nigeria) Ltd., to make it clear that he was breaking with the past. The operation was complemented by the acquisition of a quarry, called Okenla, situated some 30 km from headquarters. The quarry was to run as an independent venture, but its main client would be ROCO. Okenla would produce all the gravel and asphalt that ROCO needed and would be able to sell the surplus production to other firms as well.

His high-level contacts soon proved their worth, and the company presently got contracts for the construction of several roads in Lagos State. Now it has construction sites in several states in a radius of 300 km from the headquarters, situated in Ikeja (Lagos).

Although John asks for the opinion of his most trusted employees, all the major—and most small—decisions are taken by him. Looking at the trend of the business, he decided to invest in the acquisition of site equipment. New asphalt pavers, bitumen distributors, cranes, crawler drill rigs, and so forth were acquired, both new and used equipment, from local and overseas sources (the company had some foreign currency that could be utilized for this purpose).

A central repair yard was kept near the headquarters in Lagos. Plant equipment that needed substantial repair or maintenance was brought to the yard. A central store with spare parts for all the different types of plant equipment was kept at the repair yard.

The Information System

Fred was invited to *computerize* the company. The decision seems to have been motivated by John's belief that *the world is going computer* rather than from a felt need for information. John has developed throughout the years of experience the feeling that the information he needed to run his business is always changing, and is to a great extent subjective rather than objective. His sources are generally trusted advisers.

He does not think highly of fixed reports, but makes his decisions—often based on impressions, gossips, other people's feelings, and so forth (what can be qualified as soft information, as opposed to the hard information based on facts and figures).

Once one of his newly recruited managers was asked to prepare a quotation for a client and when they finished it, they were astonished when John asked to multiply all the figures by 2! (The client accepted the offer.)

Fred Vaughn set to work guided more from his own experience than from the information he got from John who did not seem to bother much and preferred to leave these matters in the hands of "You, computer people…."

Fred introduced an information system including accounts receivable, accounts payable, machines and spare parts inventory, and payroll. Soon after the installation, reports started reaching John's table.

Some of these reports were aggregated summaries of accounts payable and receivables, inventories, budget versus actual figures from different departments, all being by-products of the information system Fred set up, and based primarily on routine transaction paperwork processing. However, John wanted to be in full control of the decisions made, both big and small, and at times requested for detailed data. These data were given to him in the form of long listings of transactions that required a great deal of time to digest (when that is even possible).

> If John asks for any data, the computer manager keeps on sending the report or listing from them on to him periodically (usually once a month). The result is that John's table is accumulating an increasing number of long computer printouts that he has no time to look at.
>
> Fred was satisfied with his work that had automated to some extent much of the paperwork at ROCO. Nevertheless, John is not convinced of the real usefulness of the information system although be often boasts: "We are now computerized at ROCO."

Faculty leading ethics discussions need to be avid listeners that utilize the ethical principles to question opinions without passing judgment. However, faculty need to be cautious of the implicit utilitarianism of IS deployments. While acknowledging this, faculty should highlight the divergent viewpoints generated by alternative ethical principles.

In addition to the case study method, faculty leading ethics-infused sessions may also employ project-based educational and didactic approaches to enhance learning. A research-oriented approach may be used to identify extant ethical dimensions of ICTs in business. Working in groups, students are tasked with the identification of ethical issues in the IT areas: management and governance practice, software solution selection, project implementation, and general usage. Students are encouraged to use various data collection methods like observation, interviews, or surveys to discover the broad spectrum of ethical considerations in the IT discipline. A plenary session of the class where the groups present their findings concludes the project. Alternatively, the facilitator may use a consulting approach among small- and medium-sized companies (SMEs). In this setting, students are tasked with the conduct of an ethical analysis of IT management and usage practices. The findings and recommendations are presented in a written report with an executive summary shared with the management of the SME.

The teaching and application of MIS ethical principles in developing countries is marred by low digital literacy skill sets, fragmented markets, and software piracy, to name a few.

The low entry barriers of the ICT industry increase the incidence of unprofessional and unstandardized practices resulting from opportunity seekers that take the certification route to expertise development. Trends such as these have resulted in more supplier-led sales and questionable acquisitions. Inhibitive software costs (or inappropriate total cost of ownership costing) result in high piracy levels. A business executive once rationalized the use of pirated software as needful in developing economies given the revenues of the licensors. Refocusing the discussion around costs and product pricing brought about a change in perspective when asked about profitability margins if and when the company had to acquire licenses legitimately. According to the Business Software Alliance (BSA),

> Emerging economies, which in recent years have been the driving force behind PC software piracy, are now decisively outpacing mature markets in their rate of growth. They took in 56 percent of the world's new PC shipments in 2011, and they now account for more than half of all PCs in use. (BSA 2012)

Unlike mature IT markets that monitor and evaluate the costs and impacts of IT-business value (Devaraj and Kohli 2002), legal and reputation risk, and so forth, the governance and regulatory practices in developing countries are weak or nonexistent.

Conclusion

"Computers are incredibly fast, accurate, and stupid. Human beings are incredibly slow, inaccurate, and brilliant. Together they are powerful beyond imagination." Attributed to Albert Einstein, this quote not only emphasizes the socio-technical nature to IS but also summarizes the importance and role of ethics in MIS—to guide man. Table 9.1 summarizes IS ethical principles, MIS activities, and questions that may be applied in the analysis of ethical dilemmas.

Common good for the organization in SISP mandates the objectivity in all planning activities. Systems development ensures the organization will be adequately served by the solutions deployed. IT governance ensures the good of the organization is maintained through strategic

Table 9.1 MIS ethics summary

	SISP	Systems development	Management	Governance	Use
Categorical imperative (common good)	• Business and IS assessments • Benchmarking • Initiative selection	• Requirements analysis • Systems design • Testing • Change management	• Service management • Resource management • Enterprise architecture • Monitor risks	• Strategic alignment • Value delivery • Performance management	• Harming or stealing from others
	• *Will the plan generate initiatives that will ensure the organization attains its objectives?*	• *Will the various projects produce IS that will attain the stated benefits?* • *Are the applications suitable for the organization?*	• *Will the IS be well maintained, functional, and operational to attain the stated benefits?*	• *Can we validate the IS produced the stated benefits?*	• *Does the IS cause harm to its users or others?*
Golden rule (fairness)	• Business and IS assessments • Brainstorming • Initiative selection	• Vendor selection • Negotiation	• Resource management • Enterprise architecture	• Resource management	• Legitimate use
	• *Are the assessment and selection methods objective and transparent?* • *Will they ensure the most beneficial initiatives are chosen?*	• *Have all vendors been appraised equally? Are there any conflicts between parties?* • *Are we getting the best value?*	• *Does the organization have a resource catalogue for role profiles?* • *Are IS resources equally distributed across the organizations' users and locations?*	• *Are IS resources equally distributed?*	• *Have all software licenses been legally acquired?* • *Are there processes in place to guard against illegal use of software?*

TEACHING ETHICS IN DECISION MAKING

Utilitarian (greatest value)	• Business and IS assessments • Initiative selection • Benchmarking • Brainstorming	• Requirements analysis • Systems design • Bid evaluation • Vendor selection • Project management • Change management	• Enterprise architecture • Service management	• Strategic alignment • Value delivery • Resource management	• Harming others
	What initiatives will yield the most benefits?	Which IS projects will deliver the highest benefits in the shortest time? How many employees may the IS render redundant?	Which IS resources are more critical and require more attention? Does the IS generate value for the organization?	What IS projects have delivered the most benefits?	Which IS projects have failed to deliver any benefits and have caused harm or business losses?
Virtue ethics (virtue)	• Business and IS assessments • Brainstorming • Benchmarking • Initiative selection	• Develop RFP • Project management • Change management	• Enterprise architecture • Resource management • Service management • Monitor risks	• Strategic alignment • Value delivery • Resource management • Performance management • Risk management	• Legitimate use
	Has user or practitioner behaved appropriately? Are proposed initiatives the most suitable?	Has user or practitioner behaved appropriately? Has practitioner diligently defined the systems requirements?	Has user or practitioner behaved appropriately? Has practitioner diligently secured systems?	Has user or practitioner behaved appropriately?	Have the proper payments been made for use of these tools?

(Continued)

Table 9.1 MIS ethics summary (Continued)

	SISP	Systems development	Management	Governance	Use
Risk aversion (least harm)	• Business and IS assessments • Initiative selection • Benchmarking • Brainstorming	• Requirements analysis • Vendor selection • Negotiation • Project management • Change management	• Monitor risks • Service management • Resource management • IT management standards • IT usage policies	• Risk management	• Harming or stealing from others
	What initiatives have low risks?	*Which IS projects will have the least cost?*	*Which IS security policies will ensure systems are protected?* *Are security measures in place to ensure stakeholder information is secured?* *Have all iterations of the web address been registered to desist phishing?*	*Which IS resources have the lowest risks?*	*Which IS projects have failed to deliver any benefits/have caused harm or business losses?* *Have all software applications been duly licensed?*
No free lunch (ownership)	• Brainstorming	• Systems design • Programming	• Systems management • Resource management • IT usage policies	• Resource management	• Legitimate use
	Have any unique initiatives been proposed? *Have all actors been acknowledged and compensated?*	*Have any specialized systems been developed?* *Have all actors been acknowledged and compensated?* *Have all licenses been duly purchased?*	*Have any innovative management practices been applied?* *Have all actors been acknowledged and compensated?* *Is data only accessible to authorized personnel?*	*Have all actors been acknowledged and compensated?*	*Have all software applications been duly licensed?*

Initiative selection	Implementation • Project management • Change management	Systems management • Resource management	Value delivery • Performance management	System protection
• Were the initiatives in previous SISPs suitable for the business?	• Has this IS been effectively deployed? • Have previous IS projects been successful? • Have all system users been trained? • Has the system been deployed successfully across the organization (e.g., in multiple locations)?	• Have sufficient systems management competencies been developed?	• Did the IS deliver sufficient value and meet performance expectations?	• Does the security software consistently protect the organization from all types of harm?
Descartes's change (repeated action)				

alignment, value delivery, and performance management practices. This is matched with the professional conduct of those charged with the daily administration of ICT, ensuring proper implementation of data security and ergonomic practices. SISP fairness seeks justice from IS initiatives by taking human and organizational issues into consideration. In the acquisition of ICT contracts, fairness should be considered in the disclosure of license requirements and negotiation practices, given that the vendor is a commercial entity. The decisions made in the daily administration of ICT should be unbiased, satisfying the organization's goals and objectives with the oversight of resource management through effective governance. The illegitimate use of software is theft, as the owners are not rewarded for their intellectual property. The business application of IT is utilitarian as it seeks to accomplish business value through productivity and performance. In SISP, the utilitarian perspective should examine reusability as opposed to replacement. Utilitarian behaviors that seek the exploitation of IS should guide systems development, management, and IT governance practices and identify harmful IS. The *no free lunch* principle seeks acknowledgement of employee contributions to IS developments even when employment contracts deem ownership to the employer. The no free lunch principle also applies to the legitimate use of systems and the payment of license fees. The pursuit of justice through the virtue ethics approach is relevant to all actors in the conduct of MIS. In the pursuit of virtue, actors should be upright and seek outcomes that will not lead to disrepute. Even though risk is pervasive in majority of MIS activities, practices such as benchmarking, requirements analysis, and risk monitoring and management can reduce potential harm or failure. When applied, Descartes's change principle highlights areas of change for new systems' implementations using outcomes of prior experiences. In all MIS activities, the principle examines previous outcomes and experiences to ensure common good, greatest value, least harm, and so forth.

References

BSA (Business Software Alliance). 2012. *Shadow Market:* 2011 BSA Global Software Piracy Study. BSA. Retrieved from http://globalstudy.bsa.org/2011/downloads/study_pdf/2011_BSA_Piracy_Study-Standard.pdf

Cartlidge, A., Hanna, A., Rudd, C., Macfarlane, I., Windebank, J., and Rance, S. 2007. *An Introductory Overview of ITIL V3*. (A. Cartlidge and M. Lillycrop). UK Chapter of the itSMF. Retrieved from https://www.best-management-practice.com/gempdf/itSMF_An_Introductory_Overview_of_ITIL_V3.pdf.

Devaraj, S., and R. Kohli, R. 2002. *The IT Payoff: Measuring the Business Value of Information Technology Investments*. Upper Saddle River, NJ: Financial Times Prentice Hall.

Earl, M.J. 1993. "Experiences in Strategic Information Systems Planning." *MIS Quarterly* 17, no. 1, pp.1–24.

Elegido, J.M. 1996. *Fundamentals of Business Ethics*. Ibadan, Nigeria: Spectrum Books Limited.

IDC (International Data Corporation). 2014. *The Link between Pirated Software and Cybersecurity Breaches*, Framingham, MA: IDC.

IT Governance Institute. 2003. *Board Briefing on IT Governance*. 2nd ed. Rolling Meadows, IL: IT Governance Institute.

Johnson, D.G. 2000. *Computer Ethics*. 3rd ed. Upper Saddle River, NJ: Prentice Hall PTR.

Laudon, K., and J. Laudon. 2006. "Ethical and Social Issues in Information Systems." In *Management Information Systems: Managing the Digital Firm*, 1–41. New York: Prentice Hall.

Mason, R.O. 1986. "Four Ethical Issues of the Information Age." *MIS Quarterly* 10, no. 1, pp. 5–12.

Mason, R.O. 1995. "Applying Ethics to Information Technology Issues." *Communications of the ACM* 38, no. 12, pp.55–57.

O'Brien, J.A. 2006. *Management Information Systems*. 4th ed. New York: McGraw Hill.

Reynolds, G. 2011. *Ethics in Information Technology*. Boston, MA: Course Technology, Cengage Learning.

MODULE 4
Selling the Product

CHAPTER 10

Embedding Ethical Issues in Marketing Management Classes: An Instructor's Guide

Uchenna Uzo

Lagos Business School, Pan-Atlantic University

Introduction

Marketing instructors tend to pay little attention to ethical issues in marketing because few have the depth of understanding required to offer useful guidelines for managing ethical dilemmas (Kotler 2004; Elegido 2009). Understandably, the focus of marketing is not to enter into ethical squabbles associated with managing consumers but rather to understand and effectively organize to serve consumers. Yet, understanding consumers and their purchase behavior goes beyond collecting demographic data on consumer segments and organizing the marketing mix to serve those segments. It also involves *entering* into the consumer's mind to understand his or her goals, values, and ethical concerns so as to help the consumer reach human fulfillment. As Kotler, Kartajaya, and Setiawan (2010) put it:

> Instead of treating people simply as consumers, marketers approach them as whole human beings with minds, hearts and spirits…consumers are looking for solutions…they search for companies that address their deepest needs for social, economic and environmental justice in their mission, vision and values.

In other words, each individual consumer is not a *purchasing object* but rather a *person* whose purchase decision is influenced among other factors by his or her ethical frame of reference (Lee and George 2008; Chappell 1998). Thus, the point of departure of this chapter is that every marketing decision has an ethical dimension. Since ethics is about the moral quality of human actions (Mele 2009, 6), every human decision taken to understand and serve a consumer segment has ethical implications.

This chapter elaborates on this position by offering some insights on how marketing instructors can embed ethical considerations in some aspects of their marketing teaching curricula. The chapter is organized as follows. First, a brief historical overview of the field of marketing management is presented and a case is made for embedding ethics in discussions about the field. Next, typical ethical issues in marketing management for class discussion are raised and appropriate teaching strategies and methods are offered. Thereafter, a cursory look is made of developing and developed country perspectives to embedding ethics in the marketing curricular. Finally, conclusions are drawn for future thinking on the subject matter.

Description of Marketing Management

Marketing has been defined as the process of planning and executing the conception, pricing, promotion, and distribution of ideas, goods, and services to create exchanges that satisfy individuals and company's goals (Kotler 2004; Harvard Business Press 2010). Since its inception in 1937, the field of marketing has continued to shape the thinking of managers, companies, and entire industries. Over the years concepts were introduced by scholars to better how marketing works in organizations. The marketing mix was introduced by Nel Borden of Harvard Business School to describe the activities comprising a firm's marketing program used to pursue sales goals in a target market (Borden 1964). Wendell Smith developed the concept of market segmentation in 1956. Thereafter, concepts such as positioning, branding, cause-related marketing, green marketing, and digital and online marketing (Valos, Ewing, and Powell 2010; Soat 2014) were introduced to adapt the marketing field to more contemporary realities (Harvard Business Press 2010). Despite these developments in the field, scanty attention has been paid toward understanding and teaching ethical issues in marketing. Yet, any company that engages in identifying and satisfying consumer needs is forced to make choices on a daily basis that may or may not be perceived as being ethical (Alan and Wood 2009). Thus, instructors and students require more than a superficial understanding of ethical issues associated with the field so as to better prepare managers for the challenges ahead. In the next section, we shall now highlight typical ethical issues in the marketing management curricular.

Typical Ethical Issues in Marketing Management

Ethical issues associated with taking marketing decisions abound. In the foregoing, we pay special attention to the ethical issues of understanding the consumer, segmenting markets, managing channels, branding, marketing communication, and pricing. This section does not attempt to exhaustively cover all the ethical issues in marketing but rather to highlight some of the major issues in marketing that have ethical dimensions. Instructors of a full course in marketing typically begin the course by highlighting the importance of understanding the consumer. Among other things, it is usually emphasized that properly identified segments should focus on the underserved, dissatisfied, or untapped sections of the market, focus on a company's strategic objective and be flexible for social, economic, and technological changes (Foedermayr and Diamantopoulos 2009; Piercy and Morgan 1993; Yankelovich and Meer 2006).

The first question facing instructors is what ethical issues are relevant to a class discussion on understanding the consumer and segmenting the market? Since this aspect of the marketing process focuses on profiling and understanding the consumer, reflecting on the ethical principles that guide consumer behavior is important for understanding why and how consumers make purchase decisions. Drawing from the ethics literature, three fundamental principles are worthy of note. The first principle is that each consumer as a human person has an intrinsic and absolute worth irrespective of his race, age, sex, or any other particular condition and thus has a certain dignity that ought to be respected (Alan and Wood 2009; Lee and George 2008; Mele 2009). Second, each individual person has a unique and distinctive identity that leads him or her to ascribe toward certain values and virtues. Third, consumers as human beings should never be treated as a mere means to an end but rather with benevolence and care (Lee and George 2008; Wojtyla 1993). With these principles in mind, instructors can raise certain salient questions for class discussions on market segmentation. Relevant questions include the following: What values do the consumers of this potential product consider to be important for their work and family lives? How can these values be tracked during the segmentation process? What are the corporate values guiding the behavior of this organizational buyer? What consumer needs are necessary and which ones are superfluous? A discussion of these questions will enable the instructors to draw out a number of learning points on ethical considerations. One major learning point is that encouraging people to purchase and consume goods in excess of their basic needs, even to the point of causing themselves physical or moral damage, is not consistent with respecting their dignity (Guiltinan 2009; Packard 1960; Mele 2009). Second, products or services targeting consumers can move beyond avoiding the violation of consumer's basic human rights toward helping the consumers achieve transcendental goals and values. Third, marketing managers engaged in segmentation should beware of violating the privacy of potential and actual consumers. In other words, scavenging for personal details of people's lives without their consent invades their privacy (Smith and Quelch 1993, 194).

The next critical question is what are the ethical issues associated with managing channels of distribution? Instructors facilitating a discussion on marketing channels point out that channels are not just a conduit for distributing products but rather a set of interdependent organizations that work toward adding value to the products (Coughlan et al. 2006). Ethical dilemmas arising from channel relationships manifest in the areas of channel contracts, channel incentives, and power utilization within the channel. The design and execution of channel contracts is an issue that has ethical implications. For instance, in situations where distributors and manufacturers do not fully understand their contractual obligations, room is created for exploitation by both parties. One example is the *bait and switch* tactic, in which a reseller attracts consumers on the basis of a given supplier's advertising and other investments, only to substitute private-label merchandise at the point of purchase (Smith and Quelch 1993, 489). There is also the problem of allocation of territories among distributors. When contracts do not clearly specify the territories to be served by distributors, it triggers rivalry and unfair competition between distributors selling the same product. Another source of ethical concerns is the rate of information flow among members in the process of executing the contract. In situations where manufacturers hoard vital information from distributors and vice versa, mistrust is created in the relationship and this ends up leading to breaches in contractual obligations. In class discussions about channel contracts, instructors could raise ethical considerations by asking them to share experiences on the extent of involvement of all channel members in the creation of contracts. Some students typically point out that contracts tend to be pushed down from manufacturers to other channel members without much room for input from the latter. Another question for students could be how much information on competitors is a distributor willing to share with a manufacturer of a particular product? These questions can help the instructor to talk about the ethical principle of honesty in relationships. This involves speaking the truth and not concealing any aspects in the contractual relationship. Thus, telling lies, creating false expectations, distorting reality, and giving misleading feedback are examples of a lack of honesty (Alan and Wood 2009; Mele 2009, 214), which poisons contractual relationships and ends up deterring consumer's willingness to buy from distributors. Furthermore, instructors could trigger ethical considerations about channel incentives by asking students to debate on what should be the right balance of incentives for distributors and retailers. A good question for this debate is whether the incentive package should be mainly commission based or whether it should have a fixed basic component. Power relationships within the channel also have ethical implications. According to Stern and El-Ansary (1988), "Power is the ability of one channel member to get another channel member to do what the latter would not otherwise have done." Instructors could trigger the ethical issues by asking students whether product availability can be manipulated for the purpose of exploiting profits from consumers or channel members. Another useful question is to ask participants to outline tactics used by manufacturers to deal with distributors that are perceived to be nonperforming. The outcome of such debates would be anecdotal references to cases of abuses of power. The instructor could then highlight the importance of the ethical principle of justice. It could be emphasized that power is not an end in itself to be used to the advantage of the more powerful person. Thus, attempts to use power to damage the dignity of human persons are counterproductive to organizations and consumers alike.

Product decisions in marketing also have ethical dimensions. These decisions focus on issues such as new product development, product design, packaging, and quality assurance. The thesis of discussions on products is that companies create products and services to meet market needs. In other words, the development, design, and launching of new products should be triggered by clearly identified consumer needs. Ethical issues for consideration begin to appear when one considers that consumer needs vary in nature. For example, needs could be latent or manifest, present or future, continuing or declining. Thus, how can managers and product or service innovators decide whether the need is significant enough to create a new product? For example, as Guiltinan (2009) puts it, should manufacturers and product designers introduce replacement products to phase out durable and already functioning products? Other ethical concerns for class discussion center on the extent to which product developers and manufacturers have a responsibility to do what is good for consumers even if consumers do not want it. A classical issue for a class debate on the issue is the one described by Smith and Quelch (1993, 285). The authors ask:

> What about when consumers want and are willing to pay for something that does not affect the product's performance but which the company believes is not very good for the customer? Should that be incorporated into the product? For example, how should cereal producers respond to children's preference for high sugar levels in cereals? Sales probably will increase if the sugar content of the cereal is increased. But the issue is, should that be done?

The ethical principle to highlight after such a debate is that organizations as well as marketing managers are supposed to be custodians of their customers and potential consumers. In other words, in planning for products, it is important to ensure that the products and services do not only *respect* the human dignity of customers but that these also *promote* the human fulfillment of these customers. Another important ethical concern is related to the process of developing the products. Important questions to pose in class include: To what extent are customers involved in the creation of new products? How are innovative ideas rewarded in organizations? Instructors could emphasize in such a discussion that organizations ought to be structured in a way that allows employees to achieve fulfillment in their work while developing their personal capabilities. In addition, the pressure to succeed in launching new products leads some companies to conceal the defects of products to be sold. Other companies exaggerate the performance claims of the products in a desperate effort to secure market share. The ethical principle to be emphasized in discussions about such issues is that the end does not justify the means. In other words, managers responsible for product replacement strategies act in ethically questionable ways if they "psychologically condition" consumers to believe that the utility of a product is diminished simply because a new version becomes available (Giaretta 2005; Guiltinan 2009).

Marketing communication is another aspect of marketing that has ethical dimensions. Instructors usually point out that the aim of marketing communication is to substantially increase the sales volumes for products or services in the short term and build brand loyalty in the long term. Yet the quest for short-term returns tends to put marketing managers in difficult ethical situations. Instructors could ask questions such as how can you tell whether a marketing campaign for a product or service is faithful to its promise? Does the campaign encourage customers to strive for certain values or is it only focused on getting a share of the customers' wallet? Is the campaign justified in the first place? Imagine a situation where a telecommunications company launches a promotion where consumers at the bottom of the pyramid market would win an airplane if they purchased a certain amount of airtime. In such a situation, what is the company trying to achieve? Branding is also a form of marketing communication that might be deceptive or even manipulative to the consumer (Jeurissen and Van de Ven 2006). For example, what happens when Volvo, the car manufacture, fails to live up to its brand promise portrayed by its marketing campaign of safety and security? These different questions provide the opportunity to highlight integrity as an essential ethical principle for running promotions. The word integrity means *wholeness*, wholeness of virtue, wholeness as a person, wholeness in the sense of being part of something larger than the person, the community, the corporation, society, humanity, and the cosmos (Solomon 1999, 38). In other words, integrity implies a *unity of life* manifested in taking business decisions that are coherent with one's personal values. The power of a discussion on the ethical principle of integrity is that it takes the discussants beyond the case discussion to the more personal realm where they can examine other spheres of their lives (family, business relationships, etc.).

Finally, ethical issues in pricing are important but not often discussed in the classroom. Instructors emphasize that a price should come as close to a consumer's perception of value while not falling below what it costs to produce that value (Kotler 2004). Discussions generally focus on outlining pricing strategies, methods, and tactics for responding to price competition. Most instructors wishing to highlight ethical issues associated with pricing merely mention that price fixing, price gouging, predatory pricing, and failure to disclose the full price of a purchase are unethical practices (Pride and Ferrell 2008, 56). However, they do not elaborate on what constitutes fairness in pricing. This is also the case because most marketing textbooks gloss over the issue of the ethics of pricing or neglect it altogether (Elegido 2009). Instructors wishing to provoke a meaningful discussion on fair pricing could benefit from insights raised by Juan Elegido (2009) in a seminal article on the issue. The author argues that (1) the fairness of exchanges should be assessed objectively, (2) that the fair price of an article or product is one equal to its *value*, and (3) that the best indicator of that value is the price that article or product commonly fetches in the open market. A practical way of drawing from these insights in a class discussion is to ask the following questions: Are firms the rightful owners of value? Are firms entitled to charge whatever price the market can bear? Is pricing merely a pursuit for profit by exploiting consumer disadvantage such as lack of information, understanding, and so forth? A lively debate ensues once such issues are raised. Thereafter, instructors could leverage on interesting insights from "Pricing to Create Shared Value" written by Marco

Bertini and John Gourville in the June 2012 edition of the *Harvard Business Review*. The authors argue that value neither originates from nor belongs entirely to an organization. Furthermore, consumers are getting increasingly sophisticated as they have access to independent sources of information on prices and products. A well-known example highlighted by the authors is the case of Netflix, which implemented a 60 percent price increase in July 2011 for customers who both rented DVDs and streamed video. As a result, 800,000 users cancelled their service and the company's market cap plummeted by more than 70 percent. This and other examples could be discussed to highlight the implications of not charging a fair price. Instructors could conclude their discussion by highlighting some actionable points that can help organizations improve consumers' perception of fairness in pricing.

Ethics Teaching Strategy and Advice for Teachers

Various teaching strategies can be used to embed ethical issues in marketing classes. Some of them include the following: lecture method; subgroup learning through ethical discussion, exposure to alternative view points, and collaborative learning, case studies, role plays, film and video, literature, and games; personal value journals, guest speakers and practitioner participation, service-learning, and E-learning (Manolo 2013). Of particular interest is personal value journaling, which helps students and instructors to record personal thoughts and daily experiences. The process often evokes conversations with self, another person, or even an imagined other person (Hiemstra 2001). Instructors could also leverage on good teaching cases and reading material to prepare their class discussions. The book by Smith and Quelch (1993) on *Ethical Issues in Marketing* contains a collection of useful cases for class discussion. The case of Joe and Jo Camel is a good teaching case for ethical issues in marketing communication (Alan and Wood 2009). Teachers might also find it useful to adopt a framework for analyzing ethical issues in marketing. A very useful framework is the one designed by Rest (1986, 4), which outlines four stages of the ethical decision-making process. These four stages include ethical issue recognition and interpretation, moral evaluation and judgment, intention, and implementation and ethical behavior. This framework could help instructors and students to conduct a thorough and objective analysis of ethical issues in a marketing class.

Developing Versus Developed Country Perspectives

Business schools could embed ethics in marketing curricula by encouraging faculty to write or use teaching cases that highlight an ethical dilemma in at least one of their classes in an entire course. Some schools in developing and developed countries are already following this strategy. For example, the Lagos Business School in Nigeria has invested significantly in embedding ethics within its curricula. According to Adeleye, Amaeshi, and Ogbechie (2011):

> The school has also developed a required course in philosophical anthropology on the MBA programme, titled "The Nature of Human Beings." This half-course includes topics such as: man as a higher animal; man as a rational being: intelligence and will; the unity of the human person; man's freedom; man as a social being; man's development: the virtues; man's dignity (see Elegido 2009). The rationale for this course, which is taken at the beginning of the programme, is to provide students with a fuller and more realistic account of the human person, and to stimulate critical thinking when engaging with business and economic theories and concepts later on in the programme, and even after graduation.

Similarly, Sauder School of Business, University of British Columbia, offers separate scholarships for students who have demonstrated ethical leadership and are committed to the environment and have shown a passion for corporate social responsibility (CSR), business ethics, or sustainability ("Mapping the Future of Business Education" 2013). These initiatives could be replicated in other institutions.

Summary and Conclusion

It was argued in this chapter that all marketing decisions have ethical dimensions and thus instructors and students require a deep understanding of ethical issues that often come up in the course of making strategic decisions. Ethical issues associated with understanding the consumer, segmenting the market, managing the channel, setting prices, and marketing communication were discussed. Fundamental ethical principles of justice, integrity, and respect for human dignity were elaborated upon. The chapter also provided useful teaching strategies, methods, and perspectives to guide instructors in their class preparations. Future work on embedding ethics in marketing curricular could focus on discussing how to manage ethical discussions about marketing in a multicultural context. In addition, discussions about the ethical issues associated with online marketing would be very useful for present and future managers. It is hoped that instructors will find this chapter useful for their subsequent sessions on marketing.

References

Adeleye, I., K. Amaeshi, and C. Ogbechie. 2011. *Humanistic Management Education in Africa*. Basingstoke, UK: Palgrave MacMillan.

Alan, D., and N. Wood. 2009. "Incorporating Ethics into the Marketing Communications Class: The Case of Old Joe and New Jo Camel." *Marketing Education Review* 19, no. 2, pp. 63–71.

Bertini, M., and J. Gourville. 2012. "Pricing to Create Shared Value." *Harvard Business Review* 6, pp. 96–104.

Borden, N. 1964. "The Concept of the Marketing Mix." *Journal of Advertising Research* 6, pp. 2–7.

Chappell, T. 1998. *Understanding Human Goods: A Theory of Ethics*. Edinburgh, Scotland: Edinburgh University Press.

Coughlan, T., E. Anderson, L.W. Stern, and A.I. El-Ansary. 2006. *Marketing Channels*. 7th ed. Upper Saddle River, NJ: Pearson Prentice Hall.

"Mapping the Future of Business Education". 2013. *Corporate Knights Magazine* 12, no. 3, pp. 52–53.

Elegido, J.M. 2009. "The Just Price: Three Insights from the Salamanca School." *Journal of Business Ethics* 90, pp. 29–46.

Foedermayr, E., and A. Diamantopoulos. 2009. "Market Segmentation in Practice: Review of Empirical Studies, Methodological Assessment and Agenda for Future Research." *Journal of Strategic Marketing* 16, no. 3, pp. 223–65.

Giaretta, E. 2005. "Ethical Product Innovation: In Praise of Slowness." *The TQM Magazine* 17, pp. 161–81.

Guiltinan, J. 2009. "Creative Destruction and Destructive Creations: Environmental Ethics and Planned Obsolescence." *Journal of Business Ethics* 89, pp. 19–28.

Harvard Business Press. 2010. *Understanding Marketing: Expert Solutions to Everyday Challenges*. Boston, MA: Harvard Business Press.

Hiemstra, R. 2001. Uses and Benefits of Journal Writing, http://eporfolioetecmfhetu.weebly.com/uploads/8/9/0/5/8905478/uses_and_benefits_of_journa_writing._hiemstra.pdf (accessed December 2, 2009).

Jeurissen, R., and B. Van de Ven. 2006. "Developments in Marketing Ethics." *Business Ethics Quarterly* 16, no. 3, pp. 427–39.

Kotler, P. 2004. "Wrestling with Ethics: Is Marketing Ethics an Oxymoron?" *Marketing Management* 13, no. 6, pp. 30–35.

Kotler, P., H. Kartajaya, and I. Setiawan. 2010. *Marketing 3.0: From Products to Customers to the Human Spirit*. London, UK: John Wiley & Sons.

Lee, P., and R. George. 2008. "The Nature and Basis of Human Dignity." *Ratio Juris* 21, no. 2, pp. 173–93.

Manolo, M. 2013. "Teaching Strategies for Business Ethics Courses in the Undergraduate Accountancy Curriculum." *DLSU Business & Economics Review* 22, no. 2, pp. 82–94

Mele, D. 2009. *Business Ethics in Action: Seeking Human Excellence in Organizations*. New York: Palgrave Macmillian.

Packard, V. 1960. *The Waste Makers*. New York: David McKay.

Piercy, N., and N. Morgan. 1993. "Strategic and Operational Market Segmentation: A Managerial Analysis." *Journal of Strategic Marketing* 1, no. 2, pp. 123–40.

Pride, W.M., and O.C. Ferrell. 2008. *Marketing*. 14th ed. Boston, MA: Houghton Mifflin Company.

Rest, J. 1986. *Moral Development: Advances in Research and Theory*. New York: Praeger.

Soat, M. 2014. "Marketing in 2024." *Marketing News* 48, no. 1, pp. 18–21.

Solomon, C.R. 1999. *A Better Way to Think About Business: How Personal Integrity Leads to Corporate Success*. New York: Oxford University Press.

Smith, N., and J. Quelch. 1993. *Ethics in Marketing*. New York: McGraw-Hill.

Stern, L.W., and A.I. El-Ansary. 1988. *Marketing Channels*. 3rd ed. Englewood Cliffs, NJ: Prentice Hall.

Valos, M., M. Ewing, and I. Powell. 2010. "Practitioner Prognostications on the Future of Online Marketing." *Journal of Marketing Management*, pp. 361–76.

Wojtyla, K. 1993. *Person and Community: Selected Essays*. New York: Peter Lang.

Yankelovich, D., and D. Meer. February, 2006. "Rediscovering Market Segmentation." *Harvard Business Review* 84, no. 2, pp. 122–31.

CHAPTER 11

Incorporating Ethics in Teaching Consumer Behavior: An Educational Strategy Based on Principles for Responsible Management Education

Consuelo Garcia-de-la-Torre, Gloria Camacho, and Osmar Arandia

EGADE Business School Tecnológico de Monterrey

The Principles for Responsible Management Education have the capacity to take the case for universal values and business into classrooms on every continent.
—UN Secretary-General Ban Ki-Moon (2007)

Introduction

Consumers are involved in ethical marketing issues because they have been considered targets of marketing actions (Catterall, MacLaran, and Stevens 2002). They have been targets of ethical violations within marketing practices through misleading advertising, unsafe products, and manipulation, among others (Abela and Murphy 2008).

Ethics is not a standalone function, and it is embedded in all decision making (Sims and Felton 2006), including consumer behavior analysis. Given the separation of ethical issues from business issues in marketing and specifically in consumer behavior, students need to acquire skills to make ethical judgments in order to prepare them for when they need to face ethical dilemmas as marketers (Plewa and Quester 2006). Hence, given the experience of the incorporation of ethical issues in consumer behavior courses in EGADE Business School Tecnologico de Monterrey in Mexico, the purpose of this chapter is to present some alternatives for the faculty in order to teach responsible consumer behavior, through the integration of an ethical perspective following PRME principles (Table 11.1). They are inspired by internationally accepted values, such as

Table 11.1 PRME principles

Principle	Description
1. Purpose	We will develop the capabilities of students to be future generators of sustainable value for business and society at large and to work for an inclusive and sustainable global economy.
2. Values	We will incorporate into our academic activities and curricula the values of global social responsibility as portrayed in international initiatives such as the United Nations Global Compact.
3. Method	We will create educational frameworks, materials, processes, and environments that enable effective learning experiences for responsible leadership.
4. Research	We will engage in conceptual and empirical research that advances our understanding about the role, dynamics, and impact of corporations in the creation of sustainable social, environmental, and economic value.
5. Partnership	We will interact with managers of business corporations to extend our knowledge of their challenges in meeting social and environmental responsibilities and to explore jointly effective approaches to meeting these challenges.
6. Dialogue	We will facilitate and support dialog and debate among educators, students, business, government, consumers, media, civil society organizations, and other interested groups and stakeholders on critical issues related to global social responsibility and sustainability.

Source: PRME (2014b).

the Ten Principles of United Nations Global Compact (PRME 2014a), which focuses on human rights, labor, environment, and anticorruption.

This chapter is structured as follows: First, we present an introduction, and then we show a brief overview about the Principles for Responsible Management Education. Second, we develop the description on consumer behavior as a subdiscipline of marketing. We present typical ethical issues, the ethics teaching strategy, and we also offer advice for teachers. In addition, we present developing versus developed countries perspectives. Finally, we offer a summary of the chapter and also some suggestions of exercises that will enrich the integration of ethics within a consumer behavior course.

Description of the Discipline

Consumer Behavior: A Subdiscipline of Marketing

Consumer behavior is a core of marketing and is also recognized as a subdiscipline of it that focuses on the study of acquisition, consumption, disposal of products and services (Macinnis and Folkes 2009), and decision making.

During the 1950s, consumers (i.e., the man or woman who buys a product) became the center of business. Firms focused on satisfying consumers' needs and desires efficiently (Prothero 1990). During this period, marketing thought was focused on understanding, managing, and controlling consumer needs' satisfaction (Keith 1960). Hence, consumer behavior as a school of marketing thought began its growth (Macinnis and Folkes 2009). At the beginning, this school of thought focused on understanding the mass consumer market place to make decisions related to new product development, advertising, and retailing (Wilkie and Moore 2003). In order to understand consumer attitudes and motives for buying, consumer behavior scholars incorporated methods from social sciences (e.g., psychology, sociology, anthropology) into consumer research (Fullerton 2013).

In the 1960s, given the environmental concerns of the time, firms focused on satisfying consumers' needs with products and services that did not cause damage to environment (Prothero 1990). Some scholars suggest that the *marketing concept* should be replaced by the *human concept* that emphasizes environmental and societal considerations before the needs and profits of the company (Feldman 1971). Hence, "the application of the marketing concept should, therefore, put the consumer first and deliver benefits to the individual consumer, the society as whole and the company itself" (Carrigan, Marinova, and Szmigin 2005, 482). During this period, the consumerism movement emerged in the United States. It is understood as "social movement seeking to augment the rights and power of buyers in relation to sellers" (Kotler 1972, 49). This movement brought about the recognition of four important consumers' rights: (1) the right to safety, (2) the right to be informed, (3) the right to choose, and (4) the right to be heard. This movement has spread in different countries around the world, such as the United Kingdom, France, Germany, and the Netherlands, among others (Verma and Nanda 2007).

In the 1980s, environmental concerns motivated the emergence of green consumers. They are recognized as those consumers who avoid products that cause damage to other humans and environment during the manufacturing, use, or disposal process (Elkington and Hailes 1989, as cited in Strong 1996).

In the 1990s, the consumer focused on the ethical dimension of the product, besides price, quality, delivery, and environmental issues. In addition to environmental concerns, ethical consumers focused on people (e.g., human rights, labor conditions) in manufacturing, and the use or disposal of products (Strong 1996). Some consumers chose to focus on "acts beyond their immediate interests as a consumer and consider the impact of their choices on wider society" (Doane 2001, as cited in Shaw, Newholm, and Dickinson 2006, 1050). Ethical consumers choose to use products or services based on their personal and moral beliefs and values (Crane and Matten 2004, as cited in Cho and Krasser 2011).

In the new millennium, the Association of Consumer Research (ACR) promotes Transformative Consumer Research (TCR) as a research stream to address the impacts of consumption on consumers and society well-being (Mari 2008).

A consumer behavior course is an opportunity for students to understand the process that consumers follow to make better decisions about their consumption (Kimmel 1999). In addition, this course should recognize that this process is influenced by external and internal factors, such as culture, groups of reference, social status, and also the consumers' own perception, motivation, and emotions, among other examples.

Typical Ethical Issues With Examples

Consumers have the right to be informed (Verma and Nanda 2007). However, misleading advertising is a serious ethical issue that can destroy consumer trust in a firm (Ferrell and Ferrell 2009). In addition, situations that take place in our world are aggravated by consumer behaviors, such as obesity, diseases from smoking, alcohol, pollution, and other environmental issues. Hence, vulnerable consumer groups[1] (e.g., children, the poor), tobacco and alcohol consumption, nutrition and obesity, product safety, environmental concerns, and ethical concerns (Mick 2006) are some typical ethical issues within consumer behavior area.

In order to achieve a better understanding of ethical implications when teaching a consumer behavior course, we present some examples of the ethical problems that firms face when they want to understand their consumer's behavior, and that our students as future marketers would face.

Misleading Advertising

Miracle products are examples of consumer behavior snares. These products are offered via television advertising throughout the day. For example, the product known as Cicatricure is first presented as a medical product to erase scars caused by cuts, accidents, or surgeries. However, at the same time, it is presented as a beauty product that removes wrinkles almost immediately. These companies work with expired patents from recognized laboratories and neither regulations nor the offices of consumer protection do anything about this situation. However, entrepreneurs

---

[1] They are understood as "a group of people who, due to various idiosyncrasies, are sensitive and susceptible to the potential negative effect associated with using a particular product" (Morgan, Schuler, and Stoltman 1995, as cited in Cui and Choudhury 2003, 367).

should analyze from an ethical perspective the impact of their behaviors for consumers who believe in their advertising claims.

Vulnerable Consumer Groups: Children

One of the most typical ethical issues in marketing is in regards to the participation of children in marketing campaigns and marketing research. In this sense, several companies such as Nestle and Hasbro have been criticized for the way they have used children in their consumer research campaigns (Bloom and Gundlach 2001).

In this vein, authors such as Moore and Rideout (2007) consider that the usage of children in consumer research programs and later on in advertising campaigns negatively affect the personal and psychological development of the children included in such practices.

Nutrition and Obesity

According to research done in the United States by Moore and Rideout (2007), the advertising of high fat and high sugar food has resulted in several affectations for children's health in the United States. Those advertisements come up from prior research using children from all over the country as a sample population. It is important to state that in the research, the main assumption is that the motivations of consumers (children) are different from the motivations of purchasers (parents). And in this vein the article purpose is only to demonstrate the damage suffered by children when they are used unethically in advertising campaigns.

Ethical Concerns: Public Privacy Data

The dissemination and usage of personal data has become a real problem among society, thus personal data privacy is another ethical issue when we talk about consumer research (Milne 2000). According to Milne (2000), some firms are prone to pay large amounts of money for personal databases that allow them to gain a better sense of the lifestyle of their consumers.

These practices have led governments in different countries to pursue protecting laws against abusive usage of personal data. For example, in Mexico, such problems have led to Congress having to promote and approve a law to protect personal data from unethical abuse such as commercialization of personal data and abusive emailing practices (IFAI 2004).

Ethics Teaching Strategy

Since its creation in 2000, the PRME initiative was designed to ensure the adequate framework for business schools to help them introduce the ethical perspective in any business and management course, no matter their nature or characteristic. In this sense, since 2008, EGADE Business School Tecnológico de Monterrey in Mexico decided to strengthen ethics, citizenship, and sustainability in its academic curricula. As part of this policy, in order to incorporate these aspects into their courses and redesign them, professors need to become certified by taking an ethics course with a duration of 240 hours. This course focuses on the methodology of learning, which includes learning techniques to motivate the reflection in students regarding ethical aspects.

In the specific case of a consumer behavior course, which is taught in master programs such as Marketing and Business Administration, the strategy for introducing PRME principles is summarized in Table 11.2.

In addition, topics such as consumerism, responsible consumption, and social marketing are introduced in the course as an attempt to develop a responsible consumer point of view within our students. Also, we highlight their ethical responsibility to diminish negative impacts with their professional activities in their community and society.

Advice for Teachers

According to Sims and Felton (2006), the professor needs to (a) provide guidance by assisting students in staying focused on analyzing ethical issues, (b) avoid lecture-oriented environment and enhance two-sided exchanges in order to promote students' interest in their learning and also students' participation through the incorporation of new ideas and perspectives to the discussion, (c) encourage self-understanding and facilitate the understanding and respect of other's points of view, (d) foster critical thinking about decision making within firms and its impact on different

Table 11.2 Academic strategies used in consumer behavior course following PRME principles

Principle	Strategy used in consumer behavior course
1. Purpose	We present different business and social cases regarding an ethical issue from the consumer behavior perspective. Students answer different questions in this sense, and the group begins a discussion about the various perspectives.
2. Values	The students analyze the launch of different products and brands and they discuss the impact of the brands presented regarding human rights, labor, environment, and anti-corruption practices.
3. Method	We introduce case study strategy to develop a reflexive learning experience in order to help students develop ethical reasoning in their decision making regarding ethical issues in the consumer behavior area.
4. Research	The students engage in conceptual and empirical research about the implications of consumer behavior research and marketing strategies used by different companies regarding ethical issues.
5. Partnership	We invite various executives from different companies to inform the students how their companies engage the PRME principles and ethical issues from the consumer behavior and marketing perspective.
6. Dialogue	Students, who work in different firms, share their own experiences with their classmates about how their companies face ethical issues in consumer behavior area. Students are invited to attend the events organized by EGADE Business School (e.g., World Business Forum) that create a specific atmosphere that enhances the dialogue between the academia and the practitioners.

Source: Elaborated by authors.

stakeholders, and (e) evaluate students for the quality of their participation and writing rather than their opinions.

When facing ethical issues and problems, it is advisable to closely follow firm or professional codes of ethics. Different association and industry codes of ethics can be discussed in order to help students, who are future marketers, to recognize these ethics and to realize their importance.

Most of the difficulty in understanding the complexity of ethical consumerism resides in the failure to clearly and consistently grasp what it is that motivates individuals socio-politically and how it is that the purchasing context operates to reveal or not reveal the wants, desires, values, constraints, beliefs, and mindset of the individual doing the purchasing (Devinney et al. 2006) The ethical consumer focuses on small numbers of committed individuals outlining their behavior, discourses, and narratives so as to understand the effectiveness of their actions in the marketplace (Harrison, Newholm, and Shaw 2005).

Developing Versus Developed Country Perspectives

We live in an age of globalization, and every management student is going to work in a global market environment. Therefore, students need to expand their understanding of the world so they can make more informed and accountable decisions (Sims and Felton 2006). In addition, marketing managers will face ethical, moral, and social dilemmas as part of their marketing work (Catterall, MacLaran, and Stevens 2002). However, students need to follow internationally accepted values to guide their decision making because these are applicable to all cultures and geographies regardless of institutional and social context.

Summary and Conclusion

In summary this chapter offers alternatives for professors who want to incorporate ethics within a consumer behavior course. In conclusion, including ethical issues in consumer behavior courses will help students to identify them and also to recognize the consequences of their decisions to different stakeholders (Adams, Harris, and Carley 1998). The use of case studies can help students to develop ethical reasoning of ethical dilemmas embedded in real situations that students should solve (Adams, Harris, and Carley 1998) within the consumer behavior field. It is important to generate in the student his or her involvement in discussions to stimulate critical thinking and to enhance overall learning through the use of group activities and cases in order to apply the material presented in readings and lectures given by the professor (Kimmel 1999).

Suggested Exercises and Projects

Exercise: Some Questions to Ask Regarding the Labor Practices Used to Make Products that Consumers Buy

(a) Nowadays, consumers have a variety of designs and materials in their sport shoes. However, most athletic shoes are made in Asian countries where people have to work during long hours in unsafe conditions, and with a minimum wage (e.g., Nike sport shoes).

Think about the last sport shoes that you have bought: Where did you buy them? Were you accompanied or alone when you bought them? Which attributes did you consider to make your decision? Were you concerned about the workers' conditions in factories where sport shoes are made?

(b) When you buy different products: Do you consider labor issues when you are making your decisions?

Source: Devinney, Auger, and Eckhard (2010).

Other important issues than can be discussed in a consumer behavior course are those related to *green, environmentally friendly,* or *sustainable product*. In the United States alone, consumers spend more than $25 billion annually on products sold on their natural or organic credentials. However, consumers are more informed regarding these products and are able to identify if they actually are green or not. Thus, if companies advertise a product as green and it is not, firms are in risk of doing green washing that can negatively affect firms' reputation (Ferrell and Ferrell 2009).

In the next example, there are some questions to ask regarding these types of products.

Exercise: Some Questions about Environmentally Friendly Products That Consumers Buy

When you buy a product, do you consider if it is environmentally friendly?

How do you choose environmentally friendly products?

> Do you analyze if the product that you want to buy is really a green product? Can reliable sources back up its claim to be a green product?
>
> Do you question if the firm that sells products with environmental benefits ignores its negative impact in other areas (e.g., workers' well-being)?
>
> *Source*: L. Ferrell and O.C. Ferrell (2009).

Regarding ethical concerns, such as the use of personal data by firms, there is a suggested exercise.

> **Exercise: *Privacy of Personal Data in Mexican Context***
>
> Given the institutional and regional framework of Mexico, students can discuss the design of an alternative strategy to use personal data without contravening the institutional regulations and consumers' rights.
>
> The next topics could guide the discussion:
>
> 1. The new law against the abuse of personal data by firms
> 2. The need of the firms to understand the lifestyle of their customers
> 3. The implications of such laws in the understanding of consumer characteristics
>
> *Source*: Elaborated by authors.

The expected result of this exercise is not only the design of alternative strategies to understand the consumer behavior but the comprehension of the ethical implications of the usage of personal data by the firms. Also, it is possible to consider other countries in developing and expanding this exercise.

Finally, in addition, we propose that students develop their own cases (e.g., they can focus on the organization where they work) in which they analyze topics related to consumer behavior with an ethical perspective.

References

Abela, A.V., and P.E. Murphy. 2008. "Marketing with Integrity: Ethics and the Service-dominant Logic of Marketing." *Journal of the Academy of Marketing Sciences* 36, pp. 39–53.

Adams, J.S., C. Harris, and S.S. Carley. 1998. "Challenges in Teaching Business Ethics: Using Role Set Analysis Of Early Career Dilemmas." *Journal of Business Ethics* 17, no. 12, pp. 1325–35.

Bloom, P.N., and G.T. Gundlach. 2001. *The Handbook of Marketing and Society.* New York: SAGE.

Carrigan, M., S. Marinova, and I. Szmigin. 2005. "Ethics and International Marketing." *International Marketing Review* 22, no. 5, pp. 481–93.

Catterall, M., P. MacLaran, and L. Stevens. 2002. "Critical Reflection in the Marketing Curriculum." *Journal of Marketing Education* 24, no. 3, pp. 184–92

Cho, S., and A.H. Krasser. 2011. "What Makes Us Care? The Impact of Cultural Values, Individual Factors, and Attention to Media Content on Motivation for Ethical Consumerism." *International Social Science Review* 86, no. 1–2, pp.3–23.

Cui, G., and P. Choudhury. 2003. "Consumer Interests and the Ethical Implications of Marketing: A Contingency Framework." *The Journal of Consumer Affairs* 37, no. 2, pp. 364–87.

Devinney, T.M., P. Auger, and G. Eckhardt. 2010. *The Myth of the Ethical Consumer.* Cambridge, UK: University Press.

Devinney, T.M., P. Auger, G. Eckhardt, and T. Birtchnell. 2006. "The Other CSR: Consumer Social Responsibility." *Stanford Social Innovation Review* 4, pp. 30–37.

Feldman, L.P. 1971. "Societal Adaptation: A New Challenge for Marketing." *The Journal of Marketing*, 35, no. 3, pp. 54–60.

Ferrell, L., and O.C. Ferrell. 2009. *Ethical Business.* First American Edition. New York: DK Publishing.

Fullerton, R.A. 2013. "The Birth of Consumer Behavior: Motivation Research in 1940s and 1950s." *Journal of Historical Research in Marketing.* 5, no. 2, pp. 212–22.

Harrison, R., T. Newholm, and D. Shaw. 2005. *The Ethical Consumer.* 1st ed. London, UK: SAGE.

IFAI (Instituto Federal de Acceso a la Información). 2004. *Estudio Sobre Sistemas de Datos Personales.* México: Diario Oficial de la Federación.

Keith, R.J. 1960. "The Marketing Revolution." *Journal of Marketing* 24, no. 1, pp. 35–38.

Kimmel, A.J. 1999. "Consumer Behavior Classroom Exercises that Really Work." *Teaching of Psychology* 26, no. 3, pp. 203–6.

Kotler, P. 1972. "What Consumerism Means for Marketers." *Harvard Business Review* 50, pp. 48–57.

Macinnis, D.J., and V.S. Folkes. 2009. "The Disciplinary Status of Consumer Behavior: A Sociology of Science Perspective on Key Controversies." *Journal of Consumer Research* 36, pp. 899–914.

Mari, C. 2008. "Doctoral Education and Transformative Consumer Research." *Journal of Marketing Education* 30, no. 1, 5–11.

Mick, D.G. 2006. "Presidential Address Meaning and Mattering through Transformative Consumer Research." *Advances in Consumer Research* 33, pp. 1–4.

Milne, G. 2000. "Privacy and Ethical Issues in Database/Interactive Marketing and Public Policy: A Research Framework and Overview of the Special Issue." *Journal of Public Policy and Marketing* 19, no. 1, pp. 1–6.

Moore, E., and V. Rideout. 2007. "The Online Marketing of Food to Children: Is It Just Fun and Games?" *Journal of Public Policy and Marketing* 26, pp. 202–220.

Plewa, C., and P. Quester. 2006. "Case Development: An Innovative Approach to Case Studies and Experiences from a Graduate Marketing Ethics Course." *Journal of Business Ethics Education* 3, pp. 165–78.

PRME. 2014a. *Overview*. http://www.unprme.org/about-prme/index.php (accessed April 20, 2014).

PRME 2014b. *The Principles for Responsible Management Education*. http://www.unprme.org/about-prme/the-six-principles.php (accessed April 20, 2014).

Prothero, A. 1990. "Green Consumerism and the Societal Marketing Concept: Marketing Strategies for the 1990s." *Journal of Marketing Management* 6, no. 2, pp. 87–103.

Shaw, D., T. Newholm, and R. Dickinson. 2006. "Consumption as Voting: An Exploration of Consumer Empowerment." *European Journal of Marketing* 40, no. 9–10, pp. 1049–67.

Sims, R.R., and E.L. Felton. 2006. "Designing and Delivering Business Ethics Teaching and Learning." *Journal of Business Ethics* 63, pp. 297–312.

Strong, C. 1996. "Features Contributing to the Growth of Ethical Consumerism—A Preliminary Investigation." *Marketing Intelligence and Planning* 14, no. 5, pp. 5–13.

Verma, D.P.S., and S. Nanda. 2007. "Impact of Consumerism on Marketing Practices: A Study in National Capital Region." *Journal of Advances in Management Research* 4, no. 1, pp. 74–82.

Wilkie, W.L., and E.S. Moore. 2003. "Scholarly Research in Marketing: Exploring the '4 Eras' of Thought Development." *Journal of Public Policy and Marketing* 22, no. 2, pp. 116–46.

MODULE 5
People Management and Soft Skills

CHAPTER 12

Teaching Ethics in Human Resources Management

Silke Bustamante

Berlin School of Economics and Law

Introduction

Human resource management (HRM) has always been subject to ethical discussion. However, the topic has gained even more momentum as a result of the increasing importance of a skilled workforce on the one hand and increasing ethical expectations on corporations on the other. Employees as the target group of HRM play a double role when reflecting about responsibility and ethics—they are object of ethical behavior insofar as they are to be treated by *the company* and its management in a fair and just way. In the same vein, they are the subject of ethical behavior in their role as representatives of a company and as such are responsible for corporate actions and its consequences.

Ethics in HRM then has two dimensions: *Ethical Human Resource Management* and *Management of Ethical Human Resources*. The first dimension refers to the ethical treatment of employees, the latter to the efforts of leaders and personnel departments to select, train, and motivate employees such that they act in a responsible manner.

Even though the topic seems to be at the core of ethical and responsible management, research, business practice, and teaching until recently focused on issues such as ethical marketing (e.g., Brenkert 2002; Kim and Park 2011), ethical finance (e.g. Boatright 2014) and responsibility toward external stakeholders and the ecological environment (Bassen, Jastram, and Meyer 2005).

The importance of ethical HRM is underlined by altering work-related expectations of the new generation of employees (Bustamante and Brenninger 2014). Employee-directed responsibility is an important aspect in the job selection of potential employees, hence affecting the attractiveness of employers (Turban and Greening 2007; Albinger and Freeman 2000; Bustamante and Brenninger 2014). Important aspects of responsibility toward employees, such as good working conditions, employee participation, social benefits, paying more attention to employee health, and quality of life positively influence job satisfaction, employee commitment, and loyalty and thus increase motivation, productivity, and innovation (Brammer, Millington, and Rayton 2007; Collier and Esteban 2007; EC 2008). Also, societal pressures to respect human rights in the supply chain ask for assuming responsibility for employees even in subsidiaries and subcontracted companies.

The management of ethical human resources gains momentum with corporate scandals evoking the call for responsible management and ethical behavior. Ethical behavior is grounded in both *the company level*, referring to structures and systems creating the framework for ethical behavior (Enderle 1988) and in the values and motivation of individuals constituting the company (Göbel 2006). Consequently, HRM, along with teaching HRM, needs to deal with adequate institutional designs as well as with selecting, training, and motivating employees to behave in a manner that demonstrates ethical consideration.

Human Resource Management

HRM can be understood as an interdisciplinary part of management responsible for the strategic and long-term steering of the structure and the portfolio of an organization's workforce (Büdenbender and Strutz 1996). As such, it comprises the planning, provision, rewarding, and leading of human resources, as well as the design of the workplace in light of a company's goals, taking into account the capabilities, commitment, and motivation of the employees (Durai 2010; Holtbrügge 2007).

There are two main perspectives on HRM, having their roots in different approaches to management (Mac and Calis 2012). The first one, derived from the *Michigan Model*, is strategic and stresses the importance of alignment of personnel and company strategy (Fombrun, Tichy, and Devanna 1984), observing also organizational leadership and culture. A second perspective, derived from the human relations movement and taken up by the Harvard school, points to the importance of people, human relations, and personal growth as an important basis for long-term success (Agryris 1966; Beer et al. 1984). It emphasizes the relevance of providing organizational commitment through HR policies and takes into account stakeholder value for the evaluation of success (Boxall and Purcell 2011). These two perspectives are also reflected in the often-stated objectives of the HR function in companies (Scholz 2009)—economic efficiency, measured by job performance, and social efficiency, reflected in the work satisfaction of employees. Potential conflicts between the two perspectives are likely to occur, especially if company goals are in conflict with employee goals. This is where ethical considerations come into effect.

Ethical HRM

Ethical Foundation of HRM

The relationship between ethics and HRM has been discussed intensively in recent years (e.g., Greenwood 2013; Walsh 2007; Legge 2007; Koehn 2002) but there have been critical viewpoints on HRM for decades (e.g., Rowan 2000; Cornelius and Gagnon 1999; Legge 1995, 1996; Simon, Powers, and Gunneman 1993). Between others, the notion of the employee as being a (human) resource that can be "obtained cheaply, used sparingly, developed, and exploited as fully as possible" (Sparrow and Hiltrop 1994, 7) in order to reach company goals has been subject to criticism.

The idea that ethics should matter for HRM was proposed in the 1990s (Winstanley, Woodall, and Heery 1996a, b) as an off-shoot of industrial sociology (Mac and Calis 2012). It gained momentum with the debate on corporate ethics, social responsibility (Brammer 2011; Greenwood and Freeman 2011), and stakeholder theory (EC 2001, Suchanek and Lin-Hi 2006; Freeman 1984; Clarkson 1995). The crucial question was seen in how to solve the potential conflicts between the economic and social goals of HR management (Greenwood 2002). Various ethical theories and principles have been evoked for both evaluating the ethicality of different notions of HR management (Michigan versus Harvard model, see Chapter 2) and deriving principles or guidelines for ethical HR management. For example, Legge (1995, 1996) used teleological and deontological ethical theories, Budd (2004) referred to the ethics of utility, duty, liberty, fairness, virtue, and care, and Greenwood (2002) additionally alleged stakeholder theory to reflect companies' ethical obligation to care for employees.

The demand for ethical HRM can also be derived from the concept of (corporate) responsibility. Responsibility is considered as a basic demand of ethics (Göbel 2006). In the context of business ethics, it is understood as the responsibility of companies and their representatives for their actions or the consequences of their actions (Göbel 2006), which at least partly are directed to the stakeholders of a company. With respect to HRM, this implies responsibility for employees, and also for the decisions and actions of employees as company representatives.

Responsibility for employees evokes concepts such as fairness and equality (Miller 1996; Budd 2004), good employment conditions (Miller 1996), and the recognition of the voice and rights of employees (EC 2001). It is considered as one of the essential areas of corporate responsibility, next to ecological, marketplace, and community-related responsibility (EC 2008). Responsibility for the decisions and behavior of company members refers to the ideas of the HR function as a guardian of ethics (Lowry 2006) or an *ethical steward* (Winstanley, Woodall, and Heery 1996). It comprises all measures that support and motivate the ethical behavior of employees (Cooke and He 2010), such as the setting up of guidelines and codes of conduct, the training of employees, the selection of ethical employees, and also acting as a role model for employees.

Ethics and Responsibility for Employees

Based on the preceding ethical frameworks, several authors deduced moral rights of the employee that should be respected by corporations. As such, Rowan (2000) introduces fair payment, safety, due process, and privacy in the workplace as most important rights. Greenwood (2002) adds *respect for the individual* (including the right to freedom, well-being, and equality) as well as the *autonomy of the individual*.

A number of guidelines issued by political organizations and non-governmental organizations refer to these rights and elaborate more in detail fundamental principles and potential ethically relevant issues. For example, the International Labour Organization (ILO 1998) states four fundamental principles and rights of workers:

- Freedom of association and the effective recognition of the right to collective bargaining
- Elimination of all forms of forced or compulsory labor
- Effective abolition of child labor
- Elimination of discrimination with respect to employment and occupation

The International Organization for Standardization (ISO) 26000, a globally appreciated guideline for corporate social responsibility, addresses HR-related issues and expectations in two of its seven core subjects: *labor practices* and *human rights* (ISO 26000, 2010). Finally, the SA 8000 focuses on work conditions and defines minimum requirements for social and work standards (SAI SA8000, 2008). Examples for issues derived from these guidelines are as follows:

- Diversity and equal opportunity
- Work-life balance
- Social benefits and support for employees and families
- Health and safety
- Training and development of employees
- Job security and safeguarding
- Labor relations and freedom of association
- Employment and human right issues in supply chain
- No child labor or forced labor

The preceding listed issues become relevant in a number of the major tasks of HRM. For example, aspects of work-life balance, nondiscrimination, and safety are crucial for job design. Possibilities for job sharing or flexible working hours increase possibilities for working mothers or fathers and contribute to work-life balance. Tasks and responsibilities within the job influence employee satisfaction and motivation. Finally, working conditions and job design have an impact on safety at the workplace and the health of employees.

Ethics should also be incorporated in the employer marketing process. Issues such as a nondiscriminatory selection of target audience (Waymack 1990) and a truthful and honest communication of job characteristics, working conditions, and career perspectives (AMA 2004) are examples of where ethics and responsibility need to be considered.

Selection of employees, but also later assessment and rewarding, should be done in a fair and nondiscriminatory manner and based on merits (SHRM 2007). Privacy should be respected, such that mental voyeurism can be avoided (Whitney 1969). Moreover, process transparency as well as feedback support objectivity and allow job candidates and employees comprehend recruiting decisions, performance evaluation, and rewarding decisions (Winstanley, Woodall, and Heery 1996a).

Responsibility for Decisions of Employees

With increasing expectations of societies on the responsible and ethical behavior of companies, the role of HRM in motivating and influencing employees to take into account stakeholder interests and ethical expectations has also gained importance. To achieve this, HRM may revert to structural leadership instruments (via institutions) or directly try to steer employees to behave according to corporate (and societal) values.

Structural instruments comprise issuing and communicating codes of conduct, as well as guidelines for recruitment and incentive systems. Recruiting criteria may encompass characteristics and values of job aspirants, hence contributing to an ethical workforce (Redington 2005). Also, incentive systems may incorporate integrity and adherence to company values and guidelines. Moreover, in order to provide employees with the sensitivity for potentially critical situations and decisions, the contents of training could integrate issues of ethics and responsibility.

Apart from this, personal leadership and guidance are crucial for motivating employees to behave responsibly. Not only should executives try to exert influence on employees via personal communication and information, they should also—more importantly—act as role models. If, for example, an executive refrains from accepting a profitable assignment because the customer in question is known for unacceptable working conditions in third-world countries, middle managers are encouraged to decide in a similar way in the future.

Developed Versus Developing Country Perspectives

Country perspectives on ethics in HRM may vary due to economic differences and—linked to this—on sociocultural differences. Perceptions or assumption about which actions of an entity or individual are desirable, proper, or appropriate depend on some socially constructed system of norms, values, beliefs, and definitions (Suchmann 1995), which are at least partly influenced by economic and institutional development (Rossouw 1994).

Often, legal and institutional frameworks are less elaborated in developing countries resulting in lower legal protection of employees and inferior working conditions and safety standards (Dobers and Halme 2009). At the same time, moral pressure on companies from local stakeholders is not as strong as in developed countries either because the degree of organization is lower, or because priorities are placed on economic development rather than on ethics and social issues. However, companies acting in the global marketplace face expectations from global stakeholder groups and NGOs to comply with basic human rights and general ideas about responsible behavior (e.g., UN Global Compact).

Even more, transnational companies are asked to use their power and act as change agents in developing countries by positively influencing institutional frameworks and setting standards for ethical behavior (Utting 2003). More than in developed countries, ethics in HRM then does not only apply to the individual and company level, but also to the institutional or macro level.

Summing up, differences in perspectives of developing and developed countries concern:

- Cross-cultural differences in ethical frameworks, partly influenced by economic and institutional development
- Differences in pressing issues (e.g., higher importance of health and safety than work–live balance) due to lower economic and social development
- Different expectations on local and multinational companies with respect to their direct and indirect (via institutional change) responsibility for employees

Teaching Strategy and Advice for Teachers

There are different approaches for integrating ethics into the structure of the HRM syllabus. Most textbooks present ethics in HRM as a separate chapter, after having dealt with general strategic and operational issues. Teaching then might begin with objectives of HRM and its role within the company, outline strategic and operative tasks and instruments of HR, and finally reflect about responsibility for employees, ethical theories, and ethical aspects of HRM. The advantage is to be able to focus on ethical issues and revise what has been learned beforehand through ethical lenses. A second approach, more in line with the idea of mainstreaming ethics and integrating it into strategy and operations, might be to evoke ethical considerations parallel to the general teaching of HRM. A class about the goals of HRM would then comprise reflections about ethicality of different notions of HRM, about the dichotomy of objectives, and the role of ethics for solving potential conflicts. In the same way, when discussing contextual aspects of HRM, the increasing societal expectations on the responsible behavior of companies might be discussed. Finally, ethical issues should be a topic in the lessons about provision, development, and rewarding employees.

With respect to didactic methods, a mix of lecture, group discussions, case studies, experiments, and role play allows the facilitator to raise awareness for ethical issues and at the same time convey knowledge and promote problem solving. For example, there might be a moderated discussion about questions such as "Do employees have moral rights?" or "Is there a natural conflict between the strategic view of HRM and employee rights?" Work in smaller groups might be interesting for identifying ethical issues in different tasks of HRM. Role play may be applied for understanding conflicts between opposing views of employees and their superiors, for example, when overtime is seen to be necessary because a due date of an important order must be kept or when a country manager has different notions on bribing than the headquarter has. Case studies are a good method for problem solving, for example, analyzing the reasons for overt problems (such as overtime, burnout, low percentage of female employees) and designing strategies to solve these problems. Finally, experiments are effective for making students aware of automatisms in decisions leading to amoral behavior.

Projects and Exercises

Topics for moderated group discussion:

- Are there conflicts between the strategic view of human resource management and responsible behavior toward employees?
- Are there universal moral rights of employees?
- Which ethical issues might arise when multinational companies operate in developing countries?

Case studies:

- Analysis of cases reflecting conflicts in different tasks of HRM (see, e.g., Gusdorf 2010) in Groups of four based on ethical theories, guidelines of standards (SA8000, ILO)
- Nike Sweat Shop Debate: Discussion about ethical issues, conflicting interests, possibilities for action of Nike and potential limits of employee-directed responsibility in the supply chain

- Lidl Spy Affair: Which moral rights of employees were abused? How was this explained? How can incidents like these be avoided?

Role plays:

- Invent situations of conflict between line line manager or HR manager and subordinate. Make two students *play* the situation and other to reflect about their impression and ideas. Examples:
  - The project manager wants his subordinate to work overtime because an important deadline has to be met. However, the employee in question already has a private appointment.
  - HR manager tries to convince the IT manager to employ an equally qualified woman; however, the IT manager is in favor of the male job candidate.

Exercises and group work:

- Please identify potential ethical issues in the different tasks of HRM
- Analyze the diversity policy of a major globally acing company. Which structural instruments can you find that support equal treatment with respect to gender and minorities?

Summary and Conclusion

Companies are increasingly expected to behave in a responsible way, meeting not only legal requirements but also ethical expectations. HRM bears a double responsibility—it is responsible for treating employees as one of the most important stakeholder groups in a fair and respectful way, and at the same time should try to influence employees (as company representatives) to take responsibility for the impact of the company on the society and other stakeholders. Ethical considerations play a role in the most important tasks of HRM such as job design, employer marketing, employee selection and development, performance evaluation, and the design of incentive systems. Selection criteria, incentive systems, trainings, and other structural instruments may guide employees to behave responsibly toward other guidelines and standards such as ISO 26000 or SA 8000 define minimum requirements for responsible behavior toward employees, referring to, for example, working conditions, job design, and labor relations. However, the decision about what is right or wrong when there are conflicting objectives and interests requires the consideration of context and culture-specific perspectives on ethical HRM. Teaching ethics in HRM is hence a complex task. It encompasses not only the transfer of knowledge about ethical issues in the different tasks of HRM, but also conveying awareness of critical situations and providing instruments and guidelines for dealing with potential conflicts and conflicting interests.

References

Albinger, H.S., and S.J. Freeman. 2000. "Corporate Social Performance and Attractiveness as an Employer to Different Job Seeking Populations." *Journal of Business Ethics* 28, no. 3, pp. 243–53.

AMA (American Marketing Association). 2004. "Statement of Ethics". http://www.marketingpower.com/AboutAMA/Pages/Statement%20of%20Ethics.aspx, (accessed January 27, 2014).

Argyris, C. 1966. "Interpersonal Barriers to Decision Making." *Harvard Business Review* 2, pp. 84–97.

Bassen, A., S. Jastram, and K. Meyer. 2005. "Corporate Social Responsibility. Eine Begriffserläuterung." *Zeitschrift für Wirtschafts und Unternehmensethik* 6, no. 2, pp. 231–6.

Beer, M., B. Spector, P.R. Lawrence, D. Quinn Mills, and R.E. Walton. 1984. *Managing Human Assets*. New York: Free Press.

Boatright, J.R. 2014. *Ethics in Finance*. 3rd ed. West Sussex: Wiley-Blackwell.

Boxall, P., and J. Purcell. 2011. *Strategy and Human Resource Management*, 3rd ed. London, UK: Palgrave.

Brammer, S. 2011. "Employment Relations and Corporate Social Responsibility." In *Research Handbook on the Future of Work and Employment Relations*, eds. K. Townsend and A. Wilkinson, 296–318. Cheltenham, UK: Edwar Elgar Publishing Limited.

Brammer, S., A. Millington, and B. Rayton. 2007. "The Contribution of Corporate Social Responsibility to Organizational Commitment." *The International Journal of Human Resource Management* 18, no. 10, pp. 1701–19.

Brenkert, G. G. 2002. "Ethical Challenges of Social Marketing". *Journal of Public Policy & Marketing* 21, No. 1, pp. 14–25.

Büdenbender, U, and H. Strutz, 1996. *Gabler Kompaktlexikon Personal.* Wiesbaden.

Budd, J. 2004. *Employment with a Human Face.* New York: Cornell University Press.

Bustamante, S., and K. Brenninger. 2014. "CSR and its Potential Role in Employer Branding. An Analysis of Preferences of German Graduates." In *Making the Number of Options Grow. Contributions to the Corporate Responsibility Research Conference 2013*, eds. R.J. Baumgartner, U. Gelbmann, and R. Rauter. (series eds. W. Winiwarter, U. Gelbmann, and R.J. Baumgartner, ISIS reports #6 ISSN 2305-2511 /print/, ISSN 2308-1767 /online/, ISIS, Graz, Austria).

Clarkson, M.B.E. 1995. "A Stakeholder Framework for Analyzing and Evaluating Corporate Social Performance." *The Academy of Management Review* 20, no. 1, pp. 92–117.

Collier, J., and R. Esteban. 2007. "Corporate Social Responsibility and Employee Commitment." *Business Ethics: A European Review* 16, pp. 19–33.

Cooke, F.L., and Q. He. 2010. "Corporate Social Responsibility and HRM in China: A study of Textile and Apparel Enterprises." *Asia Pacific Business Review* 16, no. 3, pp. 355–76.

Cornelius, N., and S. Gagnon, 1999. "From Ethics 'by proxy' to Ethics in Action: New Approaches to Understanding HRM and Ethics." *Business Ethics: A European Review* 8, no. 4, pp. 225–35.

Dobers, P., and M. Halme. 2009. "Corporate Social Responsibility and Developing Countries." *Corporate Social Responsibility and Environmental Management* 16, no. 5, pp. 237–49.

Durai, P. 2010. *Human Resource Management.* Noida, India: Dorling Kindersley.

Enderle, G. 1988. *Wirtschaftsethik im Werden.* Stuttgart, Germany: Akademie der Diözese Rottenburg-Stuttgart.

EC (European Commission). 2001. "Promoting a European Framework for Corporate Social Responsibility." *Green Paper*, COM (2001) final. Brussels: EC.

EC (European Commission). 2008. *Commission Staff Working Document, Accompanying Document to the Communication from the Commission on the European Competitiveness Report 2008* (COM (2008) 774 final), SEC (2008) 2853. Brussels: EC.

Fombrun, C., N. Tichy, and M. Devanna, eds. 1984. *Strategic Human Resource Management.* New York: John Wiley.

Freeman, R.E. 1984. *Strategic Management: A Stakeholder Approach*. Boston, MA: Pitman.
Göbel, E. 2006. *Unternehmensethik. Grundlagen und praktische Umsetzung*. Stuttgart, Germany: UTB.
Greenwood, M.R. 2002. "Ethics and HRM: A Review and Conceptual Analysis." *Journal of Business Ethics* 36, pp. 261–78.
Greenwood, M.R. 2013. "Ethical analyses of HRM: A Review and Research Agenda." *Journal of Business Ethics*, 114, pp. 355–366.
Greenwood, M.R., and R.E. Freeman 2001. "Ethics and HRM: The Contribution of Stakeholder Theory", *Business and Professional Ethics Journal* 30, pp. 269–292.
Gusdorf, M.L. 2010. *Ethics in Human Resource Management*. Alexandria, USA: Society for Human Resource Management.
Holtbrügge, D. 2007. *Personalmanagement*. Berlin, Germany: Springer Verlag.
ILO (International Labour Organization). 1998. "Declaration on Fundamental Principles and Rights at Work." http://www.ilo.org/declaration/lang--en/index.htm, (accessed January 30, 2014).
ISO 26000 2010. Discovering ISO 26000. Geneva.
Kim, Soo-Yeon, and Hyojung Park. 2011. "Corporate Social Responsibility as an Organizational Attractiveness for Prospective Public Relations Practitioners." *Journal of Business Ethics* 103, no. 4, pp. 639–53.
Koehn, D. 2002. "Ethical Issues in Human Resources." In *The Blackwell Guide to Business Ethics*, ed. N.E. Bowie, 225–43. Oxford, UK: Blackwell.
Legge, K. 1995. *Human Resource Management: Rhetorics and Reality*. London, UK: Macmillan.
Legge, K. 1996. "Morality Bound." *People Management* 25, no. 2, pp. 34–36.
Legge, K. 2007. "The Ethics of HRM in Dealing with Individual Employees without Collective Representation." In *Human Resource Management: Ethics and Employment*, eds. A.H. Pinnington, R. Macklin, and T. Campbell, 35–51. Oxford, NY: Oxford University Press.
Lowry, D. 2006. "HR Managers as Ethical Decision-makers: Mapping the Terrain." *Asia Pacific Journal of Human Resource Management* 44, no. 2, pp. 171–83.
Mac, S.D., and S. Calis. 2012. "Social Responsibility within the Ethics and Human Resource Management Debates: A Review of Global Compact and SA8000." *Turkish Journal of Business Ethics* 5, no. 10, pp. 41–53.
Miller, P. 1996. "Strategy and Ethical Management of Human Resources." *Human Resource Management Journal* 6, no. 1, pp. 5–18.
Redington, I. 2005. *Making CSR Happen: The Contribution of People Management*. London: Chartered Institute of Personnel Development (CIPD).
Rossouw, G.J. 1994. "Business Ethics in Developing Countries." *Business Ethics Quarterly* 4, no. 1, pp. 43–51.

Rowan, J.R. 2000. "The Moral Foundation of Employee Rights." *Journal of Business Ethics* 24, no. 2, pp. 355–61.

Scholz, C. 2009. *Vahlens Großes Personallexikon*. München, Germany: Verlag Franz Vahlen.

Simon, J.G., C.W. Powers, and J.P. Gunneman. 1993. "The Responsibilities of Corporations and Their Owners." In *Ethical Theory and Business*, eds. T.L. Beauchamp, and N.E. Bowie. Englewood Cliffs, NJ: Prentice Hall.

SAI (Social Accountability International) SA8000. 2008. *Social Accountability 8000*. New York. http://www.sa-intl.org/_data/n_0001/resources/live/2008 StdEnglishFinal.pdf (accessed on January 27, 2014).

SHRM (Society for Human Resource Management). 2007. "SHRM Code of Ethics." http://www.shrm.org/about/Pages/code-of-ethics.aspx (accessed January 27, 2014).

Sparrow, P., and J.-M. Hiltrop. 1994. *European Human Resource Management in Transition*. Hemel Hempstead, UK: Prentice Hall.

Suchanek, A., and N. Lin-Hi 2008. "Die gesellschaftliche Verantwortung von Unternehmen in der Marktwirtschaft." In *Verantwortung als marktwirtschaftliches Prinzip. Zum Verhältnis von Moral und Ökonomie*, eds. L. Heidbrink and A. Hirsch, 69–96, Frankfurt am Main.

Suchmann, M.C. 1995. "Managing Legitimacy: Strategic and Institutional Approaches." *The Academy of Management Review*, 20, no. 3, pp. 571–610.

Turban, D.B., and D.W. Greening. 1997. "Corporate Social Performance and Organizational Attractiveness to Prospective Employees." *Academy of Management Journal* 40, no. 3, pp. 658–72.

Utting, P. 2003. "Promoting Development through Corporate Social Responsibility—Does It Work?" *Profit and Loss? Corporations and Development*, Global Future, Third Quarter 2003, Monrovia, USA: World Vision International.

Walsh, A.J. 2007. "HRM and the Ethics of Commodified Work in a Market Economy." In *Human Resource Management: Ethics and Employment*, eds. A.H. Pinnington, R. Macklin, and T. Campbell, 102–18. Oxford, NY: Oxford University Press.

Waymack, M.R. 1990. "The Ethics of Selectively Marketing the Health Maintenance Organization." *Journal of Theoretical Medicine and Bioethics* 11, no. 4, pp. 301–9.

Whitney, K., Jr. 1969. "Ethics for Recruiting Employees and Executives." *Management of Personnel Quarterly* 8, pp. 13–15.

Winstanley, D., J. Woodall, and E. Heery. 1996a. "Business ethics and Human Resource Management: Themes and Issues." *Personnel Review* 25, no. 6, pp. 5–12.

Winstanley, D., J. Woodal, and E. Heery. 1996b. "The Agenda for Ethics in Human Resource Management." *Business Ethics: A European Review* 5, no. 4, pp. 187–94.

Further Reading

Collings, D.G., and G. Wood. 2009. "Human Resource Management a Critical Approach." In *Human Resource Management a Critical Approach*, eds. D.G. Collings and G. Wood, 1–16. New York: Routledge.

Ferris, G.R., W.A. Hochwarter, M.R. Buckley, G. Harrell-Cook, and D.D. Frink. 1999. "Human Resource Management: Some New Directions." *Journal of Management* 25, no. 3, pp. 385–423.

Guest, D. 1997. "Human Resource Management and Performance: A Review and Research Agenda." *International Journal of Human Resource Management* 8, no. 3, pp. 263–76.

Lis, B. 2012. "The Relevance of Corporate Social Responsibility for a Sustainable Human Resource Management: An Analysis of Organizational Attractiveness as a Determinant in Employees' Selection of a (Potential) Employer, Management Revue." *Socio-economic Studies* 23, no. 3, pp. 279–95.

Montgomery, D.B., and C.A. Ramus. 2003. "Corporate Social Responsibility. Reputation Effects on MBA Job Choice." *Stanford Graduate School of Business Research Paper*, 1805. Stanford, CA: Stanford Graduate School of Business.

Pinnington, A.H., R. Macklin, and T. Campbell, eds. 2007. *Human Resource Management: Ethics and Employment*. Oxford, NY: Oxford University Press.

Valentine, S., G. Fleischman, R. Sprague, and L. Godkin. 2010. "Exploring the Ethicality of Firing Employees Who Blog." *Human Resource Management* 49, no. 1, pp. 87–108.

CHAPTER 13

Teaching Ethics in Career Management

Olusegun Babalola and Ifedapo Adeleye

Lagos Business School, Pan-Atlantic University

Introduction

An individual's career affects and is affected by almost all aspects of his or her life, therefore applying ethical reasoning and decision making to the way people manage their careers, as well as how organizations manage the careers of those in their employ, is important. Similarly, ethics is universal and permeates all aspects of life (Maxwell 2005). Thus, individuals should learn to not only make self-serving career decisions but also need to consider the effects that their career choices have on others within and outside their organizations. Organizations should also ensure that whatever career systems they have in place encourage the development of all their employees. Deliberate efforts should be made to ensure that employees do not feel pressurized into making unethical decisions in order to survive and progress in a particular organization or field. Much like the field of career studies, this chapter considers career management from two perspectives—the individual perspective and the structural and organizational perspective. The aim of the chapter is to bring to light some of the ethical considerations that could enhance or undermine career choices and progress in the long run based on both individual and collective (organizational) decisions.

Description of Discipline

The field of career studies as a management course is a relatively young one—although it has roots in the work of 19th century philosophers like Max Weber, Everett Hughes, and Emilé Durkheim—with most contemporary career management theories being established in the 1970s (Gunz and Peiperl 2007). During this time, the field has developed two distinct yet connected perspectives: the *psychological* perspective and the *social determinism* perspective. Career theorists with a psychological perspective focus mainly on individual traits and characteristics such as personality, abilities, and talent. They argue that individuals make career choices and manage their careers based on these psychological constructs. On the other hand, those with social determinism perspectives argue that societies and systems shape career choices of individuals; individual differences, though acknowledged, take a backseat from this angle.

Career studies, though similar to human resource management, is quite distinct in its pursuits. Human resource management focuses mainly on developing tools that are directly involved in the day-to-day work and nonwork-related concerns of employees and managers in organizations. Career studies instead focus on the entirety of individual work life; one of the most popular definitions of *career* is "the evolving sequence of a person's work experiences over time" (Arthur, Hall, and Lawrence 1989, 8). Thus, a person's career consists of all their different jobs and nonjobs and career theorists are concerned with how these multiple facets intertwine with all aspects of individual and societal life; career studies therefore has a *broader* scope than human resource management.

Based on this understanding of career management studies, it is easy to understand the need for individuals and organizations to recognize the importance of ethicality in career decisions. A person's career cannot be separated from the person—your career is a major part of your identity and to a large extent determines how you view yourself (Blustein and Noumair 1996). Therefore, it is important that career concerns are viewed from a long-term perspective. In order to have rewarding careers, individuals must learn to make choices that consistently display ethical reasoning and judgment. Organizations must also consider the long-term effects of their career systems on their sustainability. If people work in systems that do not encourage and foster ethicality, they will react in ways that ensure only their individual desires and survival. Eventually, this can only lead to negative consequences for not only the people themselves and their organizations, but also their customers and the larger society.

Typical Ethical Issues—With Examples

In this section, we consider two examples that highlight the role of ethics in career management and allow for reflections on the choices discussed. In keeping with the two major perspectives discussed previously, the first example will showcase careers that are highly autonomous and dependent on the individual while the second considers the organizational and societal structures and their effects on individual behavior.

Example 1: Football Management

Consider popular Manchester United forward, Wayne Rooney. Rooney gained fame as a formidable striker when he first arrived on the professional football scene in 2002. He is now one of the highest goal scorers in English soccer history with an impressive fourth position (shared with Michael Owen as at 2014). Little wonder then that very early on in his career, he caught the eye of infamous football agent, Paul Stretford. Stretford is a popular sports agent known for his unsavory ways of doing business and has even been referred to as *ruthless* (Jones 2010). Describing him as an agent purely motivated by money, Andrew Cole, a former client of his, recounted his experience with Stretford: "Stretford wasn't motivated by friendships, but money. I wasn't the only player who stopped hearing from him when I'd served my purpose. People don't speak well of him" (Cole 2010).

Wayne Rooney took Stretford as his agent in 2003 by unceremoniously dumping his then agent Peter McIntosh despite McIntosh's impressive and unprecedented Everton deal (Rooney was barely 17 when McIntosh secured the deal with the football club; they offered Rooney the most money they had ever paid to a footballer his age). McIntosh unsuccessfully sued Stretford for stealing his client but a blackmail court case in 2004 resulted in Paul Stretford being found guilty of breaching a number of agent governing rules including poaching Rooney from his previous agent, failing to represent Rooney's interests by making him sign a contract without fully explaining it to him, and signing him into a contract that was over the maximum period allowed. This and many other unpleasant details were made public during Stretford's trial. However, this does not appear to have deterred Wayne Rooney. Stretford still represents Rooney's interests to date and in 2011, he secured him a five-year contract with current club Manchester United merely two days after Rooney had stated publicly that he no longer wanted to play for the club.

Suggested Questions for Discussion

1. Would you sign a contract with an agent like Stretford? Why or why not?
2. Do you believe that Wayne Rooney is handling his career properly by allowing Stretford to continue to represent him despite Stretford's reputation?
3. What effects (if any) do you think the career decisions of players like Rooney and his agent Stratford have on the world of professional football?

Example 2: Investment Banks on Wall Street

This example looks at perceptions of Wall Street and the effect this has on the attitudes of Wall Street investment bankers.

In 2013, a staggering 53 percent of Wall Street executives stated that adhering to ethical standards would inhibit their career progression in Wall Street (Kapoor 2013). Chris Arnade, a former Wall Street employee turned journalist and photographer, describes Wall Street as "A constant battle between profit and morality" (Arnade 2013). He described his job as one in which he would create complex and confusing products that resulted in high profits for his company at the detriment of their clients. Arnade also rationalized his guilt by comparing his firm to competitors who were collecting even higher profits by selling even more complicated products. He initially believed that they would eventually have to face some sort of punishment for their actions but instead they got more money and were even applauded for their reckless behavior. He states that due to the lack of proper checks and balances—those that existed were ambiguous enough to allow for various loopholes—Wall Street traders became more and more daring and corruption became a staple in the system. He believes strongly that those who were singled out for punishment following the 2008 financial crisis were indeed genuinely surprised that they were being punished since they were simply doing what *everybody else* was doing. He also noted that the *punishments* were not effective because the real culprits were not affected; instead, a few unlucky traders were made scapegoats, ignoring the real perpetrators—the CEOs and managers. Nearly six years after the financial crisis, as seen from the recent survey results, a large number of people who work on Wall Street believe that they cannot achieve career success if they choose to also be ethical.

Suggested Questions for Discussion

1. What is your opinion on the way businesses on Wall Street operate?
2. Do you agree with Arnade's perceptions of Wall Street? Why or why not?
3. What steps can businesses on Wall Street take in order to promote ethical behavior in employees?

Ethics Teaching Strategy

Teaching ethics, particularly in management can prove to be an invaluable experience for both facilitators and their students. The success of a business ethics course however depends on the ability of facilitators to *draw out* ethical thinking and behavioral patterns from their students. If the course is to have its desired effect, which is to in fact to produce people who not only think but act ethically, it must be approached in a rigorous and structured manner. Students should be introduced to theoretical and practical foundations that can always serve as guidelines for them whenever they are faced with making ethical decisions.

The purpose of ethics as a field of study can be considered from a number of different perspectives (Rossouw 2004). Two of these perspectives are particularly relevant in teaching ethical career management—*ethical development* and *ethical control*. Ethical development is concerned with the character of individuals and its main objective is to ensure the moral development of these individuals in their roles as employees, managers, and key business and policy decision makers. Ethical control, on the other hand, focuses on the internal and external structures that govern businesses; it is concerned with policies, procedures, and standards that are put in place to safeguard against and sanction immoral business practices.

With these two perspectives laying the foundations for a career management ethics course, practical results can be more readily attained. It should be clear from the onset that the course is expected to result in the development of skills that will enable students to be ethically minded employees and managers. Rossouw (2004) refers to these skills as cognitive, behavioral, and managerial competencies. Based on our already established two-perspective career studies pattern, that is, individual (psychological) and social determinism (sociological), the first two competencies will be addressed at the individual level while the third competency will focus on sociological aspects.

Cognitive competencies should result in students acquiring and developing intellectual knowledge with regards to ethical decision making. Students should be introduced to theoretical constructs and critical thinking frameworks that can guide and develop their abilities. Students should be trained to consider the consequences of their career decisions by ensuring that they are equipped with as much knowledge about their chosen career, organization, industry, and so forth as possible. They should have an understanding of the impacts of their career decisions on others, learn to reason objectively and weigh alternative solutions to problems, and they should learn the art of moral tolerance. Developing moral tolerance will enable students to openly discuss and consider differing moral views as long as it is clear that the golden rule of ethics, the consideration for others and not only oneself, has not been ignored.

Behavioral competencies should build on cognitive competencies by translating the ability to think ethically into actually acting ethically. Like the cognitive, behavioral competencies should result in the moral development of individuals; however, in this case, the aim is to develop character and not just cognition. As discussed earlier, an individual who has gained moral cognition skills is constantly aware of and considering the impact of their actions on others; however, this may not necessarily translate into them caring enough or feeling compelled to do anything about it. Students should learn the importance of taking actions that sometimes are more for the benefit of others than themselves. In conclusion, behavioral competencies focus on the development of individual will and emotions that should lead to individuals actually behaving in an ethical manner.

The final competency is referred to as managerial. In this case, the focus is on the moral systems that students contend with as managers and business leaders. Students should learn to develop and enhance the systems in which they operate by focusing on issues such as organizational culture and attitudes with regards to the career management of employees. Are company goals and bottom line considerations consistently placed over the career needs of employees? Does the organization's career management system assist or encourage employees in improving their careers? Managerial competencies enable managers to focus on the long term rather than the immediate, thus they develop systems aimed at producing sustainable gain and competitive advantage. It also includes developing students with a leadership mindset in which they realize that they should act as role models and mentors, providing moral vision to support colleagues, subordinates, and even their superiors. The collective good is the focus in this case; managerial competencies focus on the effects that the generally accepted policies and procedures of a system have on the way individuals in that system view their chances of advancement should they choose to act ethically. For instance, the example of Wall Street employees who are in a system that they believe does not encourage ethicality if they wish to advance in their careers shows how an entire system has over time come to be associated with typically unethical behaviors.

Keeping these competencies in mind, ethics instructors can develop curricula that incorporate critical thinking, open discussions, experiential learning, and the use of real-life situations to encourage students to develop their ability to think and act outside of themselves and their needs. Students will objectively and rationally analyze their career decision-making processes so that they will not only think of immediate as well as personal and organizational gain. They will also approach managerial and leadership positions with perspectives that encourage innovative thinking as this will be required in order to understand and experience the instrumentality of morality. Personal reflection and growth is the main goal of ethics instruction; therefore, the course will typically be more effective if students are encouraged to arrive at ethical solutions on their own rather than being told what is considered ethical or otherwise.

Advice for Teachers

- Identify, at the start of the course, your ontological assumptions regarding ethics and ethics instruction as the course instructor. Also, encourage students to explore other assumptions and discuss them in the initial classes.
- An emphasis should be placed on personal reflection and growth, therefore it is important to encourage open and healthy debates. Students should be free to express themselves without fear of being branded as *unethical* for having a different opinion. Sensitivity is important so that people do not fall into the trap of simply saying what they believe is expected of them without internalizing these perspectives.
- Allow room for ambiguity as this is a reality in ethics. As a relatively young field, both in research and instruction, it is important to embrace rather than ignore the differing underlying assumptions that govern research and instruction in ethics.

Suggested Teaching Tools

- Case studies are an ideal way to encourage and enhance discussions because they present realistic situations that students can identify with.
- Relevant and recent real-life stories that have been highlighted in the media are also very useful tools. Students can analyze and discuss such stories using the theoretical

guidelines and frameworks provided, rather than just giving subjective opinions.
- Students should also be encouraged to keep learning journals as this will enhance their reflection processes forcing them to revisit class discussions and report them in their own words.
- Where exams and written tests are given, feedback is pertinent. Teachers must make time to discuss the answers that students have given, particularly those answers that do not reflect ethical thinking or behavior; this will help teachers understand and address the thought processes that led to said answers.

Developing Versus Developed Country Perspectives

This section focuses specifically on the societal effects of ethicality or nonethicality on career management. While acknowledging the fact that developed and developing societies certainly face vastly different ethical challenges in terms of careers, it is interesting to note a common theme—the problem of unethical behavior simply grows when people choose to ignore the consequences of their actions on others and the long-term effects of their decisions. Although more subtle in developed parts of the world, the problem of unethical behavior is just as grievous. In this section, we can readily identify with career theorists who argue that societal and structural systems shape careers.

Cultural systems can have a significant effect on the way individuals view their work (Hofstede 1980; Schwartz 1999). Apart from culture, the impact of economic and infrastructural development (or the lack thereof) can be more directly observed. Maslow's (1943) hierarchy of needs places physical needs at the first level of a progressive list of five needs of man. He argued that man must meet the needs in a hierarchical order starting with the first level, that is, physical needs and desire to survive, and ending with the last, that is, self-actualization (which includes morality, lack of prejudice, etc.). It is important to note that while Maslow's theory of needs is one of the most popular motivational and social behavior theories, these needs are not necessarily hierarchical (i.e., higher order needs such as self-esteem and self-actualization have been sought after in many cases where lower level physiological needs have not yet been met) (Wahba and Bridwell 1976).

In general, however, people typically focus on their immediate physical needs and thus considering the effects of one's actions on others may not be a priority when one is struggling to survive. In developing countries, the concept of career management can best be described as inchoate. People's attitude to work is evolving and careers are now no longer seen simply as a means of survival. While this makes ethical concerns about career decisions more realistic and attainable, at least at the individual level, corruption still erodes almost every level of society. Individuals therefore sometimes find the idea of ethics absurd as the opposite is the case almost everywhere they look and they are faced with what appears to be a daily battle of survival. Hence, in developing countries, it is necessary to first show individuals that despite the harsh environment, they can still operate ethically and be successful. Using real-life examples of successful indigenous individuals and organizations who have found creative ways of conducting themselves and their businesses ethically will prove to be more encouraging and convincing.

Also, in the case of developing countries, cognitive and behavioral competencies require a lot of emphasis. As a result of years of government corruption and maltreatment, people in these systems may sometimes be *forced* to think and act in ways that are purely motivated by their own self-interests. It is generally accepted that you have to be *smart*, where being *smart* means that you must do whatever you can to survive and succeed even at the detriment of others. It is therefore necessary to focus on the reorientation of individuals in these environments. Without first convincing individuals that ethics is both good and beneficial, an ethics course would simply be an exercise in futility. In conclusion, the ethical competencies discussed earlier should be enhanced with tailor-made competency sets that take into consideration the uniqueness of the environments in which individuals operate.

Class Exercises

The following exercises are based on an individual career management perspective and an organizational one.

Individual Career Choices

The following questions are intended for reflection and class discussion sessions. Each theme is intended to mirror four major decisions that individuals would typically consider when making career decisions and evaluating their careers.

Please note that these themes are not exhaustive. Discussions are to be framed within the strategies suggested in the teaching section of the chapter.

1. **Which Organization Do I Join?**
   (a) Would you join and work in an organization that is considered to be unethical by your standards as long as you do not join in their questionable practices?
   (b) Would you join and work in an organization with controversial products (because people's life choices should be solely left to them)?
2. **How Do I Serve My Organization?**
   (a) Do you believe it is your organization's responsibility to train and help you develop your skills regardless of your performance?
   (b) Would you accept an offer in an organization you have no interest in remaining in (because a bird in hand is worth more than two in the bush)?
3. **How Do I Progress In My Career?**
   (d) Would you job *hop* if it gets you to the top? (You do not owe your organization more than the required notice of your intent to leave if you have a better offer?)
   (e) Would you do *bad* things to get good results? (Because the end justifies the means?)
4. **Should I Stay or Should I Go?**
   (a) Would you leave your job for another regardless of how it affects your current employer and team?
   (b) Would you rather leave an organization than be labeled a whistleblower?

Organizational Career Practices

In this section, some typical organizational practices will be discussed. Please indicate whether you *agree* or *disagree* with these practices. Note that in this section, you are to answer as a corporation and not as an employee.

Individual Talent Management

1. Mentoring programs should be available for all employees regardless of performance or job level.
2. Prescreening processes should be as concerned with alignment of individual and organizational values as they are with individual skills and intelligence.
3. Employees should be encouraged to independently pursue career development strategies.

Team and Employee Relationship Management

4. Teamwork should be valued as much as individual performance.
5. Employees should be encouraged to share knowledge with one another and rewarded for doing so.
6. All teams should get equal opportunities regardless of team members.

Compensation Practices

7. Bonuses should be given to *all* employees when the organization declares a profit because they have all put in some measure of effort.

Performance Management and Appraisals

8. Individuals should be given the opportunity to evaluate themselves on their performance.

9. Employees should be rewarded for exhibiting organizational values.
10. Managers should be encouraged to focus attention on all their subordinates regardless of performance.
11. Using forced ranking, as long as it is done as objectively as possible, is a fair way of weeding out poor performers.

Management Practices

12. Everything we do must be clearly guided by our mission and vision statements.
13. Employees' views should be respected and they should be carried along by the management.
14. Employees should always know that their jobs are secure.

Questions 2, 10, and 12 are adapted from B. Groysberg's "People Management Questionnaire" (2006).

Summary and Conclusion

Careers, like ethics, permeate all aspects of life. It is therefore important not to seek to justify or rationalize selfish career decisions as the effects on others could be far-reaching. *Ethical development*, concerned mainly with the character of individuals, and *ethical control*, which focuses on creating systems that foster and reward ethical behavior, are two important perspectives that must be achieved in ethics instruction. Following instruction in ethics, students should be equipped with cognitive, behavioral, and managerial competencies. Finally, in developing countries, huge emphasis should be placed on highlighting the positive effects of ethicality and the development of cognitive and behavioral skills in students.

References

Arnade, C. 2013 "Here's Why Wall Street Has a Hard Time Being Ethical." http://www.theguardian.com/business/2013/nov/25/wall-street-hard-time-ethical (accessed December 22, 2013).

Arthur, M.B., D.T. Hall, and B.S. Lawrence. 1989. *Handbook of Career Theory.* Cambridge, UK: Cambridge University Press.

Blustein, D., and D. Noumair. 1996. "Self and Identity in Career Development: Implications for Theory and Practice." *Journal of Counseling & Development* 74, pp. 433–40.

Cole, A. 2010. "Rooney's Agent and How He Treated Me." *The National*, October 22. http://www.thenational.ae/sport/football/rooneys-agent-and-how-he-treated-me (accessed December 22, 2013).

Groysberg, B. 2006. "People Management Questionnaire." Boston, MA: *Harvard Business School Publishing.*

Gunz, H.P., and M.A. Peiperl, eds. 2007. *Handbook of Career Studies.* Thousand Oaks, CA: Sage Publications.

Hofstede, G. 1980. *Culture's Consequences: International Differences in Work-related Values.* Newbury Park, CA: Sage.

Jones, D. 2010. "Paul Stretford: He Mixes with Gangsters and Was Banned by the FA…Meet Wayne Rooney's Unsavoury Mr 20 per cent." *Mail Online*, October 23. http://www.dailymail.co.uk/sport/football/article-1323140/Paul-Stretford-Meet-Wayne-Rooneys-unsavoury-agent.html (accessed December 22, 2013)

Kapoor, M. 2013. A Crisis of Culture: Valuing Ethics and Knowledge in Financial Services. Report from *The Economist* Intelligence Report. http://www.economistinsights.com/analysis/crisis-culture (accessed December 22, 2013).

Maslow, A.H. 1943. A Theory of Human Motivation. *Psychological Review* 50, no. 4, pp. 370–96.

Maxwell, J. 2005. *Ethics 101: What Every Leader Needs To Know.* New York: Centre Street.

Rossouw, D. 2004. Developing Business Ethics as an Academic Field. Auckland, South Africa: BEN-Africa.

Schwartz, S.H. 1999. A Theory of Cultural Values and Some Implications for Work. *Applied Psychology: An International Review* 48, no. 1, pp. 23–47.

Wahba, M.A., and L.G. Bridwell. 1976. "Maslow Reconsidered: A Review of Research on the Need Hierarchy Theory." *Organizational Behavior and Human Performance* 15, no. 2, pp. 212–40.

CHAPTER 14

Ethics in Negotiation

Barney Jordaan and David Venter

Vlerick Business School

Introduction

While various forms of unethical behavior might arise in the context of negotiation,[1] this chapter deals with one of the most common forms of unethical negotiation behavior, deception. The term may be defined as behavior intended to "intentionally cause another person to have false beliefs" (Carson, Wokutch, and Murrmann 1982).[2] Deception may take on a variety of forms, including the withholding of relevant information, lying, or taking advantage of another's information deficit (Hames 2012, 268).

Lies and deceit come as naturally to negotiators as to people in general: "Lying is not exceptional; it is normal, and more often spontaneous and unconscious than cynical and coldly analytical. Our minds and bodies secrete deceit."[3]

---

[1] For example, intentional false statements about material facts and misleading statements about material issues (such as a party's mandate or bottom line), nondisclosure of information when the other side operates under an erroneous assumption, misleading statements about material facts, the use of threats, abuse of one's bargaining position, and so forth.

[2] Cramton defines deception as "any deliberate act or omission by one party taken with the intention of creating or adding support to a false belief in another party" (Cramton and Dees 1993, 362).

[3] In "Negotiating with Liars" by Robert S. Adler from the journal *MIT Sloan Management Review* volume 48, issue 4, Summer 2007 (quoted in Lewicki, Saunders, and Barry 2010, 183). See also Cramton and Dees (1993, 361) for an explanation of the reasons for the gap between the demands of ethics and, what they term, "the urging of self-interest."

Even the most well-intentioned negotiators routinely and unconsciously commit ethical lapses and tolerate such lapses in others (Hames 2012, 268).[4] As a matter of fact, negotiation provides ample opportunities for deception in one form or another.[5] Party A may, for example, operate on the basis of incorrect information that party B wishes to buy their farm as a lifestyle investment, whereas party B possesses inside information of a recent discovery of rich oil deposits on the property. Party B may be tempted not to disclose this information, as this would in all probability affect price. Or, party C may, knowing full well that they has no such fallback, inform party D that they will embark on a certain course of action, for example, buy from another source, should a deal not be possible.

The way negotiators translate this *potential opportunism* into real advantage or gains is what raises ethical concerns, "because it implies control or manipulation of information. Since ethics is the study of interpersonal or social values and the rules of conduct that derive from them, manipulation, truth telling and withholding information are at the core of what is or is not ethical in negotiation" (Hames 2012, 268).[6]

The issue of deception is further complicated by the fact that unlawful behavior, for example, killing another, fraud, and deliberate misrepresentation, is in most instances deemed to be unethical (Cramton and

---

[4] This has been referred to as "ethical fading," i.e., the tendency for the ethical dimensions of decisions to fade from view under certain conditions, "allowing us to diverge from our high moral standards and behave unethically—without recognizing that we are doing so" ("Will You Behave Unethically?" 2013).

[5] Whether or not they are aware of it, negotiators make a series of *micro-ethical decisions* at the negotiation table, which often involve choosing whether to disclose, conceal, or misrepresent information that would potentially benefit the other party and lessen one's own outcomes (In "Maybe It's Right, Maybe It's Wrong: Structural and Social Determinants of Deception in Negotiation" (2013) by Mara Olekalns, Christopher J. Horan, and Philip L. Smith from the *Journal of Business Ethics* [referred to in "Will You Behave Unethically?" 2013]).

[6] See also Mnookin (2000, 274): "[W]ithholding or manipulating information may confer real distributive advantages."

Dees 1993), whereas some other forms of deceit, for example, lying about one's fallback options or bottom line, may not be unlawful, but could still be deemed to be deceitful and therefore not ethical (Hames 2012, 268).[7] Compliance with the law consequently cannot be the sole measure of ethical behavior. We generally are not able to detect lies and liars, the odds of successfully doing so rarely exceeding random chance. (In Adler's "Negotiating with Liars" [quoted in Lewicki, Saunders, and Barry 2010, 185]). When we believe that we are able to protect ourselves against deceitful behavior by observing, for example, body language, we are naive.

Matters are further complicated by our cognitive styles and flawed decision making, which may lead us to participate in or condone unethical behavior:

> In the context of negotiation…a range of common cognitive patterns can lead us to engage in or condone "ordinary unethical behaviors" that we would otherwise condemn. We overlook others' unethical behavior that serves our own interests…People seem to become comfortable with behavior that gradually becomes less and less ethical, and they ignore unethical process choices if the resultant outcomes are good. One reason for these unconscious lapses emanates from evidence pertaining to our flawed decision making. We engage in systematic patterns of thinking that prevent us from noticing or focusing on useful, observable, and relevant data. We also engage in behaviors that are inconsistent with our own ethical values. These decisions not only harm others but are inconsistent with our own consciously espoused beliefs and preferences. In fact, we would condemn them upon further reflection or awareness. (Hames 2012, 272)

This begs the question how we should approach the teaching of negotiation and ethics, particularly in relation to deceitful conduct. Given that

---

[7] In Charles B. Craver's "Negotiation Ethics" (reproduced in Lewicki, Saunders, and Barry 2010, 193).

there are those (Carr 1968; Dees and Cramton 1995) who argue that ethical rules do not always apply in business negotiations, and that some measure of deception is therefore *normal* and to be expected, such consideration is essential (Carson 1993). The following examples of justification for unethical behavior are often proffered: "they had it coming"; "they deserved it"; "the tactic was unavoidable"; "the tactic was harmless"; "the tactic will produce good consequences in the long run"; "sometimes you have to be cruel to be kind" (i.e., it was motivated by altruism); "they started it"; "they were going to do it to us, so we did it to them first"; and "the situation called for it."[8]

However, the mere fact that deception may be prevalent in business dealings[9] does not justify such behavior from an ethical or moral point of view. The fact that something is *standard practice* or *part of the game* cannot be deemed to justify such behavior.

On the other hand, while we believe that all people—business people included—should behave ethically, we doubt whether merely appealing to others to behave ethically because it is the right thing to do will of itself be sufficient to change negotiation behavior, given human nature and the exigencies and realities of the business world in general. The motivation for doing the right thing must go further, we believe. Our approach when teaching ethics and negotiation, for want of a better term, is pragmatic.[10] Negotiation is essentially a process through which we try to satisfy our own interests. We can do so by trying to meet our interests regardless of the other side's (looking for our own gain), or in cooperation with them (looking for mutual gain). Whether one adopts the former or the latter approach to negotiation (our preference is for the latter), in each case it concerns a large degree of self-interest.

---

[8] See http://nego4biz.wordpress.com/2010/03/04/ethics-in-negotiation/

[9] What Carson and others refer to as "an indictment of our entire economic system that such activities are necessary in so many typical circumstances" (Carson, Wokutch, and Murrmann 1982, 20).

[10] An excellent article in this regard is "Promoting Honesty in Negotiation: An Exercise in Practical Ethics" by Cramton and Dees (1993).

Speaking to a negotiator's self-interest, in other words, showing how deception affects their reputation as negotiators and the sustainability of the agreement, as well as the quality of the outcome, holds the key to motivating them to behave ethically. First, if discovered, deception can seriously damage a party's reputation as negotiator, and consequently make it very difficult to cultivate trust (Cramton and Dees 1993, 360).[11] Second, deceit can harm or even destroy the underlying relationships that are a prerequisite for sustainable agreements. Third, deceit may be self-defeating, leading to lesser outcomes and a very difficult implementation process (Hames 2012, 283).

However, given that deceit is a reality in business negotiations, the best policy, we believe, is one of showing that you can be trusted, but not to be overly trusting. Negotiators should arm themselves with some *protective skills*, referred to later in this chapter.

Defining Negotiation

We approach negotiation from the following working definition: *Negotiation is a process in which a party engages another party or parties to advance his or her interests by motivating the other party or parties to move in their direction, therefore either departing from or amending its behavior or intended future behavior.*

This definition encompasses the three key dimensions of negotiation, that is, the problem, the people, and the process. The problem dimension concerns the merits or substance of the negotiation, that is, how the various interests can be integrated. The people dimension concerns how negotiators relate to one another in pursuance of a relationship that

---

[11] See Stark and Flaherty (2003): "Reputation plays a vital role in every negotiation. It's much easier to achieve win-win outcomes when you have a reputation for being fair, honest and willing to do the right thing. A counterpart who feels you are unfair, dishonest or unwilling to do the right thing will be less willing to make concessions or even to begin a negotiation with you in the first place. So guarding your reputation by always acting in an ethical manner is key to successful negotiation."

meets their respective needs. The process dimension concerns the activities and behaviors that could move the parties to move toward better collaboration.

This definition also captures what we regard as the key challenge in business negotiation, namely, how a party motivates another party or parties to move in its direction. This challenge poses two strategic options: To either work toward persuading the other party to move in one's direction by making it worth their while to do so, or resort to manipulation and coercion with a view to *winning* the negotiation. We depart from the view that collaboration should the preferred approach[12] in commercial negotiations. This approach is based on the assumption that the best way of achieving our goal, that is, having our interests met, requires us to assist the other party to achieve its goal, that is, satisfying the interests of the other party to the best of our ability.[13] The aim should be agreement through mutual gain, not victory over the other party. However, we do appreciate that collaboration is not always possible or feasible,[14] and that there may therefore be situations where a more assertive approach is required[15] in our endeavor to satisfy our interests. However, adopting a more assertive strategy does not mean that one now has to revert to the typical hard bargaining and sometimes deceitful tactics so typical of positional negotiation.

---

[12] Also referred to as *integrative*, *interest-based*, or *mutual gains* negotiation. This involves clarifying the parties' key interests, jointly developing options for both parties' benefit, and then trying to reach an agreement that all consider fair and in compliance with objective standards or benchmarks.

[13] What Robert B. Cialdini (2006) refers to as the principle of *reciprocity*.

[14] E.g., when the other party refuses to collaborate, or if the negotiation is once-off and does not involve longer-term commitments.

[15] Sometimes referred to as *positional* or *distributive* negotiation: a party pursues his or her own interests irrespective of the other party's concerns. To be successful, a negotiator would need to have a stronger bargaining position than their counterpart. A number of factors may play a role in determining an appropriate strategy, e.g., the context, importance of time, importance of issues, the parties' relative bargaining power, and the need for future collaboration.

Ethical Issues Arising in Negotiation

Opportunities for deception arise from a number of factors, including a large degree of information asymmetry between the parties; for example, when it is difficult to verify information, or when a party has insufficient resources to adequately safeguard it against deception; when there is infrequent interaction between the parties; when information about a party's reputation is not available or is unreliable, or when one party has little to lose or has much to gain from attempting deception (Cramton and Dees 1993, 373).

Typical Tactics

Tactics that commonly raise ethical questions include bluffing, concealment, or distortion of relevant information,[16] spying and other inappropriate information gathering techniques, the use of unconscionable threats to obtain concessions,[17] false promises; deception about future actions,[18] attacks on the other party's network,[19] misrepresentation by omission,[20] and deception about settlement preferences.[21]

What Can Be Done to Counter Such Tactics?

A number of techniques and counter-tactics are available to manage unethical behavior. Table 14.1 by no means provides an exhaustive list

---

[16] E.g., not disclosing important defects in the item bought.

[17] E.g., to publicly disclose damaging information about a party.

[18] E.g., falsely stating that one has obtained legal advice in support of one's position, or threatening to walk away to a nonexistent alternative if one does not get your way.

[19] E.g., "going over the other negotiator's head" or "behind his or her back" and negotiating directly with his or her principal.

[20] Failing to disclose information that would benefit the other party, e.g., that an item is worth far more than that party believes.

[21] E.g., overstating the importance of time, misinformation about the importance of an issue, or about one's so-called reservation price or *bottom line.*

Table 14.1 Techniques to manage unethical behavior in negotiation

Setting a personal ethical standard before negotiating, by deciding which behaviors are off-limit, and considering how to address ethical dilemmas that may be encountered.	Conducting due diligence to determine whether there are incentives for deception, e.g., time pressure or gains that could accrue to the representatives of the other party; assessing the competence, attitudes, history, and character of the other party; and assessing own biases and attitudes.
Building mutual trust. As Cramton states: "In many cases, the incentive for deception in negotiation is defensive. It arises out of a suspicion that the other party is likely to be dishonest and out of a fear that the other party will unfairly exploit any weakness that is honestly revealed. This suspicion and fear may be overcome if a climate of mutual trust can be developed."	Emphasizing the longer-term nature of the relationship that arises from the negotiation, should this be relevant.
Investing in self-protection by wisely selecting negotiation partners to avoid opportunists, to verify information provided by counterparts to the extent possible, and to secure important claims and commitments in writing.	Setting negotiation ground rules for dealing with matters that may arise, e.g., commitment of the parties to full disclosure.
Entering into contingency arrangements where necessary.	Asking probing questions.
"Calling the tactic," i.e., a party indicating that it is aware of the other party lying or bluffing, doing this tactically, but firmly to communicate its displeasure.	Requesting warranties whenever there is doubt.
Using respected intermediaries to assist in creating a deal that is beneficial to the parties involved, thereby increasing the likelihood of compliance.	Ignoring the tactic by remaining focused on the merits.
Trusting, but verifying.	Creating an atmosphere of mutual trust, as "An atmosphere of mutual trust appears to play an important role in grounding ethical behavior for many people."
Being willing to walk away from a deal if the other party's behavior remains a problem.	Not responding in kind.

but captures most of the advice offered by academics and practitioners in the field of negotiation.[22]

Self-Test

Protecting his or her own reputation and encouraging ethical behavior on the part of other parties requires that a negotiator should ensure that his or her tactics and behavior are ethical. As a *rule of thumb*, students should pose the following questions to ascertain guidelines for their behavior (Menkel-Meadow and Wheeler 2004):

(a) Reciprocity: *Would I be comfortable if the other party used the same tactics toward me?*
(b) Reputation: *How might my intended actions* impact *my reputation as a negotiator and a person?*
(c) Proximity: *Would I be comfortable if someone did the same to someone close to me, for example, a parent, a partner, or a child?*
(d) Publicity: *How would I respond if what I did or am about to do became known?*
(e) Universality: *Would I advise others to do the same thing?*
(f) Disclosure: *Would I be willing to tell someone close to me what I plan to do or did?*
(g) Legality: *Is it legal?*
(h) Values: *Is what I am doing congruent with my own value system and, where applicable, with that of the organization I represent?*

Ethics Teaching Strategy

Negotiation is a discipline that lends itself to learning through experience. Students typically engage in role plays and the analysis of case studies, both of which provide rich sources of learning and discussion. In

---

[22] The following sources are useful here: Cramton and Dees 1993, 380–388; Stark and Flaherty 2003, 2–3; In Adler's "Negotiating with Liars" (quoted in Lewicki, Saunders, and Barry 2010, 186–189; Mnookin 2000, 288–290; Hames 2012, 283–284).

addition, the use of reflective journals allows the development of *conscious conscious*, as students apply what they learn and also reflect on their real life negotiation experiences outside the classroom.

Advice for Teachers

We depart from the premise that business negotiations provide opportunities for deception and that such deception may sometimes be deliberate, but may at other times be unconscious. Given this reality, we do not believe that a moralist or Kantian approach[23] provides an adequate basis for encouraging ethical behavior among negotiators, as commercial self-interest is likely to often take preference over moral arguments. Instead, while we encourage our students to always behave in an ethical manner in negotiation, we go further than merely telling them that it is the right thing to do, which it undoubtedly is. Given human nature and the realities of the world of commerce, we try to show them that behaving ethically is in their own best interests, for the reasons given earlier.

At the same time, however, we impress on them the importance of also protecting themselves against the possibility of being deceived, that is, by way of preparation, by limiting opportunities for other parties to deceive, and by not resorting to deception themselves. In this regard, we encourage them to use the questions in the *self-test* as a framework for taking stock of their behavior and the consequences thereof.

Developing Versus Developed Country Perspectives

Deception (under which we include corruption and bribery) could severely limit or even negate the prospects of engaging in business. While this, according to Transparency International's most recent perception

---

[23] While acknowledging the gap between ethics and self-interest, Kantians assert the dominance of moral considerations over those of personal welfare (Cramton and Dees 1993, 362).

survey, is a worldwide phenomenon, developing nations generally fare worst in this regard.[24]

When students seek advice and guidance on how to deal with requests for bribes and other forms of corruption when negotiating business deals, we generally offer the following: first, they need to formulate a policy or code of ethics for the organizations they serve. They also need to do their homework by researching the anticorruption laws of the countries where they will be doing business, informing their team thereof, and planning how to deal with corruption if and when it transpires. They should also provide the other party with a copy of their organization's code of ethics, as part of the ground rules for the negotiation. When there is a request for a bribe, they need to indicate to their counterpart their desire to do business with them, but also stressing their unwillingness to act in breach of their organization's code of ethics, or to transgress the laws of the host country. It is also advisable to seek out a person from the other side with whom they are able to engage in honest business with. Finally, if all else fails, walk away rather compromise your own organization's reputation by entering into a corrupt deal.[25]

Summary and Conclusion

Deception—be it by commission or omission—and business negotiations sadly often tend to go hand-in-hand. Negotiators either find themselves on the receiving end of deceptive tactics, or may be tempted to use deception to either limit their risk exposure or to gain advantage over the other party. In order to guard against being the victim of deceit and falling prey to the temptation to deceive, our negotiation students are advised to create a negotiation environment conducive to collaboration and the establishment of enduring relationships,[26] guard against being the victim

---

[24] See http://cpi.transparency.org/cpi2013/results/ See also http://bpi.transparency.org/bpi2011/results/, which ranks countries in terms of the tendency of businesses from those countries to initiate and pay bribes.
[25] See also http://www.transparency.org/research/bps2011 for suggestions.
[26] Thus reducing the need for deception.

of deception by thoroughly preparing for a negotiation, limit the other party's opportunities for deception, and test their own tactics against the questions posed in our self-test.

In the words of Mark Twain: "Always do right. This will gratify some people and astonish the rest" (Lewicki, Barry, and Saunders 2010, 197).

Suggested Exercises[27]

Roosevelt's Dilemma[28]

Roosevelt's Dilemma offers a useful introduction to a discussion on ethics in negotiation and can be used with a group of any size. It should take no more than 15 min to complete. Each student is handed a copy of the exercise (below) and given about 5 min to consider the following questions:

(a) What is your first impression about the tactic used?
(b) Upon reflection, would you say the tactic was ethical in the circumstances?
(c) If you were the campaign manager, would you have done the same?

After having considered their own responses, students should be divided into groups of four or five and asked to share their responses with a view to reaching consensus in about 10 min. Thereafter the floor is open for discussion. Usually the students strongly disagree about the result. Some argue that the campaign manager's tactic was brilliant in that it benefited both the campaign and the photographer and therefore could not be faulted. Others argue that the photographer was misled through nondisclosure of the fact that his copyright had already been infringed. Then there are others who argue that, irrespective of the ethics of the situation, the tactic was a dangerous tactic, which, if it had been discovered, would have tarnished Roosevelt's image.

---

[27] See Carson, Wokutch, and Murrmann (1982, 16) for examples of bluffing in labor negotiations. Many further useful examples can be found in Marr and De Janasz (2013).

[28] Also referred to as "The Moffett Picture" (Asherman 2012, 31).

Once input is received from the group, the following questions are posed:

(a) Imagine that you were in Moffett's shoes and that you discovered after the fact that the Roosevelt people had not only infringed your copyright but had also been made to pay for using it. How would you feel?
(b) How else could the situation have been handled?[29]

> ## Roosevelt's Dilemma
>
> The story is told that in 1912 Theodore Roosevelt was nearing the end of a hard-fought and very close U.S. presidential election campaign. At each stop he made, pamphlets were handed out to potential voters containing his picture and a stirring speech, which he called his *Confession of Faith*. Three million of these pamphlets were printed. However, just before the campaign kicked off, someone on his team noticed at the last minute that Roosevelt's picture contained a small caption stating that the picture had been taken by a certain photographer who was based in Chicago, operating under the name of Moffett's Studios. The problem was that using the picture without the photographer's consent would infringe copyright and undermine the wonderful principles mentioned in the *Confessions of Faith*. On the other hand, trying to get the photographer's consent at that stage could have resulted in lengthy and expensive negotiation, if he were shrewd enough. Not using the pamphlets at all was not an attractive option as they were desperately needed to try to swing undecided voters. The campaign workers knew that negotiation was the only way out, yet everything counted against them: a pressing deadline, little negotiation power, and probably not enough resources to pay the photographer's asking price!

---

[29] One possibility would have been for the campaign manager to have played open cards stating that the photograph had been reproduced in error and that Roosevelt would be willing to abandon its use if that is what Moffatt wanted, but that would be a waste for the campaign and a lost opportunity for Moffett. A win-win solution would be for the photograph to be used with permission in return for the campaign offering to give some form of publicity for the studio.

> The dispirited campaign workers then approached a noted financier and campaign manager who lost no time in sending a telegram to the photographer with his proposition: "We are planning to distribute many pamphlets with Roosevelt's picture on the cover. It will be great for publicity for the studio whose photograph we use. How much will you pay us to use yours? Respond immediately". Shortly he received the reply: "We've never done this before, but we'd be pleased to offer $250". The offer was accepted straight away.

Ethical Dilemmas

The following scenarios provide a rich source for discussing ethical dilemmas. Follow the same instructions as for the Roosevelt exercise, that is, providing each student with a copy of the exercise, allowing the students to make up their own minds before debating their responses in small groups, and then engaging in a class discussion. Views tend to differ greatly. While it is difficult to label any of the possible responses as either right or wrong, we usually tell our students the following:

(a) If you were the negotiator, remind yourself of the questions that you ought to ask yourself whenever a potential ethical dilemma arises. Having asked yourself those questions, would you now deal with the situation differently?

(b) Imagine in scenario 1 that the seller knew about the planned race track and its potential negative impact on the property's value but failed to disclose it to you. Would you regard this as unethical?

(c) Imagine in scenario 2 that the buyers subsequently discover that you had withheld the information from them. Might there be any legal consequences:[30]

(d) Imagine in scenario 3 that your boss subsequently discovers what you had done. How might this impact you?

---

[30] Nondisclosure of relevant information would constitute misrepresentation with potential legal consequences.

Three Scenarios

Steal Deal

Consider the following scenario. You have been looking for a second home, nothing fancy, just some place to get away and relax. You have done a thorough search in the area and everything that meets your needs costs at least $800,000, sometimes much more. But you have just stumbled upon a handsome cottage by a small pond. The hand-painted sign says, "For Sale by Owner—Inquire Within." The elderly owner shows you around. The place is perfect. When it comes to talk price, the owner explains that he and his wife are moving back to the city to be close to their grandchildren, and they will need every penny they can get for the move. You are shocked when the man asks for only $650,000—way under market value. Assuming you can protect yourself against any unpleasant surprises—a lien on the property, for example, or environmental problems—what would you do?

(a) Quickly accept the seller's asking price.
(b) Counter with a somewhat lower offer, knowing you can always accept at $650,000 if necessary.
(c) Tell the seller that you would like to buy the cabin but that you believe it is undervalued.

Something Like the Truth

Assume that, as most people would, you brought the rustic cottage at its asking price. Now flash forward a few years. You have enjoyed the place immensely but just learned that a motorcycle racetrack will be up and running nearby in a few months. It is time to put up the "For Sale by Owner" sign. An eager couple with an expensive car has toured the property and appears ready to make an offer. One of them asks "Why would you ever want to sell such a beautiful place?" Which of these options comes closest to you response?

(a) "You know, ever since I put up the sign, I've been thinking the same thing myself."
(b) "Oh, it just feels like time to try something new."
(c) "I'm worried that the noise from the new motorcycle racetrack may be disturbing."

Doing the Devil's Bidding

Now imagine that you have been negotiating the sale of a different property, this one owned by your company. The buyer has made an attractive offer that you have tentatively accepted. Your boss is pleased with the terms as they stand but suggest that you go back to the buyer and tell her that she needs to sweeten the offer a bit to get "buy in" back at the office. "No harm in asking," he says. What would you do?

(a) Exactly what your boss suggests. It is a common bargaining tactic, after all.
(b) Tell your boss that you have already given your word to the buyer and that you are not comfortable going back on it.
(c) Ask the buyer if they can sweeten the price, while making it clear that this is not a deal breaker.

References

Asherman, I.G. 2012. *Negotiation at Work*. New York: Amacom.
Carr, A.Z. 1968. "Is Business Bluffing Ethical?" *Harvard Business Review* 46, pp. 143–53.
Carson, T. October, 1993. "Second Thoughts about Bluffing." *Business Ethics Quarterly* 3, no. 4, pp. 317–41.
Carson, T.L., R.E. Wokutch, and K.F. Murrmann. February, 1982 "Bluffing in Labor Negotiations: Legal and Ethical Issues." *Journal of Business Ethics* 1, no. 1, pp. 13–22.
Cialdini, R.B. 2006. *Influence: The Psychology of Persuasion*. New York: Collins.
Cramton, P.C., and J.G. Dees. October, 1993. "Promoting Honesty in Negotiation: An Exercise in Practical Ethics." *Business Ethics Quarterly* 3, no. 4, pp. 359–94.
Dees, J.G., and P.C Cramton. October, 1995. "Deception and Mutual Trust: A Reply to Strudler." *Business Ethics Quarterly* 5, no. 4, pp. 823–32.

Hames, D.S. 2012. *Negotiation: Closing Deals, Settling Disputes, and Making Team Decisions.* New Delhi: Sage.

Lewicki, R.J., D.M. Saunders, and B. Barry. 2010. *Negotiation: Readings, Exercises and Cases.* 6th ed. McGraw-Hill.

DeMarr, B.J., and S.C. De Janasz. 2013. *Negotiation and Dispute Resolution.* New York: Pearson/Prentice Hall.

Menkel-Meadow, C., and M. Wheeler. 2004. *What's Fair: Ethics for Negotiators.* San Francisco: Jossey-Bass.

Mnookin, R.H. 2000. *Beyond Winning: Negotiating to Create Value in Deals and Disputes.* Cambridge, MA: Belknap Harvard.

Stark, P.B., and J. Flaherty. 2003. "Ethical Negotiations: 10 Tips to Ensure Win-Win Outcomes." *The Negotiator Magazine.* http://www.negotiatormagazine.com/showarticle.php?file=article106&page=1 (accessed December 30, 2013).

"Will You Behave Unethically?" November, 2013. *Negotiation Briefings* 1, no. 11, p. 1.

Further Reading

Apart from the sources mentioned in this chapter, Bazerman, M.H. 2011. *Blind Spots: Why We Fail to Do What's Right and What to Do about It.* Princeton is highly recommended.

CHAPTER 15

Ethics in Managing Corporate Power and Politics

Duane Windsor

Jesse H. Jones Graduate School of Business, Rice University

This chapter addresses teaching the topic of the ethical management of corporate power and politics in organizations. Ethical management concerns the principled application of power and politics, as defined by personal values and widely expected norms (Cavanagh, Moberg, and Velasquez 1981). The topic of corporate power and politics lies at the interface of politics, ethics, and leadership. This interface position complicates teaching and learning, because instructors and students need to understand three literatures in some depth and also in relationship to one another in actual organizational settings. The topic of corporate power and politics is frequently separated for in-depth treatment from the topic of ethics in teaching (Alvarez 2012, 58) and is often equated in literature with Machiavellianism (Buskirk 1974; Galie and Bopst 2006; Jay 1968; Lord 2003; McAlpine 1999, 2000; Scott and Zaretsky 2013). Formal organizational policies such as corporate codes of conduct tend to be silent on power and politics, or on informal networks of interpersonal relationships (Reardon 2001) found in all organizations (see Deloitte 2005 guidance). Any corporate code selected at random will likely exhibit such silence. The *rules* of practice are unwritten (Dillon 2013) and must be learned by experience and mentoring (Moberg 2008). Politics is an art rather than a science; ethics is a value system and a framework for decision analysis. Corporate codes tend to be concerned with employee loyalty, legal compliance, and stakeholder management. Codes do however support high personal and professional standards of conduct (see Deloitte 2005).

Ethics now tends to be incorporated into books concerning organizational behavior or leadership. The emphasis in teaching corporate power and politics has been more on Machiavellian tactics (Alvarez 2012), although most typically on how to defend against dirty politics (Fisher 2007; Phipps and Gautrey 2005; Scott and Zaretsky 2013). Dirty politics is partly (but only partly) mythology (Klein 1988). The dimension of a code of conduct addressing fair treatment of employees implicitly embeds the distinction between positive and negative applications of power and politics. Positive or organizationally functional applications are associated with ethical norms and operate to improve the welfare of the organization and its stakeholders, including employees. Negative or organizationally dysfunctional applications are associated with unethical actions to improve personal interest at the expense of the welfare of the organization and other individuals.

An important consideration is identifying relevant literature, examples, and applications. There are some examples reported in the following text that can be assembled from relevant literature. There are some key foundational issues to appreciate. There are important distinctions among authority, influence, and power (Kotter 1985). Authority is formal (as in a corporate officer or manager with legitimate right to make decisions and issue orders) or informal (as in who has moral, political, or social influence with others). Power, recognized to be difficult to define and operationalize (Dahl 1957; Hay 1997), is in general terms the ability to affect people and outcomes, and can involve command of resources (Raven 1990). Much of corporate power and politics occurs covertly (influence and misconduct) rather than overtly (formal authority)—as emphasized by Machiavelli (1980). How authority and influence are exercised is greatly affected by outcomes of tournaments for promotion within a corporation. The organizational political process is dynamic and disguised, as examples will show.

Paraphrasing Dillon (2013), corporations are settings for clashing personalities, competing agendas, and turf wars (see Gandz and Murray 1980; Mintzberg 1985; Pettigrew 1973; Tivey 1978). Buchanan and

Badham (2008) address turf wars in detail. Students of organizational politics should understand the nature and importance of politics, power, influence, and authority in various organizational settings, including teams and other work units. There are several required skills for such understanding. One skill is analysis of power and influence dynamics in varying circumstances. Another is selecting ethical influence strategies and tactics dependent on circumstances. A third is realizing that responsibility may often be greater than formal authority. A fourth is appreciating the nature and importance of mentoring and networking in career development and acquisition of influence.

The rest of this chapter is structured into sections as follows: Description of the discipline; typical ethical issues, with examples; ethics teaching strategy; advice for teachers; developing versus developed country perspectives; and summary and conclusion. Following the summary and conclusion, there is a set of suggested exercises and projects, and then a bibliography of materials on power, politics, and ethics (key items being cited in the text). The chapter ends with a summary of key points.

Description of Discipline

The discipline to be described concerns the teaching for students, who will become executives and employees, of ethical management of corporate power and politics in organizations (see Alvarez 2012). There is a body of literature amounting to this discipline, but that literature is somewhat fragmented across fields of ethics, organizational behavior, and political science. One task of this chapter is to assemble a core literature for instructors so that there is a more coherent discipline that can be studied more systematically. The discipline is a kind of slice through these fields, in the sense that the discipline is about intra-organizational ethics of power and politics as applied by executives and employees (Hayes 1984). The discipline does not concern the external stakeholders of a corporation. This section addresses some key problems or issues in the discipline's core literature.

A fundamental problem is that the two key concepts of power and politics are awkward to isolate for definition and treatment even in the underlying political science literature, before one proceeds to application in organizational behavior and ethical management. The concepts of power and politics are often held to be virtually synonymous (Hay 1997) and both are awkward to define with much scientific precision (Dahl 1957). The concepts are not synonymous, although they overlap significantly, and this condition makes scientific precision difficult at best.

Two sources cited in the following text highlight the problem of defining power with any precision. Hay (1997, 45) states that "Power is probably the most universal and fundamental concept of political analysis. It has been, and continues to be, the subject of extended and heated debate." Crozier (1964, 145) finds that "Power is a very difficult problem with which to deal in the theory of organization." This controversy is not resolved in political science and organization theory.

There are a number of reasons for this condition of the literature. One reason is that *power* and also *politics* are often viewed negatively, in that power over others is suspect and *politics* is commonly used as a word conveying something underhanded or inappropriate. Another reason, as Yukl (1998, 189) points out, is that "Power is not a static condition: it changes over time due to changing conditions and the actions of individuals and coalitions." Organizational politics has a dynamic quality in this same sense.

Another reason is that *power* is partly conflated with *influence* and *authority*. For a simple setting of two actors A (an influencer) and B (the influenced) and two mutually exclusive actions X and Y (which can be alternatives rather than simply opposed), this chapter adopts the following commonly used definitions (see Dahl 1957 for the basic conceptual analysis), where the symbol = means *equals*:

- Power = A's ability or capacity to affect people or effect preferred outcomes (either directly, or indirectly through other people). Power, in this sense, tends to suggest A's control over resources (including skills and incentives).
- Influence = A's ability or capacity to get B to do X rather than Y (influence being easier if B has no initial preference between X and Y, and being more difficult if B has intense preference between X and Y). Influence can include persuasion and incentives.

Authority = A's legitimate right to act, generated either formally or informally, and whether recognized or acknowledged by B or not. A leader is someone whom others choose to follow. A manager may have formal authority due to office; but formal authority depends on willing obedience. An employee may have informal authority through influence over others without respect to office (Cohen and Bradford 2005).

For the definitions adopted earlier, one actor might be a leader and the other actor might be a follower, or each actor might be an executive or an employee. Even the definitions adopted earlier are subject to dispute. However, in essence, authority is right to act, based on some form of legitimacy (whether office or influence). Influence is the ability to persuade others. Power is capacity to alter outcomes, and that capacity typically implies the command of resources. One can argue that there is power over people, but the present author prefers influence and authority over people and power with respect to outcomes.

Corporate leadership is a political process: "… running a company is like politics. You are always trying to balance interests and personalities and trying to keep people motivated" (Jean Riboud, chief executive officer of Schlumberger, quoted in Bower and Weinberg 1988, 50–1). Organizational politics has the sense of the exercise of authority and influence to advance one's agenda for action. Standard advice in management literature is to avoid over-reliance on formal authority (Harvard Business Essentials 2005; see also Harvard Business Press 2006). In practice, many orders are given in various forms (including policies, requests, and suggestions) in any hierarchical organization; and a lot gets done in an organization through informal authority that is neither disobedience nor resistance. Superior management and also political strategy is to operate through influence as much as possible to obtain willing compliance. One can think of expenditure of resources in relationship to compliance obtained as a measure of efficiency of authority and influence.

Organizational politics is synonymous with office or workplace politics. One definition of *politics* in organizations is the set of processes, actions, and behaviors through which potential *power* is achieved and applied (Pfeffer 1992, 30). This definition includes formal authority. Another definition is any informal approach to gaining actual *power* through means other than merit or luck (Dubrin 2001, 192). This definition excludes formal authority. These definitions are typically tied to outcomes. Compliance with formal authority links desirably to work accomplished by employees. Informal approaches might link to less desirable outcomes such as promotions and assignments, control of resources including budgets, and greater prominence of particular sub-units.

The leadership and collective problem is not automatically to minimize all politics within the organization. Rather, the problem is to minimize negative politics and foster positive politics. The essence of all politics is competition for and disagreement over goals, scarce resources, and actions. Thus, all politics is about distributional conflicts (Inderst, Mueller, and Warneryd 2007): who gets what, and how—among individuals, groups, teams, subunits, and functions. The vital difference is between negative politics and positive politics.

What gives power and politics a negative interpretation is the set of conditions in organizations under which there are dysfunctional effects for individuals and organizations. Negative, or dysfunctional, politics involves individual agendas and self-interests separated from organizational welfare. Thus, negative politics occurs at the inappropriate expense of someone else or the whole organization. Negative politics is rivalry among diverse interests occurring at the expense of organizational goals and cooperation. Negative politics commonly involves undesirable tactics such as information distortion, unfair blame, withholding of cooperation, retaliation, and similar actions. Self-interested actors tend to be opportunistic and amoral in exploiting relationships (Malhotra and Gino 2011; Mudambi and Navarra 2004). Political actors may try to manage impression and reputation to personal advantage. A highly political climate in an organization will tend to the dysfunctional.

Positive, or functional, politics in contrast involves implementation of organizational goals and achievement of organizational and thus individual welfare. Functional politics is the implementation of goals in order to increase welfare. The art of functional politics is playing office politics without being dirty ethically (Fisher 2007). Functional politics is then "the art of building relationships that will help you and your team accomplish more than you could on your own"—one can think of this art as leadership with a resource multiplier (Kusy, quoted in Fisher 2007).

While positive politics may well involve the distribution of outcomes favoring some and disfavoring others, this distribution occurs within increasing organizational welfare. Outcomes, such as rewards, should be aligned with organizational goals achieved through cooperation.

An important teaching topic is about what conditions seem to favor or support positive versus negative politics in an organization. Leaders and all employees have a vital interest in promoting an organizational culture emphasizing ethics and thus positive politics. Delegation and empowerment are typically recommended approaches, partly to foster functional processes.

A large literature studies bases of power and tactics for influence and persuasion (Harvard Business Essentials 2005; Hill 2003; Hill and Lineback 2011; McFarland 2001; Sussman et al. 2002). Three tactics for transforming power into influence include framing, information, and technical authority (Harvard Business Essentials 2005). Much of tactical analysis involves anticipation of reactions by other actors much as in a game (Friedrich 1963). Dillon (2013) proposes the following approaches: (1) build relationships with difficult people, (2) gain allies and influence others, (3) obtain resources, (4) move up without ruffling feathers as distinct from corporate climbing, (5) avoid power games and petty rivalries, and (6) claim credit when due.

Pfeffer (1992) draws an important distinction between decisions and their implementation. Managers may lobby in various ways to affect decisions. But once a decision is made, executives and managers must figure out how to influence the behavior of peers, subordinates, and superiors. Power and influence are how implementation is accomplished through mobilization of political support and resources. Both personal attributes (e.g., stamina and tolerance for conflict) and structural attributes (e.g., control of resources, access to information, and formal authority) are important.

Typical Ethical Issues: Some Examples

As noted in the introduction of this chapter, a complication for teaching ethical management of corporate power and politics is that each issue or example lies at the interface of ethics, politics, and leadership. This section provides a set of typical ethical issues arising in organizations and suggests various examples of either real or disguised situations suitable for student reading to highlight one or all of the dimensions of ethics, politics, or leadership. This set of issues and examples is selective rather than comprehensive. An instructor will need to pick which issues and examples to emphasize.

One typical issue concerns how the top leadership sets ethical standards for employees. Since power is essential in social life and politics ubiquitous in organizations, the important leadership task is to create a climate or culture of high standards for ethical behavior that is self-policing and self-perpetuating (Harvard Business Essentials 2005). Unless the political climate in an organization is positive, power can be corrupting and politics can be negative. A recent example of this toxic combination is Siemens' culture of corruption reportedly practiced on a worldwide basis through multiple subsidiaries and agents (Schubert and Miller 2008). Baron (2008) provides a case suitable for students. The case shows how corruption can become pervasive within a corporation and was in effect fostered by the leadership.

Another typical issue concerns how a chief executive officer (CEO) or other manager can destroy subordinates through self-interested choices ignoring the consequences for others. Position provides power and authority. As an example, Jackall (1983, 126–7) reports on an unethical maneuver by a new CEO that ultimately drove out a vice president. The firm operated a storage depot for natural gas. Prior to the energy crisis of that period, the firm accepted a long-term contract to supply gas at a price that turned out to be about one-tenth of the market price after the energy crisis. The depot was sold to another party, which assumed the existing contract; in exchange, the selling firm agreed to buy gas from the other party at high prices to cover its own energy requirements. This rearrangement transferred the cost problem from capital accounts to operating expenses. While the CEO could project an image of asset-reduction to Wall Street, one of the firm's businesses was stuck with the operating costs following an internal reorganization. The unit's earnings fell dramatically, and ultimately the vice president in charge left the firm although not responsible for the situation. There is a useful body of literature on the ethics of organizational power and politics (Messick and Ohme 1998).

The key normative theorizing was published by three authors working jointly (Cavanagh, Moberg, and Velasquez 1981; Velasquez, Moberg, and Cavanagh 1983) and then extended by Moberg (2000, 2008; see also Caldwell and Moberg 2007). Provis (2004, 2006) and Darley, Messick, and Tyler (2001) provide comprehensive coverage of organizational politics and ethics.

In order to understand issues and examples, a student should acquire some grasp of the basics of ethical analysis. An explicit introduction to ethical analysis in relationship to power and politics is available in Cavanagh, Moberg, and Velasquez (1981). Those authors argue that management theory emphasizes outcomes while ethical constraints emphasize means—as different value propositions. They provide a normative model of ethical analysis in the form of a decision tree for incorporating ethics into political decisions (see Figure 1, 368). The model integrates three basic ethical frameworks. Utilitarianism theories evaluate behavior against social outcomes: group or social welfare is more important than individual welfare. Rights theories evaluate behavior in relationship to entitlements of individuals. Justice theories evaluate behavior against distributional effects among individuals. The model facilitates the assessment of particular political strategies and tactics against various kinds of consequences. Three major categories of ethical frameworks are consequentialism (of which utilitarianism is a major instance), duties (or Kantianism), and pluralism (under which fall religious beliefs, moral intuition, and virtue theories) (Burton, Dunn, and Goldsby 2006). A typical example concerns how the founder and head of Satyam, an important Indian company, engaged in a variety of steps that undermined corporate governance at that company and ultimately resulted in its seizure by the Indian government (Bhasin 2013). The founder, who issued a letter of explanation reprinted in the Bhasin article, had the power to effect these steps. The application of the Cavanagh, Moberg, and Velasquez's model is to ask the student to analyze how the Satyam head may have thought about or not even considered the social outcomes, individual rights, and distributive justice effects of the choices made that accumulated into a massive accounting fraud. Thus, the student can study the conditions, the steps, and the ethical analysis in this company.

A set of typical examples arise in virtually all organizational decisions across a wide range of possibilities. A *political arena* occurs whenever managers decide to influence an organizational issue involving uncertainty or conflict (Velasquez, Moberg, and Cavanagh 1983). Many issues are of this nature, separating broadly into at least resource allocation (budgeting and capital allocation), change management (reorganization and strategy redefinition), and personnel matters (promotion, demotion, and separation). As these authors point out, a *game* metaphor (i.e., organizational politics is a zero-sum game with winners and losers), while superficially applicable (Hofstede [1968] 1984; Phipps and Gautrey 2005), fails because there are not adequately specified *rules* of conduct (what means are permitted and prohibited). Firms tend to be silent on rules for influence. A game involves players, strategies, outcomes, and rules. These authors distinguish between dirty politics and organizational statesmanship. The difference lies in whether the organizational politician adheres to ethical principles. Dirty politics, negative and dysfunctional, results in reduction of organizational welfare, harm to individuals, and unfair treatment of individuals. Blazejewski and Dorow (2003) provide a detailed case study of ethics, politics, and leadership in radical change management at Beiersdorf-Lechia S.A. in Poland. All the elements of an example of organizational issue are present in this example.

There is a growing empirical literature on the ethics of organizational politics (Chang, Rosen, and Levy 2009; Darr and Johns 2004; Maslyn and Fedor 1998; Miller, Rutherford, and Kolodinsky 2008; Vigoda 2003; Vigoda and Cohen 2002). A very typical issue involves perceptions and skills. Several different kinds of examples are worth considering for selection. One typical example concerns supervisor–subordinate relationships. A study (Kacmar et al. 2013) investigated 136 pairs of supervisors and subordinates in a state agency (located in the southern United States). They found that reported perceptions of organizational politics mediated the relationship between perceptions of ethical leadership and ratings for helping and promotability. The relationship was in turn moderated by political skill. Basically, ethical leadership and political skill improved ratings for helping (of subordinates by supervisors) and promotability. Another typical example concerns team functioning (and many students will work in teams). A study (Pitesa and Thau 2013), using both experimental and field methods, found that power makes individuals more self-focused and thus more likely to act upon preferences while ignoring social influences (ethical and unethical). The findings converge across informational influence, normative influence, and compliance. Studies of teams suggest that heightened power of formal position leaders reduces team communication and team performance in undesirable ways (Tost, Gino, and Larrick 2013). Another typical example is the arrival of a new manager or executive. Studies of capital budgeting find definite evidence of political influence (Cremers, Huang, and Sautner 2011; Han, Hirshleifer, and Persons 2009) including that new insider CEOs increase capital funding of other parts of a company to garner political support (Xuan 2009).

Jackall (1983, 1988) characterizes the corporate world for managers as one of difficult *moral mazes*. This important field study (Jackall 1983) found that beyond a certain level within an organizational hierarchy managers assumed roughly equal competence. At that level, "success is socially defined and distributed" in ways contingent upon authority, political alignments (or fealty structure), and the corporation's ethos and style (Jackall 1983, 122). Social considerations greatly outweighed competence considerations. The 1983 article is a good summary and suitable for student reading.

Mentoring is a typical example of how ethics advice and political advice are or are not transferred by leadership to subordinates. Moberg (2008) examined mentoring as a natural setting for senior employees to provide ethics advice to junior employees. Using four different measures of practical wisdom, the author did not detect differences between senior and junior employees—suggesting that ethics advice is likely not transferred. However, the author did find senior employees to be more politically skilled.

Ethics Teaching Strategy

The strategy for teaching the ethics of power and politics involves combining basic readings with illustrative cases for discussion. The topic lies at the overlap of three topics: business or professional ethics, power and politics, and leadership. The instructor should blend the three topics through the selection of basic readings and illustrative cases.

Basic readings should guide students through a comparison of negative and positive politics, as well as the relations among politics, ethics, and leadership topics. The illustrative cases should help students discuss ethical issues in power and political situations.

An important point for students to understand is that Machiavelli's *The Prince* is not intended to be a Renaissance manual of political misconduct but rather a manual for the detection of such political misconduct (1980, xv–xvi) for self-protection (Buchanan 2008; McIntyre 2005; Phipps and Gautrey 2005; Scott and Zaretsky 2013). The expression "*the end justifies the means*" is commonly associated with so-called Machiavellianism (Buskirk 1974; Jay 1968; Lord 2003; McAlpine 1999), although formally the expression also conveys the essence of amoral consequentialism: Ends are ultimately more important than means. Technically, what Machiavelli wrote can be translated as *"And with respect to all human actions, and especially those of princes where there is no judge to whom to appeal, one looks to the end"* (1980, 109, in Chapter 18). In *The Prince*, Chapter 18, "In What Mode Princes Ought to Keep Faith," is the closest exposition of such practice, citing Pope Alexander VI, Rodrigo Borgia, father of Cesare Borgia, as a deceiver. Values and duties are constraints on amoral consequentialism. The essence of *Machiavellianism* is amoral realism in a ruthlessly competitive setting in which politics is warfare (Galie and Bopst 2006; Pitney 2000).

There is a vital difference between *realism* as understanding and *realpolitik* as ruthless practice (McAlpine 2000). Good counterpoints to Machiavellianism are to discuss Abraham Lincoln and Nelson Mandela as realists—who had quite a different conception of political conduct (Lee 1998). Phillips (1992) provides a detailed exposition of Lincoln's tactics for communication and persuasion. Burns (1978) introduced the modern theory of positive leadership. Politicians are good at the social skills of understanding and persuading people (Fentress 2000, 149–50, makes a comparison to mafia bosses in this regard). This teaching strategy may help students to think about good and bad examples of leadership and politics—with emphasis on the role of ethics in distinguishing such examples.

Teaching strategy then should focus on cases that illustrate key conditions in which power and politics will be key considerations. Some key possibilities are as follows. Change management (Blazejewski and Dorow 2003), empowerment (Argyris 1998), issue selling (Hamel 2000), organizational restructuring, personality clashes, policy differences, promotions (Carpenter, Matthews, and Schirm 2010; Münster 2007), and team building (Wetlaufer 1994) inherently involve politics and ethics. Strategy formulation and implementation inherently involve controversy and thus necessarily politics (Eisenhardt and Bourgeois 1988; Karnani 2008; Lewis 2002; Narayanan and Fahey 1982; Pettigrew 1977; Windsor 2010). There are relatively few cases that directly address office politics, much less ethics in office politics. Badaracco (1998) details three real cases of the ethical dimensions of organizational politics concerning tokenism, single parents, and the RU 486 abortion pill (at a French pharmaceutical firm).

- "Thomas Green" (Sasser and Beckham 2008) concerns a rapidly promoted marketing manager. Based on disagreements over work styles and market projections, his boss harshly criticizes Green. The latter thinks the sales goals set by the boss are *creative accounting* and grossly overstate the true market situation. Green becomes concerned that the boss is building a case for termination. Handling of the situation turns on Green's relationship with his boss's superior. At issue in the case is how to develop an ethical strategy for constructive conflict management and relationship building.
- "Donna Dubinsky and Apple Computer, Inc." (Jick and Gentile [1986] 2011), not disguised, concerns a disagreement that develops in 1985 between Steve Jobs (founder and chairman of Apple and then head of the Macintosh Division) and the distribution manager Donna Dubinsky (a Harvard MBA). Jobs suddenly proposed a new distribution process that would transfer much of that process into the Macintosh Division and effectively wreck the distribution unit. Dubinsky's reaction resulted in highly defensive and ultimately unsuccessful conflict. Part A of the case series ends with her threatened

resignation. At the heart of the case is whether Jobs' actions are consistent with the Apple values statement; and there is a power struggle brewing between Jobs and CEO John Sculley.
- "Amelia Rogers at Tassani Communications" (Hill and Conrad [1992] 1995) involves a conflict between an account manager and a creative director at an advertising agency in Chicago. The agency is engaged in transitioning from entrepreneurial to professional management. The marketing director of a client firm calls the account manager complaining about the creative director. This case involves client relations, managing relationships with peers and superiors, cross-departmental relationships, interpersonal conflicts, and creativity.

Advice for Teachers

Teaching ethics in relationship to organizational power and politics is a complex task. In part, as noted previously, the topic lies at the overlap of three topics: business or professional ethics, power and politics, and leadership. The instructor should have some working knowledge of all three topics. Students, other than experienced managers, tend to have relatively little knowledge, practical experience, or understanding of organizational power and politics—which is not the same thing as electoral or legislative politics. Students are likely to have specific views of ethics, varying from "business ethics is meaningless" to "the instructor's moral standards appear to be less stringent than the student's." Character is shaped by defining moments when managers (indeed all individuals) choose between right and wrong in specific circumstances (Badaracco 1998). Advice for teachers is to select one or more cases in which the student has the opportunity to appreciate defining moments for managers or other employees.

Developing Versus Developed Country Perspectives

There are differences in developing versus developed country perspectives concerning power and politics. These differences are of importance to domestic businesses and to multinational enterprises (MNEs) operating across countries. Many MNEs are headquartered in developed countries but operate in various developing countries. The internal decision process of MNEs has been characterized as highly political (Bouquet and Birkinshaw 2008): "Managers of today's multinationals are not so much economic decision makers as they are governors of a social and political strategic management process" (Bower and Doz 1979, 165).

Pfeffer (2013) argues that power is a constant across time and contexts. An alternative view is that culture may influence individuals' views of corporate power and politics in organizations. For instance, there may be more tolerance for and practice of negative politics in some cultures; and greater preference for and practice of positive politics in other cultures. These views and conditions will affect ethical management of power and politics in particular organizations.

The most comprehensive and continuing study of leadership and culture is the GLOBE (Global Leadership and Organizational Behavior Effectiveness) project begun in 1991, which studies 62 cultures or societies (Chhokar, Brodbek, and House 2008). GLOBE researchers suggest there are 10 global cultures grouped according to similarities in cultural beliefs and values.

Hofstede (2006) has been critical of some GLOBE findings. A key research finding concerns what Hofstede called *power distance*—basically the extent to which members of a given society or organization accept that power in institutions and organizations is distributed unequally. Hofstede originally proposed five dimensions of culture: power distance index, individualism versus collectivism, gender roles (masculinity versus femininity), uncertainty avoidance index, and long-term versus short-term orientation. The GLOBE project has suggested nine cultural competencies: performance orientation, assertiveness orientation, future orientation, human orientation, institutional collectivism, in-group collectivism, gender egalitarianism, and power distance. There is some overlap in the Hofstede and GLOBE classifications.

Some of these categories arguably influence the perceptions and practice of organizational power and politics in culturally contingent ways. In very general terms (there are variations within developed and developing country categories), developing countries tend to be more hierarchical (i.e., more accepting of power distance and inequality), more inclined to avoid uncertainty and ambiguity, and more group oriented (see Hofstede

1980). Developed countries (low power distance) tend to prefer participative leadership and developing countries (high power distance) to accept and tolerate autocratic leadership. There are significant implications for the teaching of ethical management. In developing countries, managers and other employees may defer to unethical orders and subordinate personal values to group loyalty. Corruption may tend to be promoted as a result. In developed countries, managers and other employees may act more on their own initiative to be unethical or be less tolerant of corruption in others.

Summary and Conclusion

The chapter is structured into sections following the introduction that address in sequence the description of the discipline; typical ethical issues, with examples; ethics teaching strategy; advice for teachers; and developing versus developed country perspectives. Immediately following this final text section, there is a set of suggested exercises and projects, and then a bibliography of relevant materials.

A vital and understudied aspect of organizational power and politics is the role of ethics. There is a large literature on office politics, but much of this literature is shaped by a Machiavellian orientation and a concern for identifying winning strategies and tactics. Corporate codes of conduct are essentially silent on politics and interpersonal networks, other than to require high standards of personal and professional behavior—not specified in any detail. The references for this chapter identify as much of the relevant literature as possible so that teachers and students can explore. Politics in organizations is ubiquitous and desirable in the forms of legitimate authority and morally shaped influence. There are two modes of organizational politics. Negative or dysfunctional politics is caused by self-interested maneuvering for advantage by individuals and units without regard for the consequences to organizational and social welfare. Understanding negative politics is essential for self-protection. Leadership should foster a climate or culture of positive or functional politics focused on open, honest discussion of issues for the improvement of organizational and social welfare.

Suggested Exercises and Projects

Diagramming Informal Networks in the Company

The formal organizational chart of a company is different from the *informal organization* of complex networks of interpersonal relationships both within and crossing functional and subunit boundaries (Krackhardt and Hanson 1993). Those authors recommend diagramming three types of informal organizations:

1. The *advice network* comprises the people to whom you would turn to get work accomplished: people whose advice you would seek.
2. The *trust network* comprises the people with whom you would share delicate information: people with whom you trust such information. Trust involves an ethics dimension.
3. The *communication network* documents the people with whom you talk about work matters.

The authors propose that managers can increase power to accomplish work by diagramming these three types of informal networks. The networks can concern business matters or office politics. The networks will change over time. Position may be more important than personal attributes in whether an individual possesses power (Kanter 1979).

For teaching ethical management of corporate power and politics, the exercise should emphasize how personal relationships depend on perceived reciprocity and honesty. Members of informal networks in organizations emphasizing positive politics are likely to value ethical behavior and avoid individuals who have a reputation for unethical behavior. Trust is a key consideration in informal networks within organizations because such networks are voluntary. Discussion should emphasize how to establish and maintain informal networks through reputation for trustworthiness and reciprocity.

Change Management Simulation Illustrating Power and Influence

Judge and Hill (2013) developed a single-player simulation illustrating exercise of power and influence in a change management setting. "Spectrum Sunglass Co." manufactures sunglasses. For purposes of the simulation, the company has 20 relevant managers, including the CEO. A player assumes the role of either the CEO or the director of product innovation. There are various scenarios in which each role can be played. The CEO or the director of product innovation wants to mobilize sufficient support (i.e., a critical mass of managers) for a new sustainability initiative. The initiative is to change raw material inputs so as to make the company's products more *green* and to address environmental waste. The time available for the critical mass to be reached is 96 weeks. Each week, the player selects levers (i.e., actions) and targets (i.e., managers to be influenced). The simulation evolves through mobilization, movement, and sustainable phases defined by number of adopters supporting the initiative. The player can obtain information about the professional and personal networks of managers. A player is assessed in terms of two dimensions: credibility and change efficiency ratio (measured as number of adopters per week). The faster the change occurs from mobilization to sustainability, the greater the credibility and change efficiency ratio of the players. A preview video is available at http://hbsp.harvard.edu/list/4345-demo-page-basic (viewed on December 26, 2013).

This exercise emphasizes credibility and change efficiency in attracting support. For teaching ethical management of corporate power and politics, the key dimension concerns how credibility may rest on reputation for reciprocity and trustworthiness. Discussion should delve into the organizational conditions that support ethical versus unethical behavior in change management.

Simplified Capital Allocation Role-Play Exercise

An explication of the role-play exercise termed "The New Truck Dilemma" (Maier, Solem, and Maier 1975) is available in Efraty and

Stratton (1995). The setting for the exercise is a telephone company work group consisting of a supervisor and five repair employees. Each repair employee uses an assigned small truck to drive to locations around a city. The work group will receive a new truck to be assigned to one of the repair employees. The supervisor is instructed to make a fair decision concerning this assignment and told to put the decision to the group without taking a position. This group decision process is thus an instance of empowerment, which is not well understood (Argyris 1998). (There is information that the group has not been satisfied with past decisions of the supervisor.) Thus, fairness is to be determined by the group in some way. Each repair employee can make arguments concerning why he or she should receive the new truck. (In the role-play exercise, a seventh person acts as observer.) The variant of this role-play exercise included in Efraty and Stratton (1995) provides the following information for each repair employee: age (all different), seniority of employment with the telephone company (all different), and type and age of current vehicle (in combination, all different). In this variant, the youngest and most junior employee has the oldest vehicle, as does the next older but second most senior employee; the oldest and most senior employee has the newest vehicle. The specific information can be shuffled about among the group members for different scenarios.

Employee
Age
Seniority
Make of Vehicle
Age of Vehicle

For teaching ethical management of corporate power and politics, the key consideration is the perception of fairness. The supervisor is to make a fair decision through putting the decision to the group without influencing the outcome. The class can discuss the meaning of fairness and how the group may come to a consensus about this meaning. Variable scenarios may help students appreciate how fairness may be viewed by different individuals in a group.

References

Alvarez, J.L. 2012. "Educating Contemporary Princes and Princesses for Power." In *The Handbook for Teaching Leadership: Knowing, Doing, and Being*, eds. S. Snook, N. Nohria, and R. Khurana, 47–62. Thousand Oaks, CA: Sage Publications.

Argyris, C. May–June, 1998. "Empowerment: The Emperor's New Clothes." *Harvard Business Review* 76, no. 3, pp. 98–105.

Badaracco, J.L. March–April, 1998. "The Discipline of Building Character." *Harvard Business Review* 76, no. 2, pp. 114–24.

Baron, D.P. 2008. *Siemens: Anatomy of Bribery*. Stanford, CA: Stanford Graduate School of Business Case P68.

Bhasin, M. 2013. "Corporate Accounting Scandal at Satyam: A Case Study of India's Enron." *European Journal of Business and Social Sciences* 1, no. 12, pp. 25–47.

Blazejewski, S., and W. Dorow. 2003. "Managing Organizational Politics for Radical Change: The Case of Beiersdorf-Lechia S.A., Poznan." *Journal of World Business* 38, no. 3, pp. 204–23.

Bouquet, C., and J. Birkinshaw. 2008. "Managing Power in the Multinational Corporation: How Low-Power Actors Gain Influence." *Journal of Management* 34, no. 3, pp. 477–508.

Bower, J.L., and Y. Doz. 1979. "Strategy Formulation: A Social and Political Process." In *Strategic Management: A New View of Business Policy and Planning*, eds. D.E. Schendel and C.W. Hofer, 152–66. Boston, MA: Little, Brown.

Bower, J.L., and M.W. Weinberg. 1988. "Statecraft, Strategy, and Corporate Leadership." *California Management Review* 30, no. 2, pp. 39–56.

Buchanan, D.A. 2008. "You Stab My Back, I'll Stab Yours: Management Experience and Perceptions of Organization Political Behaviour." *British Journal of Management* 19, no. 1, pp. 49–64.

Buchanan, D.A., and R.J. Badham. 2008. *Power, Politics, and Organizational Change: Winning the Turf Game*. 2nd ed. Los Angeles, CA: Sage.

Burns, J.M. 1978. *Leadership*. New York: Harper and Row.

Burton, B.K., C.P. Dunn, and M. Goldsby. 2006. "Moral Pluralism in Business Ethics Education: It Is About Time." *Journal of Management Education* 30, no. 1, pp. 90–105.

Buskirk, R.H. 1974. *Modern Management and Machiavelli*. Boston, MA: Cahners Books.

Caldwell, D.F., and D.J. Moberg. 2007. "An Exploratory Investigation of the Effect of Ethical Culture in Activating Moral Imagination." *Journal of Business Ethics* 73, no. 2, pp. 193–204.

Carpenter, J.P., P.H. Matthews, and J. Schirm. 2010. "Tournaments and Office Politics: Evidence from a Real Effort Experiment." *American Economic Review* 100, no. 1, pp. 504–17.

Cavanagh, G.F., D.J. Moberg, and M. Velasquez. 1981. "The Ethics of Organizational Politics." *Academy of Management Review* 6, no. 3, pp. 363–74.

Chang, C.-H., C.C. Rosen, and P.E. Levy. 2009. "The Relationship between Perceptions of Organizational Politics and Employee Attitudes, Strain, and Behavior: A Meta-Analytic Examination." *Academy of Management Journal* 52, no. 4, pp. 779–801.

Chhokar, J.S., F.C. Brodbek, and R.J. House, eds. 2008. *Culture and Leadership across the World*. Hillsdale, NJ: Lawrence Erlbaum Associates.

Cohen, A.R., and D.L. Bradford. 2005. *Influence without Authority*. 2nd ed. Hoboken, NJ: Wiley.

Cremers, M., R.R. Huang, and Z. Sautner. 2011. "Internal Capital Markets and Corporate Politics in a Banking Group." *Review of Financial Studies* 24, no. 2, pp. 358–401.

Crozier, M. 1964. *The Bureaucratic Phenomenon*. Chicago, IL: University of Chicago Press.

Dahl, R.A. 1957. "The Concept of Power." *Behavioral Science* 2, no. 3, pp. 201–15.

Darley, J.M., D.M. Messick, and T.R. Tyler, eds. 2001. *Social Influences on Ethical Behavior in Organizations*. Mahwah, NJ: Lawrence Erlbaum.

Darr, W., and G. Johns. 2004. "Political Decision-Making Climates: Theoretical Processes and Multi-Level Antecedents." *Human Relations* 57, no. 2, pp. 169–200.

Deloitte Corporate Governance Services. 2005. Suggested Guidelines for Writing a Code of Ethics/Conduct. http://www.corpgov.deloitte.com/binary/com.epicentric.contentmanagement.servlet.ContentDeliveryServlet/USEng/Documents/Board%20Governance/Ethics%20and%20Compliance/932_SuggestedGuidelinesWritingCodeEthicsConduct0805.pdf (accessed July 27, 2014).

Dillon, K. 2013. *HBR Guide to Office Politics*. Boston, MA: Harvard Business Press Books.

Dubrin, A.J. 2001. *Leadership*. 3rd ed. New York: Houghton Mifflin.

Efraty, D., and W.E. Stratton. 1995. "Leadership and Empowerment: An Experiential Exercise in Decision-Making." *Developments in Business Simulation and Experiential Exercises* 22, pp. 268–9.

Eisenhardt, K.M., and L.J. Bourgeois. 1988. "Politics of Strategic Decision Making: Toward a Mid-range Theory." *Academy of Management Journal* 31, no. 4, 737–70.

Fentress, J. 2000. *Rebels and Mafiosi: Death in a Sicilian Landscape.* Ithaca, NY: Cornell University Press.

Fisher, A. November 29, 2007. Play Office Politics without Getting Dirty. CNNMoney. http://money.cnn.com/2007/11/29/news/economy/politics.fortune/ (accessed December 27, 2013).

Friedrich, C.J. 1963. "Influence and the Rule of Anticipated Reactions." In *Man and His Government: An Empirical Theory of Politics*, 199–215. New York: McGraw-Hill.

Galie, P.J., and C.B. Bopst. 2006. "Machiavelli and Modern Business: Realist Thought in Contemporary Corporate Leadership Manuals." *Journal of Business Ethics* 65, no. 3, pp. 235–50.

Gandz, J., and V.V. Murray. 1980. "The Experience of Workplace Politics." *Academy of Management Journal* 23, no. 2, pp. 237–51.

Hamel, G. July–August, 2000. "Waking Up IBM: How a Gang of Unlikely Rebels Transformed Big Blue." *Harvard Business Review* 78, no. 4, pp. 137–46.

Han, B.D., A. Hirshleifer, and J.C. Persons. 2009. "Promotion Tournaments and Capital Rationing." *Review of Financial Studies* 22, no. 1, 219–55.

Harvard Business Essentials. 2005. *Power, Influence and Persuasion: Sell Your Ideas and Make Things Happen.* Boston, MA: Harvard Business School Press.

Harvard Business Press, comp. 2006. *The Essentials of Power, Influence, and Persuasion (Business Literacy for HR Professionals).* Boston, MA: Harvard Business School Press.

Hay, C. 1997. "Divided by a Common Language: Political Theory and the Concept of Power." *Politics* 17, no. 1, pp. 45–52.

Hayes, J. 1984. "The Politically Competent Manager." *Journal of General Management* 10, no. 1, pp. 24–33.

Hill, L.A. 2003. *Becoming a Manager: How New Managers Master the Challenges of Leadership.* 2nd ed. Boston, MA: Harvard Business School Press.

Hill, L.A., and K. Lineback. 2011. *Being the Boss: The 3 Imperatives for Becoming a Great Leader.* Boston, MA: Harvard Business Review Press.

Hill, L.A., and M.B. Conrad. (February, 1992) March, 1995. "Amelia Rogers at Tassani Communications." Boston, MA: Harvard Business School Case.

Hofstede, G. 1980. "Motivation, Leadership, and Organization: Do American Theories Apply Abroad?" *Organizational Dynamics* 9, no. 1, pp. 42–63.

Hofstede, G. (1968) 1984. *The Game of Budget Control.* London, UK: Tavistock. Reprint, New York: Garland.

Hofstede, G. 2006. "What Did GLOBE Really Measure? Researchers' Minds Versus Respondents' Minds." *Journal of International Business Studies* 37, no. 6, pp. 882–96.

Inderst, R., H.M. Mueller, and K. Warneryd. 2007. "Distributional Conflict in Organizations." *European Economic Review* 51, no. 2, pp. 385–402.

Jackall, R. September–October, 1983. "Moral Mazes: Bureaucracy and Managerial Work." *Harvard Business Review* 61, no. 5, pp. 118–30.

Jackall, R. 1988. *Moral Mazes: The World of Corporate Managers*. New York: Oxford University Press.

Jay, A. 1968. *Management and Machiavelli, An Inquiry into the Politics of Corporate Life*. New York: Holt, Rinehart and Winston.

Jick, T.D., and M.C. Gentile. (February, 1986) September, 2011. "Donna Dubinsky and Apple Computer, Inc." Boston, MA: Harvard Business School Case.

Judge, W.Q., and L.A. Hill. 2013. "Change Management Simulation: Power and Influence V2." *Harvard Business School Simulation*. http://hbsp.harvard.edu/list/4345-demo-page-basic (accessed December 26, 2013).

Kacmar, K.M., M.C. Andrews, K.J. Harris, and B.J. Tepper. 2013. "Ethical Leadership and Subordinate Outcomes: The Mediating Role of Organizational Politics and the Moderating Role of Political Skill." *Journal of Business Ethics* 115, no. 1, pp. 33–44.

Kanter, R. July–August, 1979. "Power Failure in Management Circuits." *Harvard Business Review* 57, no. 4, pp. 65–75.

Karnani, A.G. 2008. "Controversy: The Essence of Strategy." *Business Strategy Review* 18, no. 4, 28–34.

Klein, J.I. 1988. "The Myth of the Corporate Political Jungle: Politicization as a Political Strategy." *Journal of Management Studies* 25, no. 1, pp. 1–12.

Kotter, J.P. 1985. *Power and Influence*. New York: Free Press.

Krackhardt, D., and J.R. Hanson. July–August, 1993. "Informal Networks: The Company Behind the Chart." *Harvard Business Review* 71, no. 4, pp. 104–11.

Lee, B. 1998. *The Power Principle: Influence with Honor*. New York: Simon and Schuster.

Lewis, D. 2002. "The Place of Organizational Politics in Strategic Change." *Strategic Change* 11, no. 1, pp. 25–34.

Lord, C. 2003. *The Modern Prince*. New Haven, CT: Yale University Press.

Machiavelli, N. 1980. *The Prince*. "Introduction." by translator L.P.S. De Alvarez. xi–xxxiv. Prospect Heights, IL: Waveland Press.

Maier, N.A.F., A.R. Solem, and A.A. Maier. 1975. *The Role Play Technique: A Handbook for Management and Leadership Practice*. La Jolla, CA: University Associates Inc.

Malhotra, D., and F. Gino. 2011. "The Pursuit of Power Corrupts: How Investing in Outside Options Motivates Opportunism in Relationships." *Administrative Science Quarterly* 56, no. 4, pp. 559–92.

Maslyn, J.M., and D.B. Fedor. 1998. "Perceptions of Politics: Does Measuring Different Foci Matter?" *Journal of Applied Psychology* 83, no. 4, pp. 645–53.

McAlpine, A. 1999. *The New Machiavelli: The Art of Politics in Business*. New York: Wiley.

McAlpine, A. 2000. "Renaissance Realpolitik for Modern Management." In *Machiavelli, Marketing and Management*, eds. P. Harris, A. Lock, and P. Rees. London, UK: Routledge, pp. 95–107.

McFarland, J. 2001. "Four Bulletproof Strategies for Handling Office Politics." *Harvard Management Update* Article U0105B.

McIntyre, M.G. 2005. *Secrets to Winning at Office Politics: How to Achieve Your Goals and Increase Your Influence at Work*. New York: St. Martin's Griffin.

Messick, D.M., and R.K. Ohme. 1998. "Some Ethical Aspects of the Social Psychology of Social Influence." In *Power and Influence in Organizations*, eds. R.M. Kramer and M.A. Neale, 181–202. Thousand Oaks, CA: Sage Publications.

Miller, B.K., M.A. Rutherford, and R.W. Kolodinsky. 2008. "Perceptions of Organizational Politics: A Meta-Analysis of Outcomes." *Journal of Business and Psychology* 22, no. 3, pp. 209–22.

Mintzberg, H. 1985. "The Organization as Political Arena." *Journal of Management Studies* 22, no. 2, 133–54.

Moberg, D.J. 2000. "Time Pressure and Ethical Decision-making: The Case for Moral Readiness." *Business and Professional Ethics Journal* 19, no. 2, pp. 41–67.

Moberg, D. 2008. "Mentoring and Practical Wisdom: Are Mentors Wiser or Just More Politically Skilled?" *Journal of Business Ethics* 83, no. 4, pp. 835–43.

Mudambi, R., and P. Navarra. 2004. "Divisional Power, Intra-firm Bargaining and Rent-seeking Behavior in Multidivisional Corporations." *Economics Bulletin* 4, no. 13, pp. 1–10.

Münster, J. 2007. "Selection Tournaments, Sabotage, and Participation." *Journal of Economics and Management Strategy* 16, no. 4, 943–70.

Narayanan, V.K., and L. Fahey. 1982. "The Micro-Politics of Strategy Formulation." *Academy of Management Review* 7, no. 1, pp. 25–34.

Pettigrew, A.M. 1973. *The Politics of Organizational Decision-Making*. London, UK: Tavistock.

Pettigrew, A.M. 1977. "Strategy Formulation as a Political Process." *International Studies of Management and Organization* 7, no. 2, pp. 78–87.

Pfeffer, J. 1992. *Managing with Power: Politics and Influence in Organizations*. Boston, MA: Harvard Business School Press.

Pfeffer, J. 2013. "You're Still the Same: Why Theories of Power Hold over Time and Across Contexts." *Academy of Management Perspectives* 27, no. 4, pp. 269–80.

Phillips, D.T. 1992. *Lincoln on Leadership: Executive Strategies for Tough Times*. New York: Warner Books.

Phipps, M., and C. Gautrey. 2005. *21 Dirty Tricks at Work: How to Beat the Game of Office Politics*. Chichester, UK: Capstone.

Pitesa, M., and S. Thau. 2013. "Compliant Sinners, Obstinate Saints: How Power and Self-Focus Determine the Effectiveness of Social Influences in Ethical Decision Making." *Academy of Management Journal* 56, no. 3, 635–58.

Pitney, J.J. 2000. *The Art of Political Warfare*. Norman, OK: University of Oklahoma Press.

Provis, C. 2004. *Ethics and Organisational Politics*. Cheltenham, UK: Edward Elgar.

Provis, C. 2006. "Organizational Politics, Definitions and Ethics." In *Handbook of Organizational Politics*, eds. E. Vigoda-Gadot and A. Drory, 89–106. Cheltenhem, UK: Edward Elgar.

Raven, B.H. 1990. "Political Applications of the Psychology of Interpersonal Influence and Social Power." *Political Psychology* 11, no. 3, pp. 493–520.

Reardon, K.K. 2001. *The Secret Handshake: Mastering the Politics of the Business Inner Circle*. New York: Currency.

Sasser, W.E., and H. Beckham. 2008. "Thomas Green: Power, Office Politics and a Career in Crisis." Boston, MA: Harvard Business School Case.

Schubert, S., and T.C. Miller. 2008. "At Siemens, Bribery Was Just a Line Item." *The New York Times*, December 20. http://www.nytimes.com/2008/12/21/business/worldbusiness/21siemens.html?pagewanted=alland_r=0> (accessed April 18, 2014).

Scott, J.T., and R. Zaretsky. 2013. "Why Machiavelli Still Matters." *The New York Times*, December 9. http://www.nytimes.com/2013/12/10/opinion/why-machiavelli-matters.html?adxnnl=1andsrc=meandadxnnlx=1388085709-HkkwhygQ8AicbOSsR3uoNg (accessed December 27, 2013).

Sussman, L., A.J. Adams, F.E. Kuzmits, and L.E. Raho. 2002. "Organizational Politics: Tactics, Channels, and Hierarchical Roles." *Journal of Business Ethics* 40, no. 4, pp. 313–29.

Tivey, L. 1978. *The Politics of the Firm*. New York: St. Martin's.

Tost, L.K., F. Gino, and R.P. Larrick. 2013. "When Power Makes Others Speechless: The Negative Impact of Leader Power on Team Performance." *Academy of Management Journal* 56, no. 5, 1465–86.

Velasquez, M., D.J. Moberg, and G.F. Cavanagh. 1983. "Organizational Statesmanship and Dirty Politics: Ethical Guidelines for the Organizational Politician." *Organizational Dynamics* 12, no. 2, pp. 65–80.

Vigoda, E. 2003. *Developments in Organizational Politics: How Political Dynamics Affect Employee Performance in Modern Work Sites*. Cheltenham, UK: Edward Elgar.

Vigoda, E., and A. Cohen. 2002. "Influence Tactics and Perceptions of Organizational Politics: A Longitudinal Study." *Journal of Business Research* 55, no. 4, pp. 311–24.

Wetlaufer, S. November–December, 1994. "The Team that Wasn't." *Harvard Business Review* 72, no. 6, pp. 22–6.

Windsor, D. 2010. "The Politics of Strategy Process." In *Handbook of Research on Strategy Process,* eds. P. Mazzola and F.W. Kellermanns, 43–66. Cheltenham, UK: Edward Elgar.

Xuan, Y. 2009. "Empire-Building or Bridge-Building? Evidence from New CEOs' Internal Capital Allocation Decisions." *Review of Financial Studies* 22, no. 12, pp. 4919–48.

Yukl, G. 1998. *Leadership in Organizations.* Upper Saddle River, NJ: Prentice Hall.

CHAPTER 16

Ethical Dimensions of Community and Investor Relations Communication and Governance for Sustainable Management

Judith Y. Weisinger and Edward L. Quevedo

Lokey Graduate School of Business, Mills College

We need to change the terms of the conversation, to make room for a larger and more public discussion about the purpose of the corporation and larger moral and political considerations. Every corporation is embedded in a social matrix, and is accountable for multiple factors within that social setting....In a democratic society...the general public expects responsible and ethical practices and the exercise of self-restraint among business leaders in exchange for vesting an extraordinary amount of power that affects society's wellbeing in private, corporate hands. Indeed, the primary problem in this perspective is the [problem of] agency, in which all the actors are trying to protect themselves from the self-interested actions of everyone else.
    —Jay Lorsch and Rakesh Khurana, *The Pay Problem*, Harvard Magazine, March–April 2014

Overview, Introduction, and Definition of the Discipline

Community and investor relations (respectively, CR and IR), and their ethical context, constitute some of the most mission-critical domains of corporate communications. Layering ethical considerations atop these challenges weaves a rich tapestry of opportunities for communications failure and lucrative terrain for breakthrough student learning about ethics in the context of enterprise leadership and management. A variety of management skills are invoked in addressing CR and IR, including risk assessment, crisis management, risk mitigation, relationship development, systemic and critical thinking, financial security, strategic framing, and brand management and development.

In the current management milieu, properly and effectively managing an ethical approach to CR and IR requires a heightened level of authenticity and acuity than previously. In a setting in which much more is expected of the enterprise by its various internal and external stakeholders, and when financial markets and investors are increasingly calling for environmental, social, and governance (ESG) data at a very granular and transparent level, the ethical implications of these forms of communication are rife with risk, opportunity for putting a foot wrong, and creating unintended adverse consequences for the enterprise, its leaders, and its stakeholders.

CR refers to "the relationship that a company, organization, etc. has with the people who live in the area in which it operates" (*Cambridge Dictionary* 2014). IR is defined by the U.S. National Investor Relations institute as "a strategic management responsibility that integrates finance, communication, marketing and securities law compliance to enable the most effective two-way communication between a company, the financial community, and other constituencies, which ultimately contributes to a company's securities achieving fair valuation."[1] *Investor relations* is similarly defined in the United Kingdom as "the communication of information and insight between a company and the investment community. This process enables a full appreciation of the company's

---

[1] http://www.niri.org/FunctionalMenu/About.aspx

business activities, strategy and prospects and allows the market to make an informed judgment about the fair value and appropriate ownership of a company."[2]

In considering the ethical implications of communications about IR and CR, the emergent concept of *radical transparency* (RT) (Smith and Tabibnia 2012) provides one guidepost in grappling with constructing communications and engaging stakeholders. RT contemplates an approximation of one dimension of neo-classical economic theory, *perfect information*. As we are seeing RT practiced, it refers to efforts made by the enterprise to ensure that "all stakeholders knowing everything in relation to the enterprise at the same time, in 'real-time.'"

Ethical issues involving CR and IR arise in part as a consequence of conventional business operational and strategic issues, and from new, emergent patterns of expectations and obligations of business that are only now beginning to be understood. Classically, businesses must communicate effectively with communities on transitional and transactional issues (e.g., corporate expansion, new site development, mergers and acquisition activity, risk and crisis management) and with investors on governance and financial development issues (e.g., changes in securitization and financial instrument management, marketplace performance, periodic financial reporting, management and governance transitions, entry into new markets). As noted, these conventional communications are influenced by current trends in responsible management.

Responsible management frameworks, and so-called sustainable business practices, or sustainable management, are increasingly expected to be part of the everyday toolkit of the leader and manager. These frameworks can also guide the manager or leader undertaking to act ethically in the context of IR and CR communications. In the words of three respected scholars concluding a recent study:

> One theme that ran consistently through our findings was that requirements for all the C-level jobs have shifted toward business acumen and *"softer" leadership skills*. Technical skills are merely a

---

[2] http://www.irs.org.uk/about/definition-of-investor-relations

starting point, the bare minimum. To thrive as a C-level executive, an individual needs to be a *good communicator, a collaborator, and a strategic thinker.* (Kelly and MacDonald 2011; emphasis in original)

These domains inform the ethics of CR and IR through the lens of RT, which we believe provides a useful filter for evaluating CR and IR as species of ethical decision making.

Within the context of responsible management, communication with, and effective engagement of the community and investors is a lucrative area for teaching and learning about ethics as a result of several factors, including the diverse and rich ethical issues involved; the changing dynamics of stakeholder expectations that offer fertile ground for teaching that is exceptionally current and challenging; the multidisciplinary cross-cutting nature of these dilemmas and responses; and the unique opportunities to advance the assessment of learning outcomes and (where desired) clinical and applied learning experiences.

A few further words about our intentions for use of this chapter and its integration into the management curriculum follow. CR and IR are somewhat advanced concepts in the panoply of management and communication domains. The ethical dilemmas they frame require a nuanced set understanding of the stakeholder concept. We therefore recommend that this chapter be used to inform a business ethics, leadership, sustainable management, responsible business, or similar course in the latter half of the management curriculum.

We have also labored to design this chapter as the basis for architecting an entire course syllabus, if the instructor should wish. But we have also striven to modularize our approach so the elements of the chapter can be used to inform and optimize existing elements of an existing syllabus.

According to Hurst (2004, 6), "Business ethics is a form of applied ethics. It aims at inculcating a sense within an organization's employee population of how to conduct business responsibly." We would add to this notion that ethics informs the making of decisions within a systems context, taking into account a diverse set of interests and expectations, going far beyond profit motives and satisfying the demands of shareholder value. Hurst also makes the point that "[b]ecause the term 'ethics' can pose problems in an international context, i.e., the term does not translate well and it can be difficult to find a common understanding of the term, some organizations choose to recast the concept of business ethics through such other terms as integrity, business practices or responsible business conduct" (6). In our estimation, ethical IR and CR communications is an element of effective and disciplined governance, requiring the application of ethical frameworks to support good outcomes.

We operate with the view that those enterprises practicing RT communicate that they value broad, deep, and authentic information sharing as an expression of the values, philosophy, and vision of the business. When faced with a crisis, the temptation to omit a difficult piece of information, or a retrenchment in the direction of the enterprise away from a culture of openness and radical information sharing (consistent with law, policy, and other corporate guidance, of course) effects a counterweight to avoid the higher road of ethical action. Building management discipline, through modeling leadership, education programs, and clear enterprise vision and values, which constitute essential sideboards to keep to an ethical course, is essential to effective and praiseworthy ethical practices, and ultimately fundamental to operating a business for long-term profitability.

Ethical IR and CR communications have also been influenced by the emergence of the Global Reporting Initiative (GRI).[3] The GRI Guidelines provide guidance for reporting and disclosure of economic, environmental, and social metrics considered as domains of performance reporting.

Typical Ethical Issues Concerning CR and IR

Complexities and nuances in the ethics of CR and IR beyond legal minimums involve broad areas of business decision making and disclosure. Increasingly, firms find that their reputational risk profile and stock value are at risk if their threshold of ethics is coextensive with legal minimums. For investor relations in particular, the emergence of blended value, shared value, benefit corporation models, and a demand for longer term financial thinking and strategy all contribute to mandating a higher level

---

[3] See www.globalreporting.org

of ethical attention to communications. As well, the immediacy of the Internet is remapping the terrain of external communications, including supply chain and value cycle considerations, environmental content issues, carbon emission and water consumption reporting and expectations, and related elements of the social license to operate.

To demonstrate some of the typical ethical issues involving CR and IR in sustainable management, we highlight here scenarios that demonstrate complex ethical business decisions that impact the organization, its employees, its investors, and the broader community.

Deepwater Horizon Oil Spill: BP

In January 2011, the White House Oil Spill Commission issued its final report on the BP Deepwater Horizon disaster in the Gulf of Mexico, which occurred in April 2010. The Commission concluded that:

> The immediate causes of the Macondo well blowout can be traced to a series of identifiable mistakes made by BP, Halliburton, and Transocean that reveal such systematic failures in risk management that they place in doubt the safety culture of the entire industry. (National Commission on BP Deepwater Horizon Oil Spill 2011, vii)

Media coverage of the Commission's report was rife with commentary about BP's bad management and poor communication, internally and with its partners—shortcomings that the report concludes led to the oil spill disaster.[4] As of one month after the spill, BP was blaming Transocean Ltd.—the owner of the oil drilling rig—for the disaster, and Transocean was also busy deflecting blame. While it is true that, as BP claimed, it owned the oil but not the rig, and thus was only responsible for cleaning up the oil, communications expert Larry Smith states that using such a

---

[4] http://www.theguardian.com/business/2010/dec/02/bp-oil-spill-failures; http://www.nbcnews.com/id/38818600/ns/disaster_in_the_gulf/t/oil-spill-investigators-focus-communication/#.Utby62Sgkx9; http://www.huffingtonpost.com/james-hoggan/bps-crisis-communications_b_609826.html

statement to deflect blame represents a "shoddy communications strategy."[5] From a sustainability perspective, BP's communication during the disaster should have sought to inform these constituencies (accurately) about the facts about the oil spill's magnitude and its socioeconomic and environmental impact, as well as potential effects on the organization's economic viability. Instead, BP focused on laying blame outside its doors.

In fact, BP ultimately released early information to the public that significantly underestimated the extent of the spill—stating that the rig was spilling 1,000 barrels of oil per day when the figure was actually closer to 5,000. BP also underestimated the oil spill's potential damaging effects to the environment. As a result, the community and investors were at various times ill-informed about the disaster. Further, a year after the disaster, BP investors—specifically, a coalition of socially responsible investors—were still frustrated at the lack of information from BP regarding how it had strengthened its risk management process as a result of the disaster:

> BP's recently released annual report provides shareholders with an insufficient level of detail to determine how the company's safety and risk management function has been strengthened; how it is being evaluated, managed, and mitigated; how the board will oversee it; and how progress is to be assessed and measured.[6]

Despite BP's efforts, and significant financial expenditure, the broader negative effects of the oil spill are manifest. New repercussions are continuing to emerge and scientists suggest that the true impact may not be seen for another 10 years. One of the most obvious results has been the impacts on wildlife. Only six months after the spill, more than 8,000 birds and marine animals were found dead. Many local fishermen struggled to make even close to the revenue they had in the past. In fact, one estimate suggests that "over seven years, the oil spill could have an $8.7 billion impact on the economy of the Gulf of Mexico including losses in

---

[5] http://www.slate.com/articles/news_and_politics/politics/2010/05/oil_slick.html

[6] http://www.ceres.org/press/press-releases/one-year-after-gulf-oil-spill-bp-facing-investor-frustration-over-lack-of-disclosure-on-risk-management

revenue, profit, wages, and close to 22,000 jobs" (see Kroh 2012). The tourism industry, which was once a great source of economic stimulus for the region, saw a dramatic decrease after the spill.

Against this backdrop, the question of where responsibility lies for the oil spill became nearly irrelevant. But this issue of causation, a highly nuanced and complex reality at best, guided much of BP's IR and CR communications during and following the crisis stage of events. This raises the need for reevaluation of how to consider the ethics of CR and IR in this context.

Without offering a prescription or advocating for a particular path toward communication, we can suggest a few central themes, reflecting an *ethical filter* model that we will build on later as context for ethical decision making:

- When communicating in the IR or CR context, the issue of the *truth* can be a minefield. Talking points, controlling the message, and staying on point are largely outmoded notions, and insofar as they represent anachronistic notions of *controlling the message*, they almost universally will lead to adverse consequences for the enterprise. An alternative could be a 360 degree approach to revealing facts to the extent they are known, and a general technique of *taking responsibility* and *being accountable*, rather than transferring responsibility. This can be done without creating unnecessary liability. Consider if BP had, for example, communicated that "our internal experts tell us this was not our fault alone, but we feel it is our fault, and we are going to act as though it was, and here is what we intend to do…." Acting from this frame could have diffused the situation and shifted the focus from dissembling over causation to a sense of common purpose in responding to the disaster.
- The simple filter of *fairness* can also be a tool in navigating the cross-currents of CR and IR in challenging contexts. Fairness can be thought of as a systemic idea: Is our communication fair for all stakeholders insofar as it with (a) not put some

at a disadvantage relative to others, (b) enable our various stakeholders to have useful conversations and collaborate to respond to the situation or condition about which we are communicating, and (c) tend to favor, if it must, the least advantaged and most vulnerable of our stakeholders first.
- Finally, notions of *credibility* and *trust* can be useful filters. It can be useful to ask about any form of CR or IR communication, "Will these words and the context we are providing build, reinforce, and strengthen our credibility and the trust with which we are regarded, or will they corrode, weaken, and deplete these critical forms of social capital?"

Rana Plaza Building Collapse: Bangladesh

Lessons also emerge from the Rana Plaza disaster.[7] In April 2013, the Rana Plaza commercial building collapsed in Savar, Bangladesh, killing over 1,000 workers and leaving 2,515 injured. Rana is the deadliest garment-factory accident in history, as well as the deadliest accidental structural failure in modern human history. The building contained clothing factories, a bank, apartments, and several other shops, including many factories operated by Western brands such as Wal-Mart, Benetton, and several others.

The shops and the bank on the lower floors immediately closed after cracks were discovered in the building the day before the disaster. Warnings to avoid using the building after cracks appeared were ignored, however, by garment factory supervisors. Garment workers were ordered to return the following day and the building collapsed during the morning rush hour. The Bangladesh Fire Service and Civil Defense Agency reported that the upper four floors, where the factories were located, had been built without a permit. The building's architect said the building was planned for shops and offices, not factories. Other architects stressed the risks involved in placing factories inside a building designed only for

---

[7] See, e.g., *A Deeper Look: Lessons from Rana Plaza* (2013), BSR Newswire; and Quelch and Rodriguez (2013).

shops and offices, noting the structure was potentially not strong enough to bear the weight and vibration of heavy machinery.

Remarkably, the Western brands involved denied any role or responsibility, placing blame on their subcontractors who actually operated the factories. This represents a classical failure to utilize an ethical communications framework such as the *filter* framework we offer earlier. In the short term, many of these brands were able to deflect attention from their duties to understand the operating practices of their subcontractors. But in the medium term, reputations were tarnished, stock value suffered, and the social license to operate was left in tatters.

There is also value in considering three-dimensional, or relational, issues in ethical communications regarding IR and CR issues. There is a line of scholarship relating to the humanistic principle of management that focuses on the interpersonal and *agency* implications of honesty and simple fair dealing in ethical communications.

In doing so, we pay homage to the work of Domènec Melé (*Business Ethics in Action* [2009]) and others in characterizing humanistic management as applied to ethical decision making. The dimensions of human dignity, ethical reflection, and normative legitimacy suffuse this school of thought and are worthy of consideration here.

Respect for human dignity lies at the foundation of much of the work being done today in seeking higher levels of corporate responsibility in general. Integrity and deep honesty in IR and CR communications accepts that some of the stakeholders involved are attenuated from the corporate center and are exposed or vulnerable in their decision making with ethical communication values compromised.

In the go-go fast-paced world of enterprise these days, reflection and intentionality is often sacrificed for expediency. In these short cuts lie the seeds of much that is often unethical about IR and CR communications. Reflective decision making, by contrast, mandates that the ethical leader turn the communications problem carefully in their hand, prism-like, and sedulously consider the implications and consequences of various forms of actions on the various constituencies affected. When profit maximization trumps other considerations, ethical action and fair communication is almost always compromised.

Finally, returning to considerations of governance, emergent legitimacy of leaders is always on the testing block. If legitimacy results from the consistent earning, and not taking for granted the presence, of the social license to operate, then this factor must help to define ethical decision making about IR and CR issues. It is patent that investors and community members may (both in times of crisis and otherwise) challenge the enterprise's conduct and decisions. The seeking of normative legitimacy can be an aid to the leader as she contemplates the *engagement* of this dialogue, rather than its avoidance.

In summary, responsible leaders must consider the *what*, *why*, *when*, and *how* of communication about ethical CR and IR issues:

What: Identify the ethical dimensions of the event about which one must communicate. For example, in the BP scenario, a key issue had to do with communicating as accurately as possible about (1) the extent of the spill, (2) responsibility for the cleanup, and (3) identifying affected stakeholders. The *what* dimension of these issues circulates around the context of the communication, and the patterns of communication that the organization wants to be known for delivering. That is, can we be holistically ethical even when doing so would require exposing ourselves to criticism from a variety of stakeholders?

Why: Define the purpose of the communication. Is it purely informational? Is it designed to mobilize action? Is it to allay fears about a follow-on event? Considering that any such communications invoke a continuing conversation, and not on-off responses or reactions, the *why* dimension relates to the nature and tenor of the conversation the leader and the organization wish to convene.

When: Determine the optimal timing of the communication. As well, consider the other communications issuing about the event or circumstance, and when in the flow of information the communication is best delivered. Considerations include, but are not limited to, the following: Is it important that our communication come early in the flow of information, and how does our communication shift or contribute to the evolving narrative about the event or circumstance?

How: Consider the best mode of communicating. Will a press release be the most effective, or should the leaders appear at a press conference? (Recall the detrimental effect on BP's image of its chief executive officer (CEO) Tony Hayward saying to millions of television viewers, "We're sorry for the massive disruption it's caused their lives. There's no one who wants this over more than I do. I would like my life back.") The variety of communication tools available to today's leaders argue for careful contextualization of communication, as noted earlier, as part of a continuing conversation. This approach permits the leader to effectively select among a portfolio of communication techniques, and to stage the communication in the larger context involved.

Ethics Teaching Strategy

Overview

Management scholars are far from any consensus on the best way to teach ethics in schools of business and management. For decades questions have been raised about teaching ethics, particularly in the wake of seemingly endless corporate ethics scandals. One fundamental question that is routinely asked is: "Can ethics be taught?" For those who believe that it can, the question then becomes "What should be taught?" which is quickly followed by "And who should teach it?" If the reply to the latter is that ethics should be taught by business school faculty, then the pedagogical debate often leads to: "Should there be a standalone ethics course (or courses)? Or should ethics be integrated throughout the MBA curriculum?"

The very existence of this book suggests that there is considerable agreement among management and business scholars and educators that ethics, or some form of it, can and should be an essential curricular element. This section is aimed at helping those who are teaching ethics as part the curriculum in business degree programs, either as an integrated part of a standalone nonethics course, or as a section of a dedicated ethics course.

We advocate a teaching strategy that includes ethics theory content, but that does not rely upon such content to provide students with a firm grounding in business ethics. Specifically, we advocate an approach that provides students with guidance and practice about what to *do* when faced with ethical dilemmas. Teaching ethics across a management curriculum is, in our experience, best accomplished in a cross-functional context in a way that builds nimbleness of mind, truth of heart, and allegiance to principles of RT and integrity in approaching ethical decision making. Clinical experiences, real-world learning, and application in practice are crucial modalities here as in other management disciplines.

Framing scenarios for students, role play exercises requiring students to respond in crisis mode to hypothetical real-world events, and emphasizing the often conflicting expectations of various members of civil society (e.g., stockholders' preference for obfuscation vs. the potential rights of workers and their families to something approaching RT) can illuminate these often murky waters.

Our teaching strategy encompasses the *what, when, why,* and *how* of teaching ethics involving CR and IR the context of sustainable management:

1. *What*: Provide an overview of various ethics theories, but more importantly, help students to understand (and practice) how to process decision making when faced with ethical dilemmas (e.g., in the face of conflicting priorities or stakeholder perspectives).
2. *When*: This teaching strategy can be effectively used in the ethics section of a management course, as part of a standalone ethics course, or as a guiding framework for an entire course in management. (Strategy, operations management, and marketing present more granular ethical issues; leadership courses can take a more holistic or systems perspective.)
3. *Why*: Focusing on practice with ethical decision making helps to avoid students' propensity to select theories to rationalize (even bad) behavior; it also builds among students a comfort level or nimbleness, as we referred to it earlier, with confronting and effectively dealing with ethics-based management decisions.

4. *How*: Teaching ethics effectively using this strategy—foundational theories and ethical decision-making applications—involves several components:
   (a) Consider the types of learners
   (b) Consider the course and program-learning outcomes
   (c) Consider which exercises and assignments are best suited to engaging students around the proposed content in a way that reinforces their skill and comfort level with processing ethical decision making

Further, the ethical filter model discussed earlier (considering concepts of truth, fairness, and credibility and trust) lends itself to a variety of different teaching modalities, about which we provide guidance here.

Teaching From Written Cases

We counsel caution when teaching with written cases. Too often, written ethics cases can focus on theoretical successful outcomes and utilize frameworks that do not provide the depth of reflection needed to build the nimbleness of mind and action-oriented ethical approach we recommend here.

> Some enrichment of teaching cases can, however, mitigate against these limitations. Prereadings in classical and modern ethics, drawn from Rawls, MacIntyre (*After Virtue*), and Nussbaum ("Non-Relative Virtues: An Aristotelian Approach") can provide context as they draw the student into a state of mind considering human interactions and the implications of ethical behavior and decision making in a context beyond the boundaries of the enterprise. This effectively encourages students to reflect on the rapidly evolving character of stakeholder expectations regarding ethical communications we have discussed here.
>
> Then, the instructor can take key quotes from the ethicists, positioning them around the classroom in a *studio setting*. Students can then be invited to *appreciate* the quotes, as though they were in an art gallery, and stroll among the quotes reflecting and generating discussion, and then sharing key insights with the entire class. This kinetic activity, combined with more systemic reflections, can render subsequent case-based teaching sessions far more lucrative and deep.

Teaching From Living Cases

Inviting executives from corporate communications and public relations functions, and public and investor relations professionals to discuss recent cases taken from the headlines (and there are these days far too many from which to draw), can provide a more lively discussion than case method. When combined with case teaching, live cases can present counter examples and contrary conclusions that can layer and make more nuanced students' command of ethical communications techniques.

> A useful outline for such a module could include the following:
>
> - The speaker reflecting on key experiences that forged their ethical communications framework
> - Laying out of the living case, giving context and factual details, but not presenting the substance of the requisite communication in question
> - Inviting students to adopt divergent stakeholder perspectives in considering the facts and context (e.g., pressure groups, community members, stock exchange representatives or other regulatory actors, employees), and testing the truth or fairness or credibility-trust considerations in framing responses
> - Convening to fashion a press release, or communication campaign, in response to the facts and context
> - Hearing from the speaker what was actually done in the instance of the living case

Teaching From "Worst Practices"

Teaching from *worst practice* is often an abundant source of teaching as failed scenarios of CR and IR communication demonstrate how quickly an initial misstep in ethical posture can snowball and take the enterprise and its representatives amiss. The BP case is a sound example, but such instances arise frequently in the media outlets accessible to faculty and students.

Our experience in teaching from worst practices illuminates the following method as one path to effective learning for CR and IR communication:

- Identify a recent and well-publicized example of poor practice, using journalistic sources. Characteristics of useful reporting include:
  - A variety of perspectives or responses or reactions to the events and communications reflected in the reporting
  - A variety of corporate communications, spanning either different executives or sources, and over a timeline traversing the evolving character of the events in question
  - Minimal editorializing by the journalistic author, leaving room for expansion of the frame for considering ethical dilemmas without pre-emption
  - A variety of adverse consequences, both to the enterprise and its stakeholders (as in the BP case discussed earlier)
- From this context, the instructor can strongly advocate for an alternative scenario from the approach taken by the enterprise reflected in the press account. This should, as we discuss elsewhere, be based on a framework approach. Students can then role play how this alternative scenario would be discussed in the confines of a closed door board meeting to consider alternatives, represented in a meeting with stock analysis, with pressure groups, and in a press conference, taking on and rotating various roles to explore the nuances of clear, open, and even periodically *radically transparent* communications on CR and IR issues.

Experiential and Clinical Teaching Modalities

Clinical and project-based teaching on ethical communications can create unique opportunities for students to have the embodied experience of grappling with CR and IR communications scenarios. Working for a period of time in the public relations department of a firm, or in a PR agency, with the supervision of involved faculty creating a bridge to curriculum, enables exploration of *real-time* crises, observation, and critical evaluation of how they are being handled by the sponsoring firm. It also offers an opportunity to reflect on the validity of the path taken, and alternative scenarios, in consultation with supervising faculty.

Advice for Teachers

In considering the foregoing discussion, we present the following advice for teachers:

1. Become familiar with the ethics theories that are generally presented in ethics books and texts. (A course or workshop on ethics will also be extremely helpful in building the instructor's comfort level with the various theories, and their interrelationships and historical contexts.)
2. Use an ethical decision-making framework that may draw upon such theories but that transcends the theories to provide practical guidance to students on assessing the implications of their proposed ethical decisions. For example, The Harvard Business School source (Paine 2007) in our references provides a framework and an action planning chart that gives students useful guidance on what to consider when faced with an ethical decision.
3. Where possible, highlight real-life ethics decisions through various avenues: (1) include *living cases* based upon the experiences of executive guest speakers who have confronted ethical dilemmas in their organizations, (2) dissect corporate case studies with complex ethical dimensions, pushing students to justify their proposed decisions using the relevant ethical decision-making framework, and (3) structure reflective learning opportunities for students to re-examine past ethical decisions they have faced.

Developing Versus Developed Country Perspectives

Cross-cultural considerations require attention in a world where all business is both local and global. For example, in the context of teaching the

Rana Plaza case, instructors can introduce the divergent nature of the social license to operate in geographies where a desperate need for work of any kind motivates workers to forsake their own safety for the well-being of their families. Ethical communication issues in many Horn of Africa countries must be filtered through considerations of the high expectations that nations such as Namibia and Botswana have cultures that embrace indigenous RT (Shaibu 2007).

In our view, ethical CR and IR practices cannot be effectively taught without discussions that span an evocative and informed cross-cultural exploration. In the words of one prominent scholar, "The greatest challenge facing leaders in this era of globalization is working effectively through cultural barriers to achieve business goals and objectives" (Wibbeke 2009).

Conclusions and Reflections

In the contemporary management environment, ethical CR and IR communications must be framed with an increased level of authenticity and acuity. Much more is expected of the enterprise by its community-based stakeholders. The evolving social license to operate requires a heightened willingness to trade the security of limited disclosure for the longer term return of trust-building and a reputation anchored in integrity.

We advocate a basic understanding of ethics theories for the informed instructor, in conjunction with knowledge of fertile ethical decision-making frameworks and the use of real-life scenarios. RT requires practice and contextualization for a student to internalize. In order to highlight some of the ethical issues that play out in CR and IR communications within a sustainable management framework, we present several scenarios—the BP Deepwater Horizon Oil Spill and the Rana Plaza Building Collapse. These scenarios help us to consider an *ethical filter* framework of ethical decision making that encourages decision makers to consider the concepts of truth, fairness, and credibility and trust when making decisions.

Finally, we suggest that those teaching ethics focus on practicing ethical decision making, particularly through the use of scenarios, role plays, and other kinetic activities, as well as through the use of living cases and *worst cases*, along with clinical and project-based work. Cross-cultural perspectives across developed versus developing countries can be integrated by considering the degree of integration of social responsibility and sustainable management across varying economic and social contexts.

References

Cambridge Dictionary. 2014. http://dictionary.cambridge/english.org/us/dictionary/american-english/ (accessed October 24)

Hurst, N.E. 2004. *Corporate Ethics, Governance and Social Responsibility: Comparing European Business Practices to Those in the United States.* Santa Clara, CA: Markkula Center for Applied Ethics, Santa Clara University.

Kelly, G., and H. MacDonald. March 2011. "The New Path to the C-Suite." *Harvard Magazine,* http://hbr.org/2011/03/the-new-path-to-the-c-suite/ar/1

Kroh, K. 2012. "Five Reasons We Can't Forget About the BP Oil Spill." http://thinkprogress.org/climate/2012/04/20/468361/five-reasons-we-cant-forget-about-the-bp-oil-disaster/# (accessed March 7, 2014).

Melé, D. 2009. *Business Ethics in Action: Seeking Human Excellence in Organizations.* New York: Palgrave Macmillan.

National Commission on the BP Deepwater Horizon Oil Spill and Offshore Drilling. 2011. Deepwater: The Gulf Oil Disaster and the Future of Offshore Drilling. Report to the President, Washington, DC.

Paine, L. 2007. "Ethics: A Basic Framework," Case no. 9-307-059. Cambridge, MA: Harvard Business School Publishing.

Quelch, J.A., and M.L. Rodriguez. 2013. "Rana Plaza: Workplace Safety in Bangladesh." *Harvard Business Review,* September.

Shaibu, S. July, 2007. "Ethical and Cultural Considerations in Informed Consent in Botswana." *Nursing Ethics* 14, no. 4, pp. 503–9.

Smith, R., and G. Tabibnia. October 11, 2012. "Why Radical Transparency Is Good Business." *Harvard Business Review Blog Network.* http://blogs.hbr.org/2012/10/why-radical-transparency-is-good-business/

Wibbeke, E.S. 2009. *Global Business Leadership.* Oxford, UK: Butterworth Heinemann.

Further Reading

Bell, S., and S. Morse. 2008. *Sustainability Indicators: Measuring the Immeasurable.* London, UK: Earthscan.

Dunphy, D., J. Benveniste, A. Griffiths, and P. Sutton, eds. 2000. *Sustainability: The Corporate Challenge of the 21st Century.* St. Leonards, Australia: Allen & Unwin.

Elkington, J. 1998. *Cannibals with Forks: The Triple Bottom Line of 21st Century Business*. British Columbia, Canada: New Society.

Laszlo, C. 2003. *The Sustainable Company: How to Create Lasting Value Through Social and Environmental Performance*. Washington, DC: Island Press.

Sandford, C. 2011. *The Responsible Business: Reimagining Sustainability & Success*. San Francisco, CA: Jossey-Bass.

Starik, M., and P. Kanashiro. 2013. 'Toward A Theory of Sustainable Management: Uncovering and Integrating the Nearly Obvious." *Organization & Environment* 26, no. 1, pp. 7–30.

Stead, W.E., and J.G. Stead. 2004. *Sustainable Strategic Management*. Armonk, New York: M. E. Sharpe.

CHAPTER 17

Future of Ethics Education in Management Curricula

Emeka Enwere and Uchenna Uzo

In light of the recent global economic meltdown and the actions that led to it, a lot questions are being asked. More and more people have lent their voice to the few who have for a while been questioning the value graduates of business schools bring to the business world. It is quite glaring that ethics as being taught in most business schools has failed to change the general attitude of managers in mainstream business. Shareholder maximization at all cost still holds sway and is yet to be tempered by the tenets of ethics. Educators of business and management continue to overemphasize profit maximization as the goal of business (Ghoshal Birkinshaw, and Piramal 2005) thus leading firms to pursue perpetual growth in a finite world with finite resources because they cannot afford to disappoint shareholders. The focus on this way of doing business by educators and firms has led to conflict of interest situations on Wall Street, the global financial crisis, corporate malfeasance, and polarization of wealth (Schoemaker 2008). Despite the welcoming news that the global economy is in on its way to full recovery, we will end up in the same predicament if nothing is done to educate businesses differently. In the face of these challenges and opportunities, there is no better time to ask: What can business educators do to improve on how ethics is taught as their institutions evolve for the future? Although previous work has dealt with this question, answers could be more compelling. This chapter argues that a humanistic perspective to business education could serve as a useful paradigm for educators seeking to improve their teaching of ethics. The discussion in the chapter is organized as follows: First it reviews the trends shaping the future of business educators, next it explains why the humanistic perspective matters for managing these trends, and then it offers a useful framework for the sustainable insertion of ethics into management curricular.

Future Trends

A number of trends are shaping the future of business educators. Studies suggest that the global rise of online education is providing students with more learning options (Kaliski 2007). Business educators now have to contend with engaging real time and continuously with students before, during, and after their education programs. Another important trend is the transition from generic program contents to more customized programs. An illustrative example is a Financial Times survey of 45 business schools which found that open enrollment programs had grown by 10.5 percent, while the number of custom programs increased by more than 20 percent over a 3-year period (Narayandas 2007). The implication of this trend is that business educators are gradually investing in more postprogram monitoring and coaching to ensure that behavioral changes are occurring among students. There is also a rising preference for interdisciplinary work as opposed to functional specialization in business schools since the latter leads students and professors to think and teach in silos (Mintzberg 2004). Furthermore, there are wider environmental trends that are affecting the education provided by teaching faculty. These include the relentless advancement of technology, the rise in global poverty and habitat destruction (Griffith 2003). Overall, these trends suggest that business educators would need to better understand the nature of their participants as human persons so as to educate them and their businesses appropriately. This shift would require that business educators and their institutions focus on developing a more *humanistic* perspective of managing their students. In the next section, we will highlight the fundamental aspects of this perspective.

Putting the Humanistic Management Perspective to Action Among Business Educators

This perspective of management upholds the unconditional human dignity of every woman and man within an economic context (Spitzeck et al. 2009). It suggests that since every individual is unique and deserving of respect, work in organizations ought to be organized in a way that facilitates the human flourishing of individuals. In other words, it suggests that managers have to motivate people around them to acquire virtues and try to discover and promote beliefs and values within the organizational culture that fosters human virtue, in all its forms, to its fullest extent (Melé 2003). Similarly, business schools ought to respect the dignity of their employees and organize work in a way that allows them to realize their full potential. Although the ideals promoted by the humanistic perspective are quite lofty, educators require the support and commitment of their institutions to promote this perspective. Specifically, business educators could secure this commitment from their institutions by working on the following: organizing mentoring programs and embedding an ethical mindset in curricular. In the next paragraphs, we shall highlight how these activities could be implemented.

Organizing mentoring programs: As students continue to demand customization of content, mentoring programs could offer opportunities for educators to boost the personalized attention paid to students. These programs are quite useful for helping the students to reevaluate their priorities in life, set new targets, and learn from their past mistakes. A well-implemented mentoring program would position the business educator and the institution he or she represents not as one that is after profit maximization but rather one that is more interested in adding value to each individual it serves. The mentoring program is also compatible with online business education. Online educators could offer such services to online students when they make on-site visitations to the school. Agreements reached in mentoring meetings could then be discussed and monitored via e-mail. To implement this program, institutions would need to train educators adequately, create a mentoring handbook that offers useful guidelines, monitor compliance, and reward educators for effective implementation. Some business schools in Africa and Europe are already running mentoring programs. The Lagos Business School (LBS) in Nigeria has a faculty advisory system that assigns some selected faculty to mentor and coach full-time MBA students throughout the 2 years of their stay in the school. Each faculty advisor is required to meet the student at least seven times over a 2-year period and record the agreements reached after each meeting in a log book. The rate of compliance is also assessed through occasional meetings with faculty advisors. Another business school that effectively implements the advisory system is the IESE Business School in Barcelona, Spain. In the last 50 years, the school has always been guided by the mission of offering *personalized attention* to its participants. The school currently offers advisory services to its full-time MBA, Executive MBA, and Global Executive MBA students. It has also developed handbooks for students and faculty advisors that guide them through the advisory process (Adeleye, Amaeshi, and Ogbechie 2011). These are a few examples that other business schools could follow. In summary, the mentoring system could be a value-adding service offered by business educators and possibly a source of competitive advantage.

Embedding ethics in curricula: The effective teaching of business ethics could improve the moral legitimacy of business schools. This book has emphasized that business educators would need to move beyond merely teaching courses in ethics to embedding ethics in the curricular of all programs. Such an action would signify that the school supports the view that every business decision has moral and ethical dimensions. Business schools could embed ethics in program curricula by encouraging faculty to write or use teaching cases that highlight an ethical dilemma in at least one of their classes in an entire course. Furthermore, educators would require training to understand how and why ethical issues could be raised in class discussions. It would also be useful to track the frequency of ethically related discussions during a course taught by an educator. Embedding ethics in curricula will also involve communicating that the business school stands for ethical principles. This can be achieved by building a clear and meaningful ethical code of conduct to guide the activities of business educators. Academic institutions could also follow

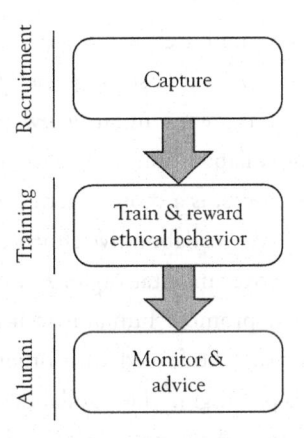

FUTURE OF ETHICS EDUCATION IN MANAGEMENT CURRICULA 327

Figure 17.1 Three-step framework for embedding ethics

the three-step framework for embedding ethics in (Figure 17.1) to ensure that the embedding of ethics in program curricular is sustained. Our framework illustrates three core stages for ensuring that institutions continue to embed ethics in their curricular.

1. *Recruitment*: Academic institutions could ensure that ethics is embedded in curricular by recruiting the right candidates for teaching positions. This would make for an easier job of inculcating ethical principles in potential leaders of the future. Secondly, using ethics as one of the criteria for student recruitment will signal its importance to future business school aspirants and will encourage a proper valuation of ethics among the populace. Business schools could, as part of their recruitment process, make potential students undergo practical ethical tests and then evaluate the outcome of such tests before offering them admission.
2. *Training*: After students are admitted, ethics could be taught not just in the classrooms but from a more holistic perspective. One way of doing this is by adding a course on ethical systems design, which will equip students with the tools they need to design appropriate ethical models when they enter mainstream business. Another way of achieving a holistic perspective is by initiating a school-wide effort to strengthen the culture of professionalism and integrity

within the MBA program itself. For example, MBA programs could find more objective ways of assessing class participation such that extroverts or introverts are not unfairly rewarded. Anything done to foster a culture of collaboration, rather than a culture of competition for scarce resources, is a more practical way of ethical training (Jonathan 2013). These collaborative efforts could also involve partnerships with nongovernmental organizations, research and regulatory agencies that promote humanistic initiatives. Furthermore, partnerships could also be forged with other business schools that are embracing this paradigm. These collaborative efforts would contribute to the creation of an enabling corporate environment where business educators are encouraged to strive for virtues and human fulfillment.

3. *Alumni*: One of the major reasons why ethical training in academic institutions has not been effective is the fact that such institutions do not make sufficient efforts to maintain active relationships with their alumni on completion of their programs. The relationships mostly die after the degree is obtained. Hence, business schools could first set up an ethical think tank and advisory unit and make this open to alumni. This could help the alumni to have recourse to the institution whenever they face an ethical dilemma. This apart from helping in preventing potential business crises will also help to strengthen the bond between such institutions and the alumni body.

Conclusion

Ethics will remain fundamental to coping with many of the challenges that corporate executives will face in the future. Yet according to Chris MacDonald, "the goal of ethics education is not to turn bad people into good ones but to create a sense of awareness about the flaws of rationalisation, and the ease with which honest folks can slide into making bad choices" (2004). Achieving this objective would require teaching ethics in a way that helps students to consider and take the right ethical decisions. Educators could profit from reflecting on the prophetic views of Ghoshal

(2005) who claimed that by propagating ideologically inspired amoral theories, business schools have actively freed their students from any sense of moral responsibility.

We hope that the issues raised in this chapter would help educators to discover sustainable ways of embedding ethics in their program curricular.

References

Adeleye, I., K. Amaeshi, and C. Ogbechie. 2011. *Humanistic Management Education in Africa*. Basingstoke, UK: Palgrave MacMillan.

Jonathan, H. 2013. "Can You Teach Businessmen to Be Ethical?" http://www.washingtonpost.com/blogs/on-leadership/wp/2014/01/13/can-you-teach-businessmen-to-be-ethical/ (accessed May 10, 2014)

Ghoshal, S. 2005. "Bad Management Theories are Destroying Good Management Practices." *Academy of Management Learning and Education* 4, no. 1, pp. 75–91.

Ghoshal, S., J. Birkinshaw, and G. Piramal. 2005. *Sumantra Ghoshal on Management: A Force for Good*. New York: FT Prentice Hall/Pearson Education.

Griffith, J. 2003. *A Species in Denial*. Sydney, Australia: FHA Publishing and Communications.

Kaliski, B. 2007. "Views on the Future of Business Education: Responses to Six Critical Questions." *The Delta Pi Epsilon Journal* 159, no. 1, pp. 9–14.

MacDonald, C. 2004. "Three Simple Reasons to Teach Ethics in Business Schools." Canadian Business. http://www.canadianbusiness.com/blogs-and-comment/are-ethics-courses-useful-chris-macdonald/ (accessed May 10, 2014)

Melé, D. 2003. "The Challenge of Humanistic Management." *Journal of Business Ethics* 44, no. 1, pp. 77–88.

Mintzberg, H. 2004. *Managers not MBAs*. San Francisco, CA: Berrett-Koehler Publishers

Narayandas, D. 2007. "Trends in Executive Education in Business Marketing." *Journal of Business to Business Marketing* 14, no. 1, pp. 23–30.

Schoemaker, P. 2008. "The Future Challenge of Business: Rethinking Management Education." *California Management Review* 50, no. 3, pp. 119–39.

Spitzeck, H., M. Pirson, W. Amann, S. Khan, and E. Kimakowitz. 2009. *Humanism in Business*. Cambridge, UK: Cambridge University Press.

Further Reading

Corporate Knights Magazine. 2013. *Mapping the Future of Business Education* 12, no. 3, pp. 52–53.

Elegido, J. 2009. "Business Education and Erosion of Character." *African Journal of Business Ethics* 4, no. 1, pp. 16–24.

Chapter Summaries

Chapter 1: Teaching Ethics Across the Management Curriculum

Management graduates need to have personal values and virtues to guide their work and behavior in order to direct the world of business in such a way as to steer clear of causing harm to others and to create value that enables and enriches the common good. They need to be able to build organizations that are ethical and responsible and therefore sustainable. This introductory chapter discusses the need to train future business managers and leaders to apply ethical reasoning in the different business situations in which they find themselves: dealing with issues raised by human resource management, management accounting, operations management, organizational politics, marketing plans, and so forth. It is thus that they will be empowered to act responsibly.

The approaches, facets, and nuances of integrating business ethics vary across the disciplines. The science required is also different. Sometimes the main challenge for faculty who wish to integrate ethics into their teaching is time—time perhaps for redesigning the course, for adequate class preparation, or for actual integration within the session. This book aims to be a helpful tool for these teachers and trainers. Its chapters are written by subject experts in various management disciplines who present the way they embed business ethics in their courses.

Chapter 2: Teaching Ethics in Business Policy (Strategy) Courses

This chapter makes the case that the business policy (strategy) course is not only an appropriate place to engage students in discussions of strategy issues; it is also one of the best places to do this. The chapter reviewed some of the reasons why some scholars might consider ethics not appropriate for a strategy course. It put forward the case that ethics is appropriate for the business strategy course. The chapter put forward some of the ways ethics can be approached with business strategy students. Three examples of classroom activities are provided.

Chapter 3: Ethical Foundations for Organizational Decision Making at the Operational and Strategic Levels

In this chapter, we discuss the current state of ethics education within the business curriculum and make the case for a more consistent approach to the discipline. Our discussion turns on organizational decision making at both operational and strategic levels to demonstrate that ethical decisions inherently involve interactions between the situations themselves and the personal convictions of the decision maker. We argue that in order to be successful in these circumstances, an ethical framework guiding organizational decisions needs to be pragmatic, reflective, nimble, and iterative.

The objective of teaching a course in ethics is to equip the student with the ability to recognize and address ethical questions, and to do so with intelligence and sensitivity to a range of personal, social, and professional considerations. As such, we employ a rich practical case study example of a typical organizational decision with multiple ethical dimensions. We utilize five critical steps to directing students through the exercise: awareness of an ethical dilemma, fact-finding, evaluating ethical approaches, pretesting the decision, and reflection on the outcome of the decision. The result is a heightened awareness among students of the many facets of operational and strategic business choices and a framework to guide their future decisions.

Chapter 4: Ethics and Agency Theory in Management

This chapter focuses on agency theory, principal–agent problem, ethical aspects of this relation, and teaching methods of all these concepts in management curriculum. Agency theory is widely discussed in economics and management, and latterly legal, sociological, and political aspects. Agency theory is interested in sharing of power, control, information, money, efficiency, and other important instruments between principals (owners, shareholders, stakeholders, etc.) and the agents (CEOs, managers, board of directors, etc.). The heart of principal–agent theory is the trade-off between the cost of measuring behavior and outcomes and risk sharing of the principal and agent.

Business management academic programs need to be designed to emphasize the challenge of ethical problems based on these principal–agent frictions. Experiential learning exercises—lecture, case study, role play, behavioral modeling, and business simulations—can play an important role in teaching ethics focused on the principal–agent problems. However, many ethical problems do not have specific *correct* solutions like some other problems in a number of courses.

The theoretical background of the agency theory is outlined in the first part of the chapter. The discipline is explained shortly and some of the agency problems are explained. Typical ethical issues of theory are discussed by some cases. The chapter is ended with advises about ethics teaching strategies, comparing of developed versus undeveloped countries, and an exercise on agency problem.

Chapter 5: Embedding Ethics and Social Responsibility in Management Accounting Courses

In this chapter, you will learn how management accountants directly or indirectly influence important strategic and operational decisions made by managers. The chapter begins with a description of the management accounting discipline and has detailed descriptions of typical decision-making scenarios, highlighting businesses' positive and negative contributions to society. For example, management accountants may or may not include information about ethics, sustainability, and corporate social responsibility (CSR) when they share financial and nonfinancial performance measurements with managers. This choice has the potential to influence managers' behavior and, thus, how firms impact stakeholders.

This chapter explains why ethics, sustainability, and CSR data should be provided by management accountants to managers to support decision making and resolve conflicts among many stakeholders. End of chapter materials include four learning activities that you can use to prepare management accountants and managers for their critical roles in organizational decision making.

Chapter 6: Ethical Dimensions in the Teaching of Economics and the Tradition of Critical Political Economy

The chapter begins with a reflection on how, the macroeconomy being largely part of the business environment rather than something on which businesses can directly act, considerations regarding the role of ethics in respect of the study of economics are of a different nature than those in say human resources management or marketing where direct moral guidance to daily managerial actions can be sought. For the most part therefore the integration of ethical concerns into the teaching of economics to business students cannot be expected to bear the immediate fruits that might be expected in other management disciplines. Nonetheless it will be argued that moral concerns have a place in the teaching of economics. We will explore how under the influence of positivism there has been a complete excision of *any* considerations of ethics from the teaching of mainstream neoclassical economics and we will argue that this is not only philosophically indefensible but has also been highly damaging in practice. An appeal for an approach to teaching economics in full recognition of the normative issues raised by economic policy will be made and examples of how this can be done in practice in the everyday teaching of the subject will be given. It will be suggested not only that this can make the teaching of economics much more interesting and palatable for students but also that such an approach lies in the grand tradition of critical political economy.

Chapter 7: Teaching Ethics in Operations Management

In this chapter, we discuss ethical issues that arise in the context of operations management (OM) and how students' awareness of these issues can be heightened. Ethics is largely equated with the pillars of CSR and thus sustainability. We cover three relevant areas of OM decision making: strategy deployment in response to legal frameworks, development of sustainable products, and services and measures to cope with the scarcity of natural resources. We propose an inductive teaching process where examples and case studies serve as primary learning vehicles for students to put themselves in the shoes of business decision makers and to discuss possible ethical conflicts. Conflict resolution can be obtained by referring to an extended version of the categorical imperative that calls for decision makers to assume responsibility for their acts so as to assure the livability of the planet. We complement this approach by noting that it is essential for the teacher to emphasize how individual, seemingly small contributions from the bottom-up can contribute to resolving problems on a much larger scale.

Chapter 8: Teaching Ethics in Supply Chain Management

The current global business environment creates a situation where corruption, high taxes, and intense competition make firms more vulnerable to unethical or illegal practices both within their native country and overseas. This situation is even more pronounced in the field of supply chain management since multiple companies work together to produce a good or service. This chapter addresses the nuances of ethics in supply chain management in a manner that can be presented to students studying in this field.

We begin the chapter by reviewing three disciplines: supply chain management, ethics, and curriculum techniques. We integrate the ideas from each of these disciplines to develop a concept-based ethical decision-making model that allows the student to analyze the most salient components of ethical decision making in a supply chain management environment. We offer two examples and use the decision-making model to illustrate how ethical issues arise in supply chain management and how students can analyze and better understand how to avoid unethical situations. We supplement these examples with recommended teaching strategies, thereby providing advice for teachers on concept integration, and outlining how the country's state of economic development can alter the ethical perspectives of supply chain decision makers.

Chapter 9: Teaching Ethics in Decision Making: Embedding Moral Reasoning in the Management of Information Systems

The ubiquity of information and communications technology (ICT) initiatives like the Internet and mobile networks have triggered ICT-related ethical controversies like data security and privacy. However, the realm of ethical issues is not restricted to Internet and mobile resources, but encompasses the spectrum of information systems (human, organizational, and digital resources) deployed to serve business and society and their management.

The teaching of ethics in the realm of management information systems (MIS) is the focus of this chapter that shares insights into the hidden ethical dilemmas in MIS activities—strategic planning, systems development, management, governance, and application (use). The chapter commences with a cursory introduction of MIS activities and related ethical principles before delving into the moral dilemmas attributed to the deployment of digital resources. The discussion on dilemmas not only highlights the issues hidden in the conceptualization activities but also exposes usability issues including occupational health risks and cybercrime.

For information systems (IS) faculty leading ethical discussions, the chapter provides case-based and self-study approaches that not only deepen student learning and engagement, but also demonstrate moral reasoning and ethical decision analysis by highlighting the intersection between MIS activities and ethical principles.

Chapter 10: Embedding Ethical Issues in Marketing Management Classes: An Instructor's Guide

This chapter argues that all marketing decisions have ethical dimensions and thus instructors and students require a deep understanding of ethical issues. It then identifies the lack of development of ethics in marketing as the discipline evolved since its inception in 1937. Afterward, ethical issues associated with understanding the consumer, segmenting the market, managing the channel, setting prices, and marketing communication are discussed with a view of raising these as salient questions for class discussions. Fundamental ethical principles of justice, integrity, and respect for human dignity are also elaborated upon. This chapter elaborates on its position by offering some insights on how marketing instructors can embed ethical considerations in some aspects of their marketing teaching curricula. It does this by providing useful teaching strategies, methods, and perspectives as well as suggested academic materials and frameworks that could aid the process. In particular, personal value journaling was recommended. Finally, it asks business schools to encourage faculty to write or use teaching cases that highlight an ethical dilemma as well as encourage ethical behavior by providing scholarships for students who have demonstrated ethical leadership.

Chapter 11: Incorporating Ethics in Teaching Consumer Behavior: An Educational Strategy Based on Principles for Responsible Management Education

In the beginning of the new millennium, and as a consequence of unethical corporate scandals, the topic of business ethics became more important for various stakeholders (e.g., government, firms, business scholars, educators, accrediting bodies). For example, in the specific case of educators, Association to Advance Collegiate Schools of Business—International (AACSB) has suggested that teaching ethics should be a priority for business schools. Moreover, employers have made demands upon business schools to elaborate upon the training of their students in ethics and social responsibility, in order to influence good business practices. This situation has modified the teaching experience in business schools and it represents a provocative challenge in terms of strategy and methodology (e.g., EGADE Business School Tecnologico de Monterrey, Mexico). Ethics is not a standalone function—it is embedded in all decision making; and consumer behavior analysis is not the exception. Hence, the purpose of this chapter is to present some alternatives for the faculty in order to teach responsible consumer behavior, through the integration of an ethical perspective following PRME principles.

Chapter 12: Teaching Ethics in Human Resources Management

Due to an increasing pressure on companies to deal with stakeholders in a responsible way and the growing importance of attracting and retaining talent, the discussion about ethics in human resources management (HRM) has gained momentum. The chapter distinguishes two dimensions of HRM: the ethical treatment of employees and the steering of a company's workforce in a way that employees behave in a responsible way toward other stakeholders. For each of the two dimensions, ethical issues as well as moral rights and standards are identified. Also, potential differences in moral expectations and in pressing issues in developing and developed countries are outlined. Based on this, the chapter proposes different teaching strategies for ethics in HRM and describes which didactic method may be appropriate for which didactic situation.

Chapter 13: Teaching Ethics in Career Management

This chapter focuses on career management and ethics from the point of view of individuals and organizations. An underlying theme is that career management is the joint responsibility of both the career owners, that is, the individuals, and the organizations that employ them. Thus, it is important to consider how to ethically manage careers from both perspectives in order to build sustainable careers and career systems. Drawing from Rossouw's perspectives for ethical study, *ethical development* and *ethical control* are discussed in considerable detail as major focus points in the instruction of ethics. Ethical development focuses on developing individuals' character while ethical control focuses on the structures and systems that exist to govern business practices. Also discussed are three main competencies that should be achieved by the students at the end of an ethics course—cognitive, behavioral, and managerial skills. Cognitive skills are concerned with gaining intellectual knowledge and frameworks for ethical decision making while behavioral competencies focus on translating thought to action. The final competency, managerial, helps students develop skills that will enable them to handle situations they face as managers as well as develop ethical career systems in their organizations.

Chapter 14: Ethics in Negotiation

Deception is a common tactic in all forms of negotiation, business negotiation being no exception. Even the most well-intentioned negotiators routinely and unconsciously commit ethical lapses and tolerate such lapses in others. As a matter of fact, negotiation provides ample opportunities for deception in one form or another. Some would argue that ethical rules do not always apply in business negotiations, and that some measure of deception is therefore "normal" and to be expected. However, the mere fact that deception may be prevalent in business dealings does not justify such behavior from an ethical or moral point of view. The fact that something is "standard practice" or "part of the game" cannot be deemed to justify such behavior.

On the other hand, while we believe that all people—business people included—should behave ethically, we doubt whether merely appealing to others to behave ethically because it is "the right thing to do" will of itself be sufficient to change negotiation behavior, given human nature and the exigencies and realities of the business world in general. The motivation for doing the right thing must go further, we believe. Our approach when teaching ethics and negotiation is to emphasize that negotiation is essentially a process through which we try to satisfy our own interests. We can do so by trying to meet our interests regardless of the other side's (looking for our own gain), or in cooperation with them (looking for mutual gain). Whether one adopts the former or the latter approach to negotiation (our preference is for the latter), in each case it concerns a large degree of self-interest.

For us, focusing on a negotiator's self-interest, and showing how deception affects their reputation as negotiators, the sustainability of the agreement as well as the quality of the outcome, holds the key to motivating them to behave ethically. However, given that deceit is a reality in business negotiations, negotiators should not be naive. The best policy, we believe, is one of showing that you can be trusted, but not to be overly trusting: "trust, but verify." Negotiators therefore should arm themselves with some of the "protective skills" referred to later in this chapter.

Chapter 15: Ethics in Managing Corporate Power and Politics

Teaching about the ethical management of corporate power and politics lies at the interface of politics, ethics, and leadership. While there is a considerable literature on the topic of organizational power and politics, application to in-depth teaching of ethics can be neglected because ethics is taught separately. Ethics concerns principled application of power and politics, subject to personal values and widely expected norms. Formal organizational policies tend to be silent on power and politics. Paraphrasing Dillon, corporations are settings for clashing personalities, competing agendas, and turf wars. The leadership and collective problem is not automatically to minimize all politics within the organization. The problem is to minimize negative politics and foster positive politics. The essence of politics is competition for and disagreement over goals, scarce resources, and actions. The chapter provides a description of the discipline, typical ethical issues with examples, ethics teaching strategy, advice for teachers, and developing versus developed country perspectives. There are differences in developing versus developed country perspectives concerning power and politics due particularly to *power distance* acceptance. There is a set of suggested exercises and projects. A bibliography provides considerable materials on organizational politics, power, and ethical politics.

Chapter 16: Ethical Dimensions of Community and Investor Relations Communication and Governance for Sustainable Management

Effective and authentic approaches to community and investor relations (IR and CR) communications require a spectrum of management and leadership skills, including risk assessment, crisis management, risk mitigation, relationship development, systemic and critical thinking, financial security, strategic framing, and brand management and development.

We explore ethical issues involving CR and IR in the context of conventional business operational and strategic issues, and from new, emergent patterns of expectations and obligations of business being imposed by internal and external stakeholders. We introduce the concept of radical transparency and traverse a normative approach to ethical IR and CR communications. We use the BP Deepwater Horizon and Rana Plaza collapse as teaching cases. A multi-dimensional *ethical filter* model is proposed as a tool for navigating ethical IR and CR communications with integrity and rectitude. This framework proposes that *truth telling*, sense-making, and formal notions of fairness and credibility can effectively countervail corporate instincts to dissemble or shade the facts. We provide teaching advice, including teaching from written cases, living cases, and *worst practices*. Clinical and experiential learning modalities are explored. Advocacy for cross-cultural exploration of ethical communications is offered.

Chapter 17: Future of Ethics Education in Management Curricula

Ethics as taught in business schools has so far failed to impact mainstream business as evidence by the recent economic crises. There is currently a real need for a complete overhaul of the current system and curricula for teaching ethics. At the same time a number of trends are already shaping the future of business education toward a more *humanistic* perspective of managing students. This presents a great opportunity to implement the necessary changes to the current system of teaching ethics in business schools in order to achieve the goal of raising more ethical leaders.

This chapter argues that a humanistic perspective to business education could serve as a useful paradigm for educators seeking to improve their teaching of ethics. Based on this tenet, it then offers a useful framework for the sustainable insertion of ethics into management curricular through organizing mentoring programs and embedding an ethical mindset in curricular.

About the Authors

Arnd Huchzermeier chairs the Production Management Department and the Center for Collaborative Commerce at WHU—Otto Beisheim School of Management in Germany. Prof. Huchzermeier has developed a case course on "Operations Strategy and Sustainability," which he taught successfully at the graduate and master level. In the first part of the course, students are introduced to the concept of "Management-Quality for Industrial Excellence" with many examples derived directly from the INSEAD-WHU Industrial Excellence Award competition that Prof. Huchzermeier codirects. The main objective is to show how effective strategy cascading and execution, including change management projects, are conducted in benchmark firms. In the second part, 16–20 benchmark case studies are discussed focusing mostly on ethical issues, for example, integrated reporting, green washing, product safety, and so forth. Prof. Huchzermeier has published in numerous international academic journals, acts as senior editor for top publications in the area of supply chain management and OM-marketing interface, and has received prestigious science awards.

Barney Jordaan holds a doctorate in law from Stellenbosch University and was admitted as an attorney of the Supreme Court of South Africa in 1982. He was professor of law at Stellenbosch University until 1997, when he entered full-time practice as a specialist in the areas of employment law and labor relations, but later also in the areas of negotiation, mediation, and conflict management. He holds a number of academic appointments: He is professor extraordinaire at the Graduate School of Business of Stellenbosch University (USB), teaching fellow at the Graduate School of Business of UCT, and with effect from September 1, 2014, professor in negotiation at Vlerick Business School, Belgium. His research and teaching focuses on negotiation, mediation, and conflict resolution.

Apart from his academic involvement, Barney is a director and cofounder of a leading firm of employment relations, employment law, and organizational growth specialists, with offices in Cape Town and Johannesburg. He is a senior mediator, having been involved in the field since 1989. He is certified by the International Mediation Institute in The Hague, and chair of the International Bar Association's mediation across border subcommittee. Since May 2011, he has been acting as external consultant to the World Bank Group's Office of Mediation Services. He is listed in the 2011–2013 *Who's Who Legal (Commercial Mediators) of the International Bar Association*, one of five in the RSA.

Cathleen S. Burns, PhD, CPA, is a senior instructor of accounting at the Leeds School of Business at the University of Colorado Boulder (CU) and Owner of Creative Action Learning Solutions, LLC, an executive training and higher education consulting business. Cathleen has been teaching management accounting for 25 years and has been the recipient of 14 local, state, regional, and national teaching awards.

She has developed and delivered custom executive education programs for large organizations including Boeing, DigitalGlobe, Key Equipment Finance, Shell, Molson Coors, Basic American Foods, Western Union, WhiteWave–Dean Foods, KPMG, and Deloitte. Cathleen serves as the Pedagogy Task Force Chair for the joint American Accounting Association (AAA) and American Institute of CPAs (AICPA) Pathways Commission for enhancing the quality and integrity of the educational process for future accountants. Cathleen taught the first offering of a graduate accounting and MBA course in Integrated Reporting at CU in spring 2012.

Cathleen received a BS in Applied Science from Miami University, an MBA from Xavier University, and a PhD from New Mexico State University. Cathleen has also been a faculty member at the University of Missouri Columbia and New Mexico State University.

Consuelo Garcia-de-la-Torre holds a PhD in Management, HEC University of Montreal. She is currently a full-time professor at the EGADE Business School, Tecnológico de Monterrey, in Mexico. She is a member of the Mexican National Research System (SNI 1), director of Humanism and Management Research Center at EGADE, and fellow of the Academy of Management. She is a member of the Humanistic Management

Network and chapter head of Mexico. She has published articles and book chapters regarding corporate social responsibility (CSR) in prestigious scientific publications nationally and internationally. Currently, she is vice president of the Academy of Administrative Sciences in Mexico, ACACIA. Also, she is a visiting professor at various international universities. She is currently regional president PRME Latin America and the Caribbean.

David Venter practiced psychology for 15 years before serving in the South African government as the Director General responsible for communication during the transition from apartheid to democracy. In his latter role, he was greatly privileged to spend 10 years working very closely with Nelson Mandela, and later with Thabo Mbeki when President Mandela left office. During these years and the time he spent in Namibia with Martti Ahtisaari, he was extremely fortunate to experience how two of the foremost negotiators of our time—both Nobel Prize recipients for their negotiation expertise—successfully deal with seemingly intractable problems. On leaving the public service in 1996, he successfully assisted in establishing three negotiation training and consulting companies before joining the faculty of the Vlerick Business School in Belgium where he was awarded numerous best teacher awards during his tenure of more than 8 years. In addition to teaching in Belgium, he teaches in St. Petersburg in Russia, at Peking University in China, the Judge Business School at Cambridge, Trinity College in Ireland, MCC in Hungary and Rumania, the South African universities of Cape Town and Stellenbosch. Apart from teaching, he has also regularly consulted to a very wide array of national and multinational companies.

Donna Sockell, while at the Leeds School of Business (2005–2013), developed the curriculum for and founded the Curriculum Emphasis on Social Responsibility (2007) and the Center for Education on Social Responsibility (CESR) (2010). Serving as CESR's first executive director, Donna oversaw the infusion of values, ethics, and CSR discussions throughout the graduate and undergraduate curriculum, touching nearly 4,000 students yearly. Under Donna's leadership, Leeds ranked sixth nationally in undergraduate sustainability education in 2013 and achieved Net Impact's gold status.

An award-winning teacher and curriculum designer in Business and Society and Industrial Relations, Donna published over 25 articles in scholarly venues during her 14 years as a professor at Columbia and Rutgers Universities. Donna also designed and taught the required ethics course for four New York Commodities Exchanges.

Donna presents to academics (including the AACSB), businesses, and community groups about values-driven, socially conscious decision making. Her work has been cited in outlets including *The Wall Street Journal*, *BusinessWeek.com*, *The Chronicle of Higher Education*, *The Guardian*, and *Le Monde*. Her firm, SB Educational Consultants, provides advice on educational design for colleges and businesses.

Donna received her undergraduate degree in economics (Union College, in 1977) and her master's (1979) and doctorate (1982) in industrial relations (Cornell University).

Duane Windsor, PhD (Harvard University), is Lynette S. Autrey Professor of Management in the Jesse H. Jones Graduate School of Business at Rice University. He is an alumnus of Rice University (BA) and has been on the Rice faculty since 1977. He has had experience teaching power and politics, leadership, and ethics in the Rice MBA program. His research focuses on CSR and stakeholder theory. His articles have appeared in *Business & Society*, *Business Ethics Quarterly*, *Cornell International Law Journal*, *Journal of Business Ethics*, *Journal of Business Research*, *Journal of Corporate Citizenship*, *Journal of International Management*, *Journal of Management Studies*, *Journal of Public Affairs*, *Philosophy of Management*, and *Public Administration Review*. Dr. Windsor served as editor of *Business & Society* during the years 2007–2014. He coauthored a book with Lee E. Preston titled *The Rules of the Game in the Global Economy: Policy Regimes for International Business* (Kluwer Academic Publishers 1992), the second edition of which was published in 1997.

Edward Quevedo is a member of faculty of Sustainable Enterprise and visiting assistant professor at the Lorry I. Lokey Graduate School of Business at Mills College (Oakland, California, United States) and is the director and senior research fellow in the Mills College Center for Socially Responsible Business.

Ed also holds an appointment as Associate within Reos Partners LLP, an international diplomacy agency. Within Reos, Ed and his colleagues advise and counsel national and regional governments and other civil society organizations on complex problem solving and conflict resolution. The problem patterns they address include energy, environment, development, peace, health, education, food, finance, and social cohesion.

During his career, Ed has held several academic appointments, including Presidio Graduate School in San Francisco, California, from 2010 through 2013, where he served as interim dean of the faculty. Ed's agency career has been highlighted by strategic planning and futuring processes, including engagements by BMW Group AG, Gallo Family Vineyards, and the Cities of Calgary (Alberta), and Amsterdam (Holland), among many others.

Ed is also a practicing natural resources and water rights attorney. He makes his home in Northern California, where he continues to learn from his children and the local communities he is privileged to serve.

Emeka Enwere is a marketing professional and currently heads business development in West Africa for Comviva Technologies Limited, a leading global telecom value-added service (VAS) provider. Having started his career as a consultant, he displays a deep and varied experience across functions and industries as evidenced in his numerous pursuits. Emeka is an online publisher of two blogs and currently writes business school cases and book chapters.

He holds an MBA in marketing and entrepreneurship from London Business School.

Eva Kohl is the head of Dean's Office at WHU—Otto Beisheim School of Management. The Dean's Office is responsible for managing and coordinating diverse projects for further development of the school. Among other projects, the Dean's Office is driving the development of a school-wide concept, steering and reporting regarding sustainability. This includes sustainability in all core areas of activity, like academic programs, research, corporate connections, as well as administration and organization. Eva Kohl has a degree in business and was working in a strategy consulting company before joining the higher education sector.

ABOUT THE AUTHORS

Gerald (Jerry) Burch is an assistant professor at Tarleton State University. He earned his PhD in Management-Organizational Behavior from the Virginia Commonwealth University, a master of science from the Naval Postgraduate School, and a bachelor's degree from the University of Texas at Austin. His primary areas of research include the use of affect by business leaders, supply chain management, and creativity and innovation. To improve in his role as scholar and educator, Jerry has conducted Scholarship of Teaching and Learning research where he has developed the Conception Focused Curriculum (CFC) model designed for teaching students at the conception level. He has used this curriculum model to deliver curriculum to undergraduate and graduate students in the areas of business statistics, organizational behavior, and operations management. His research has been published in several journals including *Organizational Dynamics*, *Entrepreneurship Research Journal*, and his seminal article on CFC will be published in the *Journal of Management Education*. Jerry can be contacted at gburch@tarleton.edu.

Gloria Camacho has a PhD in Management Sciences from EGADE Business School. She is a researcher in Humanism and Management Research Chair and an adjunct professor at Universidad Cristóbal Colón in Veracruz, Mexico. Her research interests are sustainable marketing, responsible consumption, corporate sustainability, and CSR. She has participated in national and international conferences and has several publications in her research topics.

Ifedapo Adeleye is a senior lecturer in strategy and human resources management at Lagos Business School (LBS). A major strand of his current research and consulting activities focuses on how organizations can drive performance through talent management. He also has a keen interest in responsible management and sustainable HRM. Dapo has authored over 20 journal articles, teaching cases, and book chapters, and presented his work at conferences around the world. He received his PhD in HRM from Manchester Business School and is a certified Senior Professional in Human Resources of the Society for HRM, United States. He can be reached on +234-805-805-8091 or via e-mail: iadeleye@lbs.edu.ng.

ABOUT THE AUTHORS

Jan Bell is a professor of accounting, Babson College, and currently on assignment to Babson Global to assist foundations start new private universities that focus on creating entrepreneurial, virtuous leaders. At Babson, Bell codesigned, coordinated, and taught in the sophomore year integrative, signature learning experience. In this position, she embedded sustainability and ethics into traditional, required courses.

Bell's recent publications focused on incorporating sustainability into the curriculum and business decision making. She has published teaching cases and applied articles for practitioners and has written a chapter in a text meant for educators and curriculum designers in *The New Entrepreneurial Leader*. She also engages in and supports traditional research in this area, and in 2010, she hosted the Global Accounting and Organizational Change conference under the theme of "Accounting's Role in Promoting Social Change." In the past 5 years, she has published more than 20 journal articles and interdisciplinary cases and won awards for case writing and best papers.

Dr. Bell earned her PhD from University of California, Los Angeles, and holds a CPA certificate from Tennessee, where she earned her bachelor's degree and worked for KPMG. Bell taught at Columbia University, Santa Clara University, and California State University Northridge.

Joanna Shaw is an assistant professor of human resource management at Tarleton State University (a part of the A&M University System) in Stephenville, Texas. Joanna's teaching interests include business ethics and a variety of human resource management courses. Her latest publication was focused on student engagement. You can reach her at jshaw@tarleton.edu.

Judith Weisinger is an associate professor of business at the Lorry I. Lokey Graduate School of Management at Mills College (Oakland, California, United States). She conducts research on organizational diversity, with current interests in the management of diversity and inclusion and the role of social capital in organizations, with an emergent interest in diversity and social capital in social enterprises. Her research is published in various journals, including *Human Resource Management*, the *Journal* of *Management Inquiry*, the *Irish Journal of Management*, the *Nonprofit & Voluntary Sector Quarterly*, and *Nonprofit Management & Leadership*, among others. She is coeditor of a special issue of the *Nonprofit & Voluntary Sector Quarterly* devoted to "Diversity in the Nonprofit and Voluntary Sector" (forthcoming 2014).

Judith teaches in the areas of leadership and ethics, organizational behavior, and human resources management and has taught management courses at the undergraduate, graduate, and executive levels. She has also consulted various organizations on topics such as team-building as well as diversity and inclusion. She currently resides in Oakland, California, and enjoys spending time with family and friends.

Kemi Ogunyemi holds a degree in Law from University of Ibadan, Nigeria, an LLM from University of Strathclyde, UK, and MBA and PhD degrees from LBS, Pan-Atlantic University, Nigeria. As a senior lecturer, she leads sessions on business ethics, managerial anthropology, and sustainability management at LBS and is the academic director of the School's Senior Management Programme. She is also currently the PRME promoter for the School. Her consulting and research interests include personal ethos and organizational culture, responsible leadership and sustainability, and work-life ethic. She has authored over 20 articles, case studies, and book chapters, and the book titled *Responsible Management: Understanding Human Nature, Ethics, and Sustainability*.

Kemi worked as director, team lead, and mentor in various projects of the Women's Board (Educational Cooperation Society) before joining LBS. She is a member of the Business Ethics Network of Africa (BEN-Africa), International Society of Business, Economics and Ethics (ISBEE), and European Business Ethics Network (EBEN). She was also a part of the faculty team that developed the UNGC-PRME Anti-Corruption Toolkit.

Melissa L. Cast is a PhD candidate at New Mexico State University. Her interests broadly include the micro application of Organizational Behavior and Human Resources topics to contexts unexplored in the management literature. In particular, she is interested in the collaboration of private sector nonprofits and public sector government entities and the resulting implications for employees, volunteers, and management involved in such collaborations. She was recognized for "Outstanding Research" in August 2012 by the New Mexico State University Management Department.

Michael E. Cafferky is the Ruth McKee Chair for Entrepreneurship and Business Ethics at Southern Adventist University where he has served since 2003 teaching strategy and business ethics. Prior to this he served for 20 years in the healthcare industry in middle and senior management. Michael is a graduate of Anderson University Falls School of Business (DBA), Andrews University Theological Seminary (MDiv), and Loma Linda University School of Public Health (MPH). He is the author of eight books including the college textbook *Management: A Faith-Based Perspective* (Pearson 2012) a peer-reviewed, full-length principles of management textbook written from a Christian worldview and Breakeven analysis (Business Expert Press 2010). He is coeditor of the Scriptural Foundations for Business monograph series (Andrews University Press 2013). In 2011, Dr. Cafferky received the President's Award for Excellence in Scholarship from Southern Adventist University. In 2013, Dr. Cafferky received the Sharon G. Johnson Award from the Christian Business Faculty Association, in national recognition for his efforts in integrating faith and business scholarship. He has lectured on religion and business in several countries including the United States, Canada, Mexico, Australia, Russian Federation, South Africa, France, Rwanda, and Ghana.

Olayinka David-West is a senior fellow at the LBS, Pan-Atlantic University, Lagos, Nigeria, where she has been a faculty member since 2003. Olayinka completed her DBA at Manchester Business School, UK, MSc at City University, London, UK; and BSc at University of Lagos. Her research interests focus on adoption and utilization, information technology (IT) management practices, and benefits of information systems in diverse business industries and across societal sectors. In recent years, she has investigated technology-related services like electronic and mobile banking. She has professional certifications in systems audit and the enterprise governance of IT.

Olayinka is passionate about sharing the mysteries of IT with business managers and leads sessions in the management of information systems (MIS).

Olusegun Babalola is a PhD candidate at the LBS specializing in organizational behavior. Her research interests are career management and development, specifically how individual differences and situational contexts affect individuals' orientations toward their careers. Olusegun is a Nigerian representative of the 5C group (The Cross-Cultural Collaboration on Contemporary Careers).

Osmar E. Arandia has a PhD in Management Sciences, with specialty in strategy and Humanistic Management. He is currently Vice President of Strategic Development at the Universidad Cristóbal Colón in Veracruz, Mexico. Also, he is currently professor of social responsibility, nongovernmental organization (NGO) marketing, business ethics, and strategy in various post graduate programs in Mexico. His research interests are humanistic management, business ethics, CSR, sustainability, and strategy.

Patrick O'Sullivan, formerly a senior lecturer and MBA Programme Director at Cardiff University Business School, was appointed as full professor and director of Studies at Grenoble Graduate School of Business within Grenoble Ecole de Management (GEM) in September 2006. From September 2009 to September 2012, he has been head of Department of People Organisations and Society in GEM heading up a diverse team of colleagues across a range of disciplines including organizational behavior, human resource management, economics, politics, and ethics. He has extensive experience in teaching at all levels and in academic administration. His teaching specialties include business ethics, critical scientific methodology, and political economy of the European Union as well as managerial economics, and in recent years he has acquired wide international teaching experience in these subjects having taught in UK (Cambridge University), Germany (Frankfurt University), Poland (Warsaw University), Finland (Aalto University), Nigeria (LBS), Georgia (Caucasus Business School),

Thailand (Webster University) and France (GEM) as well. His research interests include critical scientific methodology, business ethics, transport policy issues, and system timetabling and planning, a field in which he has some consultancy experience. His publications include classic academic articles, case studies, a methodological monograph (book), a custom textbook for Cardiff University, and most recently he has been principal editor and written four chapters of an advanced textbook titled *Business Ethics: A Critical Approach Integrating Ethics across the Business World* (2012).

Silke Bustamante is a professor of management at the Berlin School of Economics and Law and course director of the Division of Service Management. Her research focuses on corporate responsibility, particularly on cultural aspects and role for trust and reputation, and corporate and international strategy. She was visiting professor at Kobe University in Japan and the UADE in Buenos Aires, Argentina. Earlier, she worked for several years as a consultant for the Boston Consulting Group in international strategic projects.

Between 1995 and 1999, Silke Bustamante did a PhD program on applied microeconomics and wrote her doctoral thesis on "Multimarket Contact and Organizational Design." She also worked as research assistant at the Social Science Research Center Berlin. Silke Bustamante studied business administration and cultural studies in Passau and graduated in 1995 from Passau.

Stefan Spinler is the director of the Kühne Institute for Logistics Management and holds the Chair of Logistics Management at WHU—Otto Beisheim School of Management in Germany. One of the focal areas of Prof. Spinler's research is related to sustainability in OM and supply chains. The key findings of this research are translated into courses such as Logistics and Supply Chain Management and Real Options Analysis where dedicated sessions focus on ethical issues in supply chains. The courses are taught at the undergraduate as well as graduate and MBA level. Relevant publications include a study on the electrification of La Poste's vehicle fleet, which was a finalist in 2011 of INFORMS' prestigious Daniel H. Wagner Prize for Excellence in Operations Research

Practice, the development of a supply chain framework for school feeding, and a review of contributions of an Operations Management lens to sustainability.

Thomas G. Pittz is a PhD candidate at New Mexico State University. His research interests lie at the nexus of the fields of strategy, entrepreneurship, and nonprofit management. He is particularly interested in studying how organizations collaborate across sectors to explore and assimilate new knowledge. He has contributed work as a corresponding author for peer-reviewed journal articles in entrepreneurship, book chapters on sustainability and ethics, and has presented works-in-progress at major management conferences.

Uchenna Uzo is a professor of marketing in the LBS. He received his BSc and MSc in Sociology from the University of Lagos, Nigeria and his Masters of Research in Management as well as PhD in Management from the IESE Business School, Barcelona. He is a member and reviewer of the Academy of Management and also a Research fellow of the Scandinavian Consortium for Organizational Research (SCANCOR). He is also a member of the European Group of Organizational Studies (EGOS) and the American Marketing Association. In addition, he has served as a visiting research scholar at Stanford University, United States.

He teaches courses in marketing management, personal selling, sales, and channel management. His research and consulting assignments span several industries focusing mainly on retail marketing management, sales, and distribution channel management. He currently sits on the board of a retail marketing company and is the author of several business case studies. His academic articles have been published in the *Strategic Entrepreneurship Journal* and his case won the 2013 EFMD Case Writing Competition in the *African Business Cases* category.

Umit Ercan is a PhD candidate in Defense Management Program of the Defense Sciences Institute of Turkish Military Academy. His graduate school education was also in Defense Sciences Institute of Turkish Military Academy and Naval Post Graduate School of United States. He studied on cultural differences and leadership on his master thesis.

He has a major of law from Marmara University, Turkey, and system engineering from Turkish Military Academy. Mr. Ercan teaches the legal perspective of military operations at the NATO school of partnership for peace and military justice lessons in Turkish Military Academy. He is writing his PhD dissertation on Agency Theory and Corporate Ethics. Umit can be reached at ercanumit@yahoo.com.

Unsal Sigri (PhD in Management) is an associate professor of management at the Baskent University, Ankara, Turkey. He has been also working as a lecturer at Turkish Military Academy since 1998. He worked as a visiting professor in the Azerbaijan Military Academy, Baku, Azerbaijan, in 2001, and as a research scholar at St. John Fisher College, Rochester, New York, United States, in 2010. Dr. Sigri teaches Management, Leadership, Group Dynamics, Social Psychology, Organization Development and Change, Cross Cultural Management, Conflict Resolution, Negotiation, and military sociology. He has been working in different international academic projects within Research Committee 01 "Armed Forces and Conflict Resolution" of the International Sociological Association and ERGOMAS—European Research Group on Military Studies. He also worked within international organizations including NATO, United Nations, and EU. He teaches at TOBB Economy and Technology University, Turkish Military Academy and NATO School of Partnership for Peace and NATO Center of Excellence on Defense against Terrorism as a visiting professor. Unsal can be reached at usigri@baskent.edu.tr.

Walter Kendall is an associate professor of marketing at Tarleton State University (a part of the Texas A&M University System) in Stephenville, Texas, United States. His teaching interests include marketing management, marketing research, logistics, and international marketing. Logistics and transportation are the primary foci of his research endeavors. He can be contacted at kendall@tarleton.edu.

Index

Absolutism *vs* relativism, 27, 28
Accountability, 60
Adverse selection, 61
Advice for professors on curriculum scaffolded, 92, 93
Agency relation, 56
Agency theory, 55
   developing *vs* developed country perspectives, 70, 71
   ethical issues in, 62, 63
      case study in teaching, 66–69
   ethics of agent-owner relation of, 56
   ethics teaching strategy for, 63–66
   links to mainstream organization perspectives, 57
   problems with, 56, 58–62, 72
   re-establishes incentives and self-interest importance, 62
   sides of, 57
All-knowing teacher, 46
Alumni, 328
American Institute of Certified Public Accountants (AICPA), 94, 98–115
Analyze, design, develop, implement, and evaluate (ADDIE) model of instructional design, 94–96
Annual budgeting, 87, 88
Art, 6–10
Asian financial crisis (1997), 132
Association of Consumer Research (ACR), 216
Association to Advance Collegiate Schools of Business (AACSB), 40
Authority, 281
Autocratic leadership, 292

Bankruptcies, 62, 68

Borden, Nel, 202
Branding, concept of, 202
Brand piracy, 26
Bribery, 24
Building Ethical Leaders Using an Integrated Ethics Framework (BELIEF), 4, 5
Building management discipline, 307
Business(es), 22
   ethics, 306
      bifurcation of, 39
      education, 145
      principles of, 23
   schools, 72, 210, 219
      as broken individuals, 40
      questioning value graduates of, 323
Business behaviors, minimum moral standards of, 23
Business curriculum, 18
   strategy importance in, 20, 21
Business decision makers, 79, 80
Business decision making, 81, 82
Business educators, 323
   future trends of, 324
   humanistic management perspective to action among
      embedding ethics in curricula, 326–328
      organizing mentoring programs, 325, 326
Business ethics teaching across management curriculum, 4–6
Business people, 262
Business policy strategy, 17, 18, 29
   focus of, 19
   seeks to assist student develop conceptual thinking skills, 19
Business Software Alliance (BSA), 191
Business students, reputation of, 40

Business-to-consumer (B2C)
e-commerce, 185
Business undergraduates, 41

Career(s), 257
  definition of, 246
  studies, 246
Career management, 10, 245
  advise for teachers, 252, 253
  developing *vs* developed country
    perspectives, 253, 254
  ethics teaching strategy, 249–252
  individual career choices, 255
  perspectives of, 246
  roots of, 246
  typical ethical issues, 247–249
Care ethics, 160, 161
Carlyle, Thomas, 134, 135
"Categories of the understanding,"
    126
Cause-related marketing, concept of,
    202
Caux Round Table Principles for
    Business (1994), 24
Change management, 289
Cheating culture, 2–4
Child labor and working conditions,
    24
Classical family organizations, 71
C-level executive, 306
C-level jobs, 305
Common good approach, 161, 182,
    183
Community relations (CR). *See also*
    Radical transparency (RT),
    concept of
  advice for teachers, 319
  definition of, 304
  developing *vs* developed country
    perspectives, 319, 320
  ethical communication, 307
  ethical dilemmas, 306
  ethical issues, 305
  ethics teaching strategy
    experiential and clinical teaching
      modalities, 318, 319
    teaching from living cases, 317
    teaching from worst practices,
      317, 318
    teaching from written cases, 316
  implications of communications
    about, 305
  typical ethical issues, 307–314
Competitor intelligence gathering, 26
Computers, 191
Concept-based curriculum approach,
    160, 162
Concept-based ethical decision-
    making model, 163, 168, 176
Consumer(s), 80, 141, 147, 165, 169,
    172, 173, 201–203, 205–207,
    211
  behavior, 8, 203, 214, 216
    during 1950s, 215
  advice for teachers, 219–221
  developing *vs* developed country
    perspectives, 221
  ethics teaching strategy, 219
  meaning of, 215
  empowering through product
    transparency, 149, 150
  ethical, 216
  focus in 1990s, 216
  groups, 27
  as human beings, 204
  involved in ethical marketing, 213
  perception of fairness in pricing,
    209
  perception of value, 208
  rights, 216
  typical ethical issues
    ethical concerns, 218, 219
    misleading advertising, 217,
      218
    nutrition and obesity, 218
    vulnerable consumer groups, 218
Consumerism, 216, 219, 220
Consumerism movement in United
  States, 216
Contract theory, 161, 163
Corporate codes of conduct, 277,
    278, 292
Corporate ethics scandals, 314
Corporate leadership, 281
Corporate organizations, 186
Corporate power and politics, 9, 10
  advise for teachers, 290
  description of discipline, 279–283

developing vs developed country perspectives, 290–292
emphasis in teaching, 278
ethics teaching strategy, 287–290
typical ethical issues, 283–287
Corporate scandals, 62
Corporate social responsibility (CSR), 80, 81, 84, 85, 96, 149, 150, 170, 210
 costing of products, services, or activities, 86
 decision making, 88, 89
 developing vs developed country perspectives, 95
 management control, 89, 90
 planning, 87, 88
 teaching strategy, 93–95
Corporate value, 21
Corporate world, 287
Corporations, 278
Corruption, 24, 120, 159, 292
Counterfeit goods, 26
Cradle-to-cradle approach in industrial ecology, 151, 152
Critical political economy, 132, 133
Critical social theory, 132, 133
Culture, 70

Data security, 185
Deceit, 259, 261, 263, 269, 339
Deception, 259, 260, 262, 268, 269
Decision making, 10, 88, 89
Decisions, 163
Deregulation, 132
Descriptive ethics, 39
Developed vs developing country perspective on strategy, 26–28, 46, 47
Development economics, 131
Digital marketing, 202
Dirty politics, 286
Discipline, description of, 56–58
Double standards, 24, 27
Dysfunctional politics, 282, 292

Economics, 122, 130, 134
Economic science, 42

Economy, 119
EFMD. See European Foundation for Management Development
Embeddedness, 61
Embedding ethics framework, 326–328
Employees
 directed responsibility, 230
 ethics and responsibility for, 232–234
 responsibility for decisions of, 234, 235
Empowering consumer through product transparency, 149, 150
Empowerment, 289
Enron scandal, 62, 68, 69
Enterprise resource planning (ERP) systems, 149
Environmental, social, and governance (ESG), 304
ESADE Business School, 5
Ethical behavior in organizations
 competitive forces impact on, 21
 organizational factors affecting, 3
Ethical choice, 41, 42
Ethical consumers, 216, 220, 221
Ethical decision making, 4, 6, 7, 41–43, 45, 46, 145, 160, 164, 174
Ethical dilemmas, 272
Ethical fading, 260
Ethical finance, 229
Ethical human resource management, 229, 230
Ethical issues
 fruitful for classroom discussions, 27, 28
 in global strategy, 24–26
Ethical management, 277
Ethical managers, 120
Ethical organizational decision making framework, 43–45
 typical ethical concerns in, 45
Ethical rules, 71
Ethical standards, 26
Ethical strategy, 22

Ethical values, 22
Ethics across the Curricula (EAC) committee, De Paul University, 5
Ethics, concept of, 80, 81, 85, 93–95, 121, 122, 160, 161, 214, 260, 278
  arbiter in business schools, 40
  education, goal of, 328
  importance in strategy, 20–24, 26
  in information age, 180
  meaning of, 58
  in real-world environment, 40
  in teaching of economics, 133–135
Ethics teaching
  objectives of, 39
  reason for, 2
European commission, 133
European Foundation for Management Development (EFMD), 4
European Union, 146

Faculty, 5
Fair competition, 147
Fair dealing, 23
Fairness, 9, 24, 25, 182, 183
  to others, 90, 91
Fairness approach, 183
Fair Trade movement, 131
Fiduciaries, 61
Finance, 10
Financial market regulation, 132
Financing, 1
Firm, 19
  competitive pressures on, 21
Formal contract, 164
Formal organizational policies, 277
Friedmanite mainstream, 134, 135
Friedman, Milton, 122–124, 131
Functional politics, 282

Generally accepted moral principles (GAMPs), 23
  principles of, 24, 25
Giving voice to values (GVV) approach, 4
Global economic meltdown, 323

Global economy, 323
Global Leadership and Organizational Behavior Effectiveness (GLOBE) project 1991, 291
Globally responsible leaders (GRLE) group, 4
Global Reporting Initiative (GRI) 2013, 85, 307
Global warming, 141
Goal conflict, 59
Golden rule principle, 183
Green marketing, concept of, 202

Hardball competition, 24
Hollinger scandal, 62
Honesty, 23
Honor agreements, 23
Human relations movement, 231
Human resource management (HRM), 1, 9, 10, 119, 120, 134
  definition of, 230
  developed *vs* developing country perspectives, 235, 236
  employees as target group of, 229
  ethical foundation of, 231, 232
  ethical, importance of, 230
  ethics and responsibility for employees, 232–234
  ethics, dimensions of, 229
  focuses on developing tools, 246
  functions of, 231
  perspectives of, 230, 231
  responsibility for decisions of employees, 234, 235
  responsibility toward employees, aspects of, 230
  teaching strategy and advice for teachers, 236, 237
Human sciences, 127
Hume, David, 133

Incentive alignment, 150
Individual level responsibility
  fairness to others, 90, 91
  fraud cases in accounting department, 92
  performance management, 91

Industrial Excellence Award (IEA), 148, 149
Industrial/organizational (I/O) model, 21
Influence, 280
Information age, 180
Information and communication technologies (ICTs), 181, 184, 190, 196
  deployed to enhance productivity and performance, 179
  low entry barriers of, 191
  occupational health risks from, 185
  utilization ethical dilemmas, 186
Information systems (IS) initiative, 179
  management of, 181
  meaning of, 180
Information technology (IT) management, 181
Institute of Management Accountants (IMA), 85
Instructors, 49, 51, 93, 94, 101, 102, 167, 175
  advise for engaging in strategy students on ethical issues, 29–34
  ethic of answerability as, 41
  guides supply chain management students, 176
  marketing (*see* Marketing instructors)
Interfaith Declaration Report (1993), 24
International Integrated Reporting Council (IIRC), 85
Investment strategy, 1
Investor relations (CR). *See also* Radical transparency (RT), concept of
  advice for teachers, 319
  definition of, 304
  developing *vs* developed country perspectives, 319, 320
  ethical communication, 307
  ethical dilemmas, 306
  ethical issues, 305
  ethics teaching strategy, 314–319
    experiential and clinical teaching modalities, 318, 319
    living cases teaching, 317
    worst practices teaching, 317, 318
    written cases teaching, 316
  implications of communications about, 305
  typical ethical issues, 307–314
Islamic finance, 132
Issue selling, 289
IT-business value, 191
IT governance, 182, 185, 191–196
IT infrastructure library (ITIL), 182

Kant, Immanuel, 125, 126, 133, 153, 182, 183
Keynes, J. M., 131
Krugman, Paul, 131

Lagos Business School (LBS), Nigeria, 4, 210, 326
Leadership, 4, 5, 11, 18, 66, 80, 182, 210, 251, 252, 277, 278, 282–284, 286–288, 290–292, 306, 307
  activities and performance motivation, 23
  bad, 143
  corporate (*see* Corporate leadership)
  enterprise, 304
  low-cost, 19
  organizational, 231
  personal, 235
Leadership for Change (LC) program, 5
Legality, concept of, 163
Life-cycle case study, 30, 31
Logical positivism, 123
Lucas, Robert, 131, 132
Lying, 259

Machiavellianism, 288
Macroeconomics, 10, 121, 122
Management, teaching ethics in (*see* Teaching ethics in management)
Management accountants, 80, 82, 88, 95
  fail to include social and environmental information, 85, 86

forward-thinking, 84
reports, 83
Management accounting, 10, 82–85
　information, 82, 83
　reports, 82
Management of ethical human
　　resources, 229
Management of information systems
　　(MIS), 8, 10
　activities of, 181
　ethical issues in, 183–186
　ethical principles in, 182, 183
　ethics, 192–195
　and governance, 181, 182
　integrating business ethics in,
　　186–191
　moral dimensions of, 180
　organizations ability to deliver
　　effective, 181
　practices, 182
Managerial competencies, 250, 251,
　　257
Managerial economics, 7
Managers, 41, 45, 55–57, 59, 60,
　　82–92, 107, 110, 119, 147,
　　148, 161, 182, 184, 203, 211,
　　246, 249, 250, 270, 278, 281,
　　286, 287, 290, 292, 305, 323,
　　325
　destroy subordinates through self-
　　interested choices, 284
　ethical, 120
　ethical behavior, 3, 4
　ethical behavior of, 21
　individual, 19, 119, 120
　information and advise used by,
　　83, 84
　leadership activities and
　　performance motivation
　　tactics, 23
　lobby, 283
　managerial competencies, 251
　marketing, 204, 206, 207, 221
　middle, 235
　personal values and virtues, 3
　professional, 62
　responsible for product replacement
　　strategies act, 207
　self-interest of, 62
　supply chain, 162
　of today multinationals, 291
　uses of accounting information, 80
Marketing and Business
　　Administration (MBA), 2–4,
　　326
　curriculum, 1
　students, 146
Marketing, concept of, 10, 216
　communication, 207
　decisions, 210, 211
　definition of, 202
　focus of, 201
　instructors, 201–211
　mix, 202
　product decisions in, 206
Marketing management, 8, 202, 203
　developing *vs* developed country
　　perspectives, 210
　ethics teaching strategy and advice
　　for teachers, 209, 210
　typical ethical issues in, 203–209
Marketing plans, 1
Market segmentation, concept of, 202
Marx, Karl, 130, 132
Mentoring, 287
Michigan model, 230, 231
Microeconomics-based theory of firm,
　　21
Mill, John Stuart, 129
Moral development, 32–34
Moral hazard, 59, 60
Multinational corporations, 27
Multinational enterprises (MNEs),
　　290, 291
Myrdal, Gunnar, 127, 128

Natural resources, finite, 152, 153
Nature of human beings (NHB), 4
Negative politics, 282, 292
Negotiation(s), 10, 260, 262
　advise for teachers, 268
　business, 262
　common cognitive patterns, 261
　definition of, 263, 264
　developing *vs* developed country
　　perspectives, 268, 269

ethical issues in
   methods to counter tactics, 265–267
   self-test, 267
   typical tactics, 265
   ethics teaching strategy, 267, 268
Negotiators, 91, 259, 260, 269
   harm with some protective skills, 263
   self-interest, 263
No free lunch principle, 183
Nongovernmental organizations (NGOs), 121, 147, 235
Normative discourse, 123, 125
Normative ethics, 39
Normative political economy in classroom, 128–132
Northern Illinois University, 4, 5

Online educators, 325
Online marketing, 202
Operational actions, 19
Operational performance, 21
Operations management (OM), 1, 8, 10, 141
   advise for teachers, 153, 154
   developing *vs* developed countries, 144, 145
   ethics in, 142, 154
   ethics teaching strategy
      business ethics education, 145
      management of closed loop supply chains, 151–153
      strategy deployment and execution for sustainable performance management, 146–149
      sustainability, focus areas of, 146
      sustainable products creation, 149–151
   meaning of, 142
   sustainable, 142
   typical ethical issues
      dimensions of, 143, 144
      meaning of, 142
Opportunistic exploitation, 24
Optimal teaching approach, 45
Organizational career practices, 256, 257

Organizational decision making, 42, 43, 81, 85
Organizational design, 24
Organizational leaders, 84
Organizational politics process, 1, 278–281, 285, 286, 289
Organizational restructuring, 289
Organizational statesmanship, 286
Organizations, 57, 245–247

Pan-Atlantic University, 4
Pareto value judgment, 131
Parmalat scandal, 62
Participative leadership, 292
Patent infringement, 26
Peak oil, notion of, 152
Personality clashes, 289
Personal values, 21
   of leaders, 23
Planning for products, 206, 207
Policy differences, 289
Political actors, 282
Political arena, 286
Political colonialism, 131
Politicians, 288
Politics, 277, 280, 281
Positioning, concept of, 202
Positive discourse in human sciences, 126
Positive politics, 282
Power, 205, 278, 280–282, 291
Power distance, 291
Principal–agent problem, 55
Principles for responsible management education (PRME) initiative, 4, 10, 11, 40, 47, 219
   principles of, 214, 220
Privacy breaches, 185
Process design, 88
Product defects, 89
Product design, 88
Product dumping, 24
Professional ethics, 62, 180, 186, 287, 290
   definition of, 58
Professionalism, 60
Promotions, 289
Psychological perspective of career management, 246

Pursuit of virtue, 183
Pyramid markets, 89

Radical transparency (RT), concept of, 305, 306, 315, 320
Realism, 288
Realpolitik, 288
Recruitment, 234, 327
Red light, green light teaching technique, 31, 32
Reporting relationships, 23
Report to the Nations on Occupational Fraud and Abuse (2012), 92
Resource-based theory of firm, 21
Resource management, 192–195
Resource perspective, 21
Responsible, concept of, 169
Responsible consumption, 219
Risk sharing, 59
Roosevelt's Dilemma, 270–272

Sarbanes–Oxley, 2
Scaffolded education approach, 81
Scaffolds, 92
Scandals in China, 2–4
Science, 6–10
Self-test approach, 9
Service management, 182, 192
Sharing economy, 150, 151
Siemens bribery scandal, 144
Skill, 6–10
Small-and medium-sized companies (SMEs), 190
Smith, Adam, 63, 128, 129
Social considerations, 287
Social determinism of career management, 246
Social marketing, 219
Softer leadership skills, 305
Sourcing decisions, 88
Stakeholders, 3, 6, 9, 27, 45, 46, 49–51, 84, 86, 96, 112, 113, 144, 153, 154, 163, 167–170, 172, 176, 183, 184, 214, 220, 221, 229, 231, 232, 235, 238, 239, 305, 306, 310–313
 characteristics of, 46, 47
 external, 279, 304
 interests, 80, 234
 management, 278
 organizational, 93
 roles of, 65
Stiglitz, Joseph, 131
Stigmatization of goodness phenomenon, 41
Strategic action, 21
Strategic commitments, 17, 18, 22
 cluster of, 29
 in developing countries, 28
Strategic decision making, 43
Strategic information systems planning (SISP) process, 181, 191–195
 activities of, 183, 184
 challenge of, 184
 fairness, 196
Strategic leaders, 17
Strategic management, 18
Strategic planning, 87
Strategic thinking, 21
Strategy, discipline of, 17, 18
Strategy formulation and implementation, 289
Strategy for teaching, 45
Strategy students on ethical issues
 advice for instructors
 engaging, 29–34
Strengths-weaknesses-opportunities-threats (SWOT) framework, 18
Success, 287
Supplier ethics management (SEM), 170
Supply chain management, 8, 10, 159, 163
 advise for teachers, 175
 amalgamation of disparate companies, 176
 developing *vs* developed country perspectives, 175, 176
 ethics teaching strategy, 174, 175
 management of actions, 162
 meaning of, 162

objective of, 162
success of, 162
typical ethical issues
 contractually based ethical issues in, 164–170
 ethical issues based on working conditions, 170–174
Sustainability, 80, 81, 146, 169
Sustainable business practices, 305
Sustainable management, 305
Systems development, 181, 192–195
Systems software bugs, 185

Teaching
 advise for, 46
 ethics in management, 1, 2
 of macroeconomics, 131
 strategy for (*see* Strategy for teaching)
Team building, 289
Technical skills, 305, 306
Tradition of critical political economy, 127, 128
Tradition of purely positive economics, 122–128
Transformative Consumer Research (TCR), 216
Transparency, 10, 60
Truthfulness, 23

Turf wars, 279
Tyco scandal, 62

Unethical behavior, 4, 63, 69, 143, 251, 253, 261, 262, 265
 definition of, 259
 management techniques in, 266
United Nations Global Compact (1999), 24
Utilitarian approach, 183

Value in social theory, 127, 128
Value judgments, 122, 123, 125–127
Value(s)
 importance in strategy formulation, 22
 producing activities of firm, 20
Vandals, 2–4
Vicens Vives Program (VVP), 5
Virtue ethics approach, 183
Von Hayek, Friedrich, 131

Wealth creation, 2
Welfare economics, 131
Well-written contracts, 165
World Bank, 133
Worldcom scandal, 62
WTO, 131

This book is a publication in support of the United Nations Principles for Responsible Management Education (PRME), housed in the UN Global Compact Office. The mission of the PRME initiative is to inspire and champion responsible management education, research, and thought leadership globally. Please visit www.unprme.org for more information.

The Principles for Responsible Management Education Book Collection is edited through the Center for Responsible Management Education (CRME), a global facilitator for responsible management education and for the individuals and organizations educating responsible managers. Please visit www.responsiblemanagement.net for more information.

—Oliver Laasch, University of Manchester, Collection Editor

- *Business Integrity in Practice: Insights from International Case Studies* by Agata Stachowicz-Stanusch and Wolfgang Amann
- *Academic Ethos Management: Building the Foundation for Integrity in Management Education* by Agata Stachowicz-Stanusch
- *Responsible Management: Understanding Human Nature, Ethics, and Sustainability* by Kemi Ogunyemi
- *Fostering Spirituality in the Workplace: A Leader's Guide to Sustainability* by Priscilla Berry
- *A Practical Guide to Educating for Responsibility in Management and Business* by Ross McDonald
- *Educating for Values-Driven Leadership: Giving Voice to Values Across the Curriculum* by Mary Gentile, Editor (with 14 contributing authors)
- *Teaching Anticorruption: Developing a Foundation for Business Integrity* by Agata Stachowicz-Stanusch and Hans Krause Hansen
- *Corporate Social Responsibility: A Strategic Perspective* by David Chandler
- *Responsible Management Accounting and Controlling: A Practical Handbook for Sustainability, Responsibility, and Ethics* by Daniel A. Ette

Announcing the Business Expert Press Digital Library

Concise e-books business students need for classroom and research

This book can also be purchased in an e-book collection by your library as

- a one-time purchase,
- that is owned forever,
- allows for simultaneous readers,
- has no restrictions on printing, and
- can be downloaded as PDFs from within the library community.

Our digital library collections are a great solution to beat the rising cost of textbooks. E-books can be loaded into their course management systems or onto students' e-book readers.
The **Business Expert Press** digital libraries are very affordable, with no obligation to buy in future years. For more information, please visit **www.businessexpertpress.com/librarians**. To set up a trial in the United States, please contact **Adam Chesler** at adam.chesler@businessexpertpress.com, for all other regions, contact **Nicole Lee** at nicole.lee@igroupnet.com.

CPSIA information can be obtained at www.ICGtesting.com
Printed in the USA
LVOW04s0050220215

427841LV00008B/40/P